Pattern and Process in Human Geography

Vincent Tidswell
University of Hull

University Tutorial Press

Published by
UNIVERSITY TUTORIAL PRESS LIMITED
842 Yeovil Road,
Slough, SL1 4JQ.

ISBN 0 7231 0770 X

Published 1976
Reprinted 1977
Second Edition 1978
Reprinted 1979

Printed in Great Britain by
REDWOOD BURN LIMITED
Trowbridge & Esher

Preface

This book aims to introduce A level students and first year undergraduates to the ways in which the professional geographer thinks and works.

Many current ideas of geography are explored through the use of case studies undertaken by individual research workers. From a synthesis of such studies, an appreciation of the general processes contributing to landscape patterns is gained and an evaluation of general laws or 'probability norms' attempted. Specific and worked examples of commonly encountered techniques are included in their appropriate context.

There can be no simple answers to complex problems. The reader is stimulated to think logically, within a structured framework, about problems confronting geographers.

No book is written without the help of generous friends and colleagues. I am grateful to sixth form teachers and college lecturers for their constructive and incisive comment. In particular I wish to thank Hilary Arnold and Sheila Barker, Keith Hilton and David Lewis. I am indebted to my colleagues: Jeffery Moore for his writing and running of computer programs and Howard Thomas for his attempts to ensure the validity of the statistical methods employed. For the preparation and drawing of all the diagrams, and the design of the cover, I thank Vince Driver.

As always my wife, Patricia, has helped me through many difficulties, whilst Chris Kington of U.T.P. has skilfully handled the diagrams and text with expertise. For remaining errors and omissions, I alone remain responsible.

Vincent Tidswell.

March 1976.

Using this Book

As explained in the preface, this is not so much a book of answers or prescriptions but more a collection of approaches to problems.

If the early pages of Chapter 1 prove rather difficult then turn to the section entitled *The Scientific Method of Enquiry* pages 10–13. Return to the remainder of the chapter later as you work through the book, but do so as soon as possible.

Chapter 2 is concerned with the basic steps of data collection and data description and you should familiarise yourself with this before moving to specific areas.

The remainder of the book is sectionalised into topics familiar to you. For each topic you will find an introduction to current ideas and methods of enquiry. Carefully study the diagrams in association with the text as certain key ones provide a framework to help structure your thinking. Within each section are contained summaries of important case studies. The original sources are listed at the end of the relevant chapter. Read the full account of those cases which particularly interest you. To obtain them give the specific reference including the page numbers to your local *public library* requesting them to obtain a photocopy from The British Library. You will be required to sign a copyright declaration and normally to pay a modest fee.

The methodology employed by individual research workers may help guide your own enquiry. Sources of data are provided at the ends of chapters whilst in the text you will find examples and work to involve you. All the techniques used in this book are indexed in Appendix IV, page 326.

After completing each section, it will be profitable to summarise the important ideas introduced, evaluate the evidence from reality which supports these ideas and isolate the unresolved questions. At the end of the entire book, it will be especially valuable to reconsider some fundamental issues such as the role of perception in decision-making. For example, are there common elements in the decision areas of: choosing a crop, locating a factory or deciding where to shop?

Contents

1. Ideas and Approaches in Modern Geography

Introduction

You will be familiar with the well known idea 'History is about chaps; geography about maps'. It is doubtful whether or not this was ever true in the past. Certainly today, geography is concerned with both maps and chaps, for the geographer's distinctive interest lies in the spatial distribution of man's activities which he represents in maps, and also in offering an explanation for such distributions which result from the decisions of man.

It is naïve to think that any explanation in the complex realm of human activity can ever be complete. Nevertheless we can use the most sophisticated data available combined with techniques of analysis to approach the problems posed and so improve the quality of our geographical thinking. The principal aims of this book are to introduce you to methods of geographical enquiry and familiarise you with the more significant theories and ideas at present contained within the field of human geography. Resultant models may then be tested against reality. Appropriate statistical techniques are applied only when they help identify or elucidate the problem in hand.

Through this approach you should come to appreciate how a geographer thinks and works and hence apply his methodology to investigations initiated by yourself.

The Philosophy of Modern Geography

Geography, in common with many other subject disciplines, has undergone rapid changes in recent years. Because of the bewildering range of statistical techniques which cloak the fundamental change in philosophy, the latter is often overlooked. Yet it is the philosophical change which is all-important. What then is its nature?

The great aim of geography in the past was to 'describe and interpret the variable character, from place to place, of the earth as

1

the world of man' (*Hartshorne*). This was attempted through the medium of regional geography and in particular focused upon the differences between regions, and the uniqueness of regions. 'Geography is the study of aerial differentiation in all its aspects' (*Hartshorne*). Such regional studies are known as *idiographic* studies and perhaps the outstanding example is the classical landscape descriptions of Vidal de la Blache, whose work served as a model of studying regional geography for half a century. These studies tended to be based upon the framework of the physical landscape and often were too concerned with seeking causes for distributions of human activity within the physical environment.

Whilst the part played by the physical environment remains important, it is clearly more significant in regions of physical extremity than on the remainder of the earth's surface. This role of the physical environment will also depend upon the scale of the problem being investigated. For example, rainfall regimes are more significant at world or continental level than is usually the case at the smaller national level. Regardless of scale and severity, the physical environment is only one of a number of factors contributing to explanation, and in many cases may be entirely subordinate.

This change of emphasis in moving beyond the earth sciences towards the social sciences in the search for explanation is the first important characteristic to note. Alongside this move is a growing consciousness that many relationships are man–man rather than man–land ones, and are rarely simple. Since the landscape around us largely results from decisions taken by people, there is now a realisation that explanation of it depends as much upon human or *behavioural* forces and *stochastic* (chance) influences, as upon physical and economic ones. Not only is the role of physical forces being re-assessed but a more realistic appraisal of classical economic attitudes is taking place. For example, the concept of the all-knowing '*economic man*' is currently being replaced by the more realistic concept of '*bounded rationality*' as will be demonstrated later.

The second major change in philosophy has far-reaching consequences: this concerns the preoccupation with a search for order in the landscape and the identification of patterns which repeat themselves. Studies associated with this regularity of pattern are called *nomothetic*.

This search for regularity and order is all-important and contrasts markedly with the earlier approach which confined itself to the unique. Allied to this is the identification of certain key relationships between two or more sets of phenomena or *variables*. Such key relationships should exist independent of particular localities and should continue to operate on a variety of scales. It is when general relationships can be deduced that it becomes possible to develop a body of theory as in other sciences. Using this information it is possible to make valid predictions from that theoretical base. Because of the nature of the phenomena with which we deal, this task is itself more difficult than in the physical sciences or indeed the physical branch of geography where, for example, it is possible to talk of the 'laws' of hydraulic geometry.

Human geography today may be regarded as a social science and it is suggested that within this sphere *norms of probability* may be substituted for the '*laws*' of the physical sciences. The term *probability norm* means that, given certain assumptions, it is reasonable to expect certain relationships to exist between two sets of phenomena. An example is: the intensity of agricultural land use decreases with increasing distance from the market. This expected relationship will be fully examined in Chapter 5 where you are shown how to measure the strength of the association. You will meet many more cases later in the book.

It is from the identification of significant relationships that the key ideas – or *concepts* – emerge upon which our discipline may be organised. Although as yet in an early stage, Ambrose has identified and discussed four important concepts: gradient, network, least cost location and cumulative causation. These four concepts, together with many others such as *optimiser* and *satisficer* will be explored and used as you work through the text. A consequence of this conceptual approach is that we now look more closely at the *processes* at work in the human landscape rather than stop short at description of forms and patterns, however good these descriptions have been in the past. Furthermore there can be transference of ideas from one set of problems to another as will be exemplified in later chapters. It will be shown, for example, how the concept of interaction, incorporated in the gravity model, has relevance in a number of different contexts.

The complex and imponderable nature of many problems in human geography has already been mentioned. This difficulty results from attempting to handle the total environment containing diverse physical and human elements at any given point of time. Such elements, and the linkages between them, also change over time and this dynamism adds further to our difficulties. Sheer scale together with the rapidly changing and multivariate nature of reality renders the total scene too complex to comprehend and handle, hence the need for what is termed a *systems approach* to geography and to build *models* as simplifications of reality. At the same time it is essential to focus on individual problems and approach these in a truly scientific way.

More recently the picture has been further clouded by serious questioning of what constitutes reality. This may hitherto have been regarded as a metaphysical question, but if we are truly to grapple with problems of explanation, then the attributes of what is described as the *decision-making environment, ie.* the image of the environment as perceived by the decision-maker (whether subsistence farmer or industrial tycoon) must be identified.

The Role of Perception

The importance and implications of perception have been highlighted by Ambrose when he writes: ' If they (men) were conditioned by what actually and objectively does exist, no city would ever have been built where earthquake and flood could damage it, no explorer would ever choose the wrong route through a range of mountains and no farmer would ever choose a combination of crops that did not perfectly suit the physical conditions of his farm and the economic conditions of the market'.

Decisions then seem to depend upon an *image* of the environment rather than as it actually is. This image will depend basically upon awareness which results from a number of factors.

The first of these factors may be called *direct experience* of a particular phenomenon. Its impact may vary with the frequency and intensity of such an experience. An example of this is introduced in Chapter 6 and perhaps you can recall from your own fieldwork experiences, situations where your preconceived mental image of a landscape feature required re-adjustment after a visit. For example, how did the image of the surface features of a glacier conjured up by verbal description match the visual portrayal of a coloured slide? If you have been fortunate enough to walk on a glacier's surface how was your previous impression further modified?

A second factor is *indirect experience* for which we are dependent upon the communications media. How does the viewing of a film

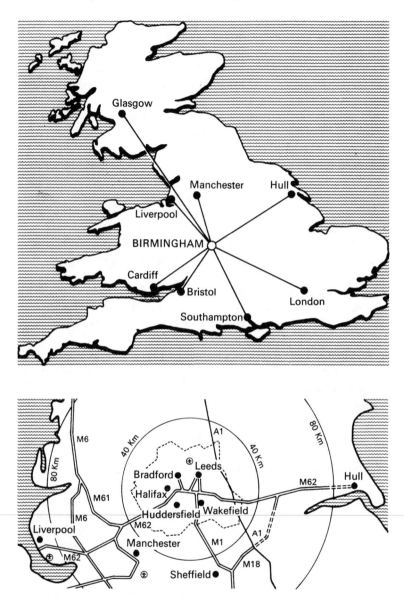

Figs. 1.1 and *1.2* The Crossroads of Britain: whose viewpoint? (*Based on Times Newspaper*)

improve your image of far-away places? How strongly are you influenced by the new-type *topological* maps showing relative location such as the 'over ground' maps of British Rail? What is the impact of advertisements as shown in Figs. 1.1 and 1.2? When you see these two maps juxtaposed, is the mental image created by one corrected by the mental image created by the other? How easily would the decision-maker be persuaded by any one of these advertisements viewed in isolation? What criteria are used to justify the term 'crossroads of Britain'?

A third group of factors is far more elusive to identify and incorporates *attitudes and values*, in turn influenced by cultural background and socio-economic status; age, experience and education; personality and temperament which are reflected in ambition and aspiration. If you come from the south of England is your image of 'The North' that of 'Coronation Street'? What is the northerner's view of 'down south'? Is the farmer's view of the Lake District the same as that of the tourist?

An important summary of how attitudes to the landscape vary is provided by Lewis's study of the Great Plains. Equally valuable are the studies of White and Gould of residential desirability for differing regions of the British Isles. Suitable reading is suggested at the end of this chapter but later in this book you will find the perceptions of climatic hazard and of the journey to shop are discussed and assessed in context.

Although a difficult one, the concept of perception of the environment must be appreciated if an understanding of the decision-making processes at work is to be approached.

The Methodology of Modern Geography

1. GENERAL SYSTEMS APPROACH

Systems analysis more properly belongs to a higher level of academic research than we hope to cover in this volume. Nevertheless at this level its value lies in providing a logical and sequential framework within which to think, and a realisation of the functioning of the whole rather than a number of individual parts.

It is difficult to arrive at a simple definition of a system. A system consists of a number of so-called *elements* between which there are identifiable *linkages* and relationships and from the interaction of which emerge a number of outcomes. This input–throughput–output arrangement is well illustrated in a simple system already known to you, namely, the hydrological cycle. The input is precipitation, the throughput is what happens to that precipitation in given circumstances and the output is channel discharge and evaporation, each with its feedback into the system.

It is more difficult to conceive systems within the sphere of human geography, but an attempt has been made to illustrate this in the contexts of agriculture (Chapter 3) and transport networks (Chapter 14).

A systems approach is really an attempt to appreciate the wholeness of an entity. A system focuses upon the functioning processes and relationships within it, as well as the resultant forms. Used as a thinking model this approach necessitates five steps:

1. Identification of the elements or component parts.
2. Appreciation of the relationships between these parts.
3. Evaluating the results of the interaction of the components.
4. Identification of the impact of (a) the end product of the system or (b) a new input from outside the system.
5. Understanding the dynamic nature of the system.

An example of this framework is given near the beginning of Chapter 3 which should be read in conjunction with Fig. 3.1 (Page 37).

2. THE USE OF MODELS

Models seem to combine ubiquitous application with elusive definition. A model can after all be 'a theory or a law, an hypothesis or structured idea, a role, a relation, or equation, a synthesis of data, a word, a map, a graph or some type of hardware arranged for experimental purposes' (*Haggett*).

What then are the attributes of models and why are they useful?

ATTRIBUTES OF A MODEL

In order to build a model, irrelevancies or '*noise*' are excluded and attention is confined to those features which are of particular interest or significance to a specific problem. Thus models are selective and provide only a partial view of the real world. At one end of the scale a model could be so simple and selective as to be of little value, whilst at the other end of the spectrum it may be so complex as to be almost indistinguishable from reality. Since a model ignores certain elements so that it may concentrate on others the builder must exercise judgment and skill in its construction: criteria for selection are normally conditioned by the nature of the problem and the basis of existing geographical knowledge and theory, combined with a degree of intuition.

Although simplified and selective, a model is structured and the relationships between its components are clearly identified. For example, in the von Thünen land use model (page 81) all variables are laid to rest except distance. It is the relationship between distance from market and intensity of land use which is expounded.

The structure of a model can be readily modified as a result of testing against reality and hence it is dynamic in nature. Especially is this so since reality itself is constantly changing; as the real world changes so do models relating to it. The variation in the form of the gravity model (page 225) provides an example of this. In the early literature the simple gravity model merely employs the distance between two towns; other versions use the square of the distance whilst more sophisticated versions add a *constant* to reflect not the mere physical distance, but the time taken to traverse it.

A third characteristic is the predictive nature of models enabling the projection of normative patterns. A *normative* pattern is one that should exist given certain assumptions compared with the *descriptive* pattern *ie.* that one which actually exists on the ground. An example of their predictive nature is provided in the Monte Carlo Simulation model in Chapter 9.

THE USEFULNESS OF MODELS

Earlier in this chapter it has been argued that the scale of reality is too great to handle and its complexity too diverse to comprehend. The model through its selectivity facilitates the isolation of the problem and of its component and relevant factors. The scale and complexity of reality are thus reduced and our understanding of it helped. The structured nature of the model provides a theoretical framework within which hypotheses may be formulated and tested as part of a sound scientific enquiry. Conformity to the model will help the development of geographical theory whilst deviations from the expected may form the basis of later investigation. This indication of the direction of further enquiry thus saves valuable time. An example of this process in action is shown in Chapter 12 where the work of Bracey is compared with the application of Reilly's law of retail gravitation in the same study area.

Perhaps the greatest value of the model is that it may reveal an order in the pattern, enabling generalisations to be formed, theories to be formulated and eventually valid predictions to be made. Peter Haggett succinctly sums up their usefulness:

'Models are made necessary by the complexity of reality. They are a conceptual prop to our understanding and as such provide for the teacher a simplified and apparently rational picture for the classroom, and for the researcher a source of working hypotheses to test against reality. They convey not the whole truth but a useful and apparently comprehensible part of it'.

3. THE USE OF QUANTITATIVE TECHNIQUES

It is most unfortunate that the recent developments in geographical thought and methodology have been dubbed 'The Quantitative Revolution'. Statistics have been described as a powerful aid to judgment, but the techniques they employ can never be an end in themselves. It is imperative to recognise and maintain the subservient role of statistical methods by employing them only when they are useful in helping identify a pattern or solve a geographical problem.

Statistical methods have been the concern of geographers for many years and simple examples familiar to you include frequency diagrams, graphs and flow line maps. Used in the correct context, the armoury of recently acquired techniques is invaluable. Sampling enables rapid collection of data; derivation of indices overcomes difficulties arising from differences in scale. Correlation and regression analysis not only establish whether or not a relationship exists between two variables, but indicate the strength of that relationship and whether or not it could have arisen by chance.

Allied to the geographer's use of statistics is his application of mathematical theory and methods. The outstanding example here is the application of graph theory and topological transformations in network analysis, together with matrices for storing and manipulating the information.

There is no real dichotomy between the so-called qualitative, literary approach and the quantitative statistical approach – the one is an extension of the other and represents a necessary expression of the evolutionary change in philosophy already discussed. The aim to be more precise in measurement of data and relationships between sets of data is an essential prelude to the core of modern geography: the scientific method of enquiry.

4. THE SCIENTIFIC METHOD OF ENQUIRY

From the time of the earliest fieldworkers, such as the Forsters in the eighteenth century, geographers have followed a logical sequence of events. Careful observations were recorded and analysed and conclusions deduced from the original evidence. Why then is there a need to change?

Basically there are three reasons for a change of approach. The first of these is that the scale and complexity of reality – mentioned earlier – prevents accurate observation and recording of the totality. Secondly, no matter how careful the observer, he will have his own distinctive viewpoint revealed as previously discussed in considering perception level, and this will obstruct any truly objective assessment. If however attention is focused on one or two components relevant to a specific problem, then the task becomes more manageable. Stated more simply, it is important that when conducting an investigation you need to know what you are looking for and to eliminate irrelevancies. The third reason for change is probably the most significant: the aim of geographical study today is no longer the regional monograph but the recognition of pattern regularities, and understanding of the functional processes and hence the development of a body of theory from which valid predictions may be made. The latter is the essence of all sciences and the method by which such theory is built up is known as the scientific method of enquiry.

The scientific method is a way of approaching problems and involves a logical sequence of steps leading to certain conclusions based upon precise and stated evidence. If the conclusions are satisfactory then an explanation at a given level of truth is offered and certain predictions may be made from the evidence. This route is illustrated in the flow diagram in Fig. 1.3A and exemplified in the context of agricultural geography in Fig. 1.3B. This example is elaborated and worked in Chapter 4. The steps may be identified as:

1. Definition of the problem – this will arise from our study of the landscape around us and models may well help isolate the problems within it.

2. Formulation of hypotheses – to help solve the problem as defined. It should be remembered that an hypothesis is the term used to describe the starting point for investigation or a possible solution to a problem. The hypothesis should be stated in the form of a relation-

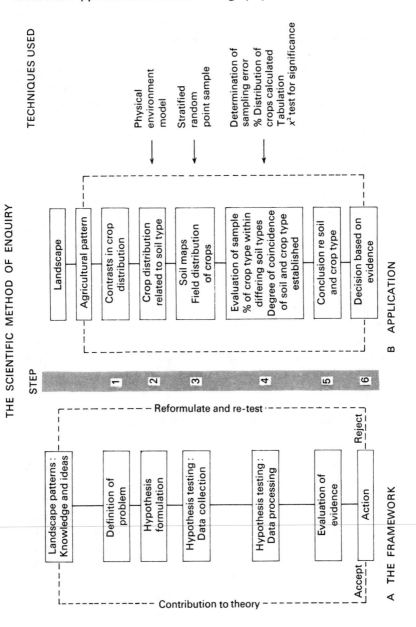

Fig. 1.3 The Scientific Method of Enquiry

ship between two *variables*. For example, agricultural land use is related to soil type. A newcomer to this approach may be puzzled by the source of hypotheses which may normally be derived from assumed relationships within geography – as in the example quoted above – or from the principles of another discipline applied to geographical situations. The classical example of this latter case is the gravity model. The third source is intuition or 'hunch' about a relationship; this usually springs only from prolonged contact with the problem in hand and you should not be discouraged if this source proves elusive.

3. Testing the hypothesis: data collection – this normally involves use of published data such as maps and census returns in conjunction with original fieldwork to supplement this data. Sampling is often a swift method of collecting data, especially when the scale of the problem is a large one (see Chapter 2).

4. Testing the hypothesis: data processing – using quantitative techniques as appropriate in order to facilitate interpretation and expedite testing. Such processing may involve the conversion of data into a numerical index for feeding into regression analysis and rank correlation. The results of such analyses should be tested for statistical significance *ie.* tested to ascertain whether or not such a result could have arisen as a chance happening.

5. Evaluation of evidence – leading to acceptance or rejection of the hypothesis at a given level of significance.

6. Implications of conclusion – it may be possible to confirm an hitherto unproven assumption and hence add to the body of theory. As you read on you will see how geographers have both used and contributed to existing theory. Much of the current work is a search to establish a viable body of geographical theory. Alternatively a weakness in the original hypothesis may be uncovered so that it is necessary to return to step 2; or again new problems may be revealed requiring a complete re-cycling of the process.

This method of enquiry, incorporating fieldwork as an integral part rather than as a separate entity, permeates the whole of our approach to geographical problems. Thus a changed philosophy and methodology came together and from this union may spring refreshing attitudes. It is in this spirit of enquiry that the changed philosophy and methodology are expressed and from which intellectually satisfying results and questioning attitudes may emerge.

Suggestions for further reading

A. Related to recent changes in Geography

Chorley, R. J. and Haggett, P. (1965) ed. *Frontiers in Geographical Teaching*, Chapter 1. Methuen.

Chorley, R. J. ed. (1973) *Directions in Geography*. Chapters 4 and 5. Methuen.

Chorley, R. J. and Haggett, P. ed. (1967) *Models in Geography*. Chapters 1 and 14. Methuen.

Cooke, R. U. and Johnson, J. H. ed. (1969) *Trends in Geography*. Chapters 1 and 8. Pergamon.

Hagerstrand, T. (1967) 'The computer and the geographer'. *Transactions of Institute of British Geographers*, no. 42, pages 1–19.

Henderson, H. C. K. (1968) 'Geography's balance sheet'. *Transactions of Institute of British Geographers*, no. 45, pages 1–9.

Keuning H. J. (1977) 'Aims and scope of modern human geography'. *Tijdschrift voor economische en sociale geografie*, vol. 68, no. 5, pages 262–274.

Rutherford, J., Logan, M. I. and Missen, G. J. (1966) *New Viewpoints in Economic Geography*, Chapter 1. Harrap.

B. Related to Perception

Ambrose, P. (1969) *Analytical Human Geography*. Chapter 5. Longman.

Goodey, B. (1971) *Perception of the Environment – an Introduction to the Literature*. University of Birmingham, Centre for Urban and Regional Studies.

Gould, P. R. and White, R. (1974) *Mental Maps*. Penguin.

Lanegran, D. A. and Palm, R. (1973) *An Invitation to Geography*. McGraw-Hill.

Lewis, G. M. (1962) 'Changing emphasis in the description of the natural environment of the American Great Plains area'. *Transactions of Institute of British Geographers*, no. 30, pages 75–90.

C. Related to The Scientific Method of Enquiry

Fitzgerald, B. P.(1974) *Developments in Geographical Method*. Chapter 1. O.U.P.

Harvey, D. W. (1969) *Explànation in Geography*. Chapter 4. Arnold.

2 . Data Collection and Description

It is clear from what you already know about the scientific method of enquiry that collection of data is necessary at an early stage.Such data may be derived from published sources and obtained through original fieldwork. Despite the plethora of data already available, it is often necessary for data to be supplemented by fieldwork. Hence the investigator needs to be alerted to collect such data on a comparable basis to that of the published material. For example, the Census of Distribution (see p. 227) provides information about numbers and types of shops in larger towns. If similar information about smaller towns within the study area is required, then fieldwork classification and criteria should correspond to those of the official publication.

Data collection should also take into account the processing and methods of interpretation which are to be employed at a later stage. If rank correlation is to be used then *ordinal* or ranked data will be sufficient since, although no absolute values are given, orders of magnitude are stated. Because of their strength of measurement and flexible methodology in processing, *interval* or *ratio* data are of greater value. In both these types precise numerical values are given; the distinction between them is that ratio data have a true zero point of origin, whilst interval data do not. An example will clarify this difference: temperatures in degrees Centigrade are interval data because o degrees Centigrade is an arbitrary base whereas rainfall in millimetres has a true zero. Thus $10°C$ is not twice as hot as $5°C$, but 1000 mm of rainfall is twice as much as 500 mm.

No attempt is being made to give comprehensive coverage or full explanation of statistical methods, and only those more widely used are included in this book. These are indicated in Fig. 2.1. This chapter confines itself to the preliminary steps of collection and description; the relationships between data are examined in their appropriate contexts in the problems investigated in subsequent pages. References to more advanced texts are given at the end of this chapter.

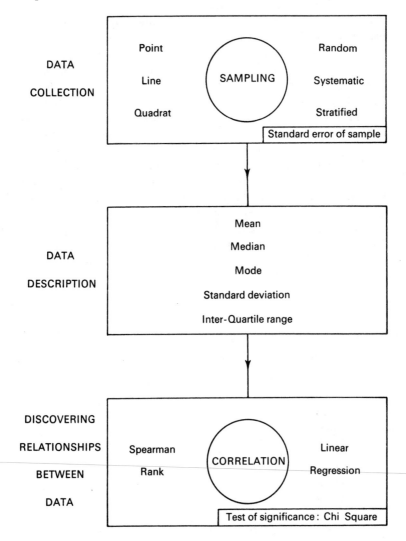

Fig. 2.1   Collecting and using data

Data Collection: Sampling Techniques

ADVANTAGES OF SAMPLING

The collection of data is both time-consuming and costly. Therefore it is often useful to take a sample from the total population in order to *estimate* what is happening within the whole. One example will be familiar to you: every ten years a complete census of the entire population of the United Kingdom is taken. At the mid-point between censuses, a 10% sample census is undertaken to estimate changing trends within the total population. Also in your own fieldwork you have no doubt surveyed land use along a transect rather than map the entire area.

The great advantage of sampling is that it enables the rapid collection of data, and provided certain safeguards are undertaken the results can be remarkably accurate. An example of such accuracy is shown in Table 2.1 which compares the percentage of land use within twelve categories for Chicago obtained by sampling techniques with actual measured values. Furthermore the limits of the estimate can be determined by calculating the *sampling or standard error*.

Table 2.1

The value and usefulness of sampling as a method of investigation

Land use in the Chicago standard metropolitan statistical area

Type of land use	Sample value	% measured value
Estate	0·1	0·4
Single family residence	31·7	30·5
Multifamily residence	0·6	0·6
Commercial	1·7	1·9
Manufacturing	1·2	2·0
Mining	0·0	0·0
Transport, communications	0·3	0·3
Public buildings	0·7	0·7
Open space (recreational)	17·4	18·2
Agricultural and vacant	39·6	39·3
Access streets	4·1	4·0
Through streets and highs	2·3	2·1

Source: Berry and Marble, *Spatial Analysis.*

THEORY BEHIND SAMPLING

First it must be understood that sampling can never give a completely accurate answer, but it can provide a *best estimate* of that answer. Sampling assumes that the total population from which it is taken conforms to what is known as the *normal distribution* shown in Fig. 2.2. Notice that the shape of this distribution is symmetrical

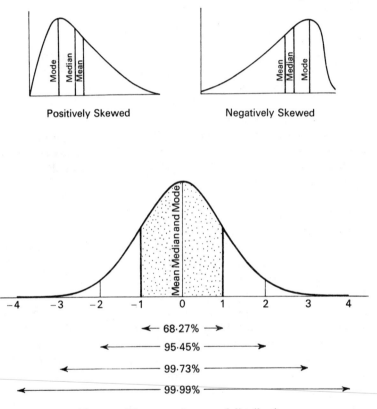

Fig. 2.2 The normal curve of distribution

about the mean value. This symmetry has important implications since 68% of the area under the curve lies within one *standard deviation* of the *mean* and 95% within two standard deviations. (For an explanation of the terms mean and standard deviation, see pages 28, 30).

The larger the population, the more likely it is to conform to this normal distribution. It is also reasonable to assume that the accuracy of the estimate will increase with the sample size. This remains true until a certain size is reached beyond which the law of diminishing returns begins to become significant. For example, the *increased* accuracy resulting from a sample size of 1000 compared with the estimate derived from a sample size of 500 may not justify the additional time and expense needed to undertake the larger sample survey. The optimal size for a sample is discussed below, but the minimum size normally accepted is 30.

It is essential to eliminate any bias in the selection of items in the sample: each person or unit of land must have exactly the same opportunity of being selected.

METHODS OF SAMPLING

The variety of sampling methods is outlined in Fig. 2.1 and basically one uses either points, lines or areas, each of which may be arranged in either a random, stratified random or systematic way. By far the most widely employed type is point sampling.

1. Point Sampling

Three designs of point sampling are shown in Fig. 2.3. A random point sample is generated by establishing the co-ordinates of the points by using random numbers. An extract of these is given in Appendix I on page 320, together with instructions for their use. For this purpose the numbers may be used in groups of four to establish co-ordinates as in the familiar grid reference on an Ordnance Survey map – the point marked by X in Fig. 2.3A is established by 1992. A set of point locations entirely free from bias is generated in this way.

A modification of this is the systematic point sample where the co-ordinates of the first point are established randomly and subsequent points arranged at a pre-determined fixed interval as in Fig. 2.3B.

It is sometimes necessary to divide a study region into a series of sub-regions called *strata* and to allocate points to each stratum. In Fig. 2.3C all the strata are equal in area and hence have the same number of points allocated to them. When this is not the case, as in the soil types examined in Chapter 4 then the number of points is allocated on a proportional basis. Within each stratum the points must be established on a random basis in the way described earlier.

Such a design is known as stratified random.

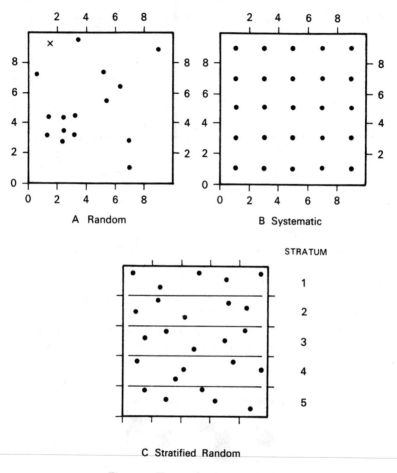

Fig. 2.3 Types of point sampling

2. Line Sampling
Instead of using points, a random line or transect may be created by random co-ordinates fixing its terminals. Once again this may be random as shown in Fig. 2.4A or systematic as in Fig. 2.4B.

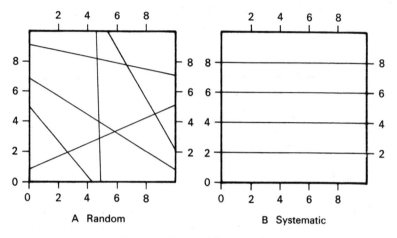

Fig. 2.4   Types of line sampling

3. *Quadrat Sampling*

In addition to points and lines, areas free from bias may also be chosen for close investigation. Such areas are square in shape, hence the term *quadrat* sampling. Fig. 2.5 shows a randomly generated sample which is easily achieved either on a co-ordinate basis as before, or by numbering the quadrats and calling random numbers. The size of the quadrat will depend upon the nature of the problem being investigated, but the kilometre square or ¼ kilometre square is often a useful guide.

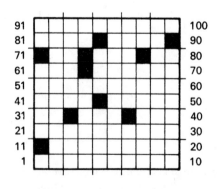

Fig. 2.5   Quadrat sampling

ESTABLISHING A SAMPLE FROM NUMERICAL DATA

In establishing a sample population for questionnaire purposes the electoral roll is a convenient basis from which to work, provided you are satisfied that your investigation is concerned with adults as defined by the electoral laws. A short extract of the electoral roll for part of a typical English parish is included below. All the people should be re-numbered and random numbers called to establish the sample population. This could then be treated as a random point sample. Alternatively random numbers could be used to select the first name and thereafter every fifth name be chosen. What kind of sample would this be? The methods described may be applied to any list such as farms or industrial firms.

Data extract from the electoral roll of an English parish

Electoral roll no.		Number for use with random tables
140	Bowen, Emma, The Laurels	001
141	Bowen, Marjorie, The Laurels	002
142	Booker, Frederick J., Sunnybank	003
143	Bradley, Ann, Ivy Cottage	004
144	Bradley, Arthur J., Ivy Cottage	005
145	Bradley, John, Ivy Cottage	006
146	Brooks, Caroline, Bush Bank	007
147	Brooks, Hugh, Bush Bank	008
148	Burton, Alfred T., The Coach and Horses	009
149	Bull, Margaret, 7 Station Road	010
150	Bull, Charles, 7 Station Road	011

SELECTION OF SAMPLING TYPE AND SIZE OF SAMPLE

In establishing a sample design three basic questions need to be answered:

Should the sample be random, stratified random, or systematic?
Should points, lines or quadrats be used?
What size of sample is necessary?

The response to these questions will be largely conditioned by the kinds of data you are handling and the kinds of problems you wish to solve. The following guidelines are suggested, but *geographical judgment* must be exercised in the final choice.

Random? Stratified Random? Systematic?
When the distribution of the data itself is random then any method may be employed. When is this likely to be the case?

If an area has a known regular pattern, such as the Prairies, the Dutch Polders or a pattern of grid-iron towns then a systematic sample would be biased, so that a random one must be used.

If linear trends are present such as in an area of scarp and vale topography, then a stratified random sample is expedient so that an estimate of the characteristics of each type of landscape may be obtained.

To select from a list of items, a systematic method is appropriate.

Point? Line? Quadrat?
A point sample is easily generated and the standard error quickly calculated. It is very helpful for choosing both map locations and items from a list. It should be remembered, however, that when conducting fieldwork, you will need to visit the sample points on the ground and thought should be given to minimising the amount of travel.

A line sample is useful for transect mapping, for example, along a road or river valley. However, the calculation of the standard error is more complex as will be seen later.

Quadrats are normally employed to isolate small areas of complex morphology for detailed investigation as within the inner areas of cities.

For most purposes a point sample is adequate and its simplicity is a strong recommendation.

SIZE OF SAMPLE
If the sample size is too small, then it becomes difficult to have a range of values near the true mean. In such an event, the sampling error would be so great as to prove worthless. An example of this is included on page 53. At the other extreme, as explained earlier, a sample could be so large that it represents little economy of effort, accordingly a compromise solution should be reached. The point at which the law of diminishing returns begins to operate in a significant way is shown in the example from the work of Hammond and McCullagh in Table 2.2.

Table 2.2

The relationship between sample size and standard error

Number in sample	Item 1	Item 2	Standard error
50	20%	80%	5·7%
100	20%	80%	4·0%
200	20%	80%	2·8%
400	20%	80%	2·0%

Source: Hammond and McCullagh. *Quantitative Techniques in Geography*, page 128.

Would the effort of doubling the sample number from 200 to 400 be justified by the decrease in the standard error from 2·8% to 2·0% in the example cited above? The answer must really depend upon the required reliability of the estimate for the particular investigation.

It is possible to ascertain the number required in a sample to achieve a pre-determined standard error. The procedure is complex but is lucidly explained by Hammond and McCullagh.

For most practical purposes a sample of 50 or 100 points is normally adequate and has the advantage that the results are already expressed in percentage terms.

A comparison of the different methods described above when they have been applied to an extract of the Second Land Utilisation Map of the Hartlepools area is provided in Table 2.3. In the point

Table 2.3

Summary of results of differing types of sampling applied to the same land use map

Type of sampling	Category of land use (%)					
	Arable	Pasture	Market garden-ing	Wood-land	Settle-ment	Others
Point						
Random	39	53	4	1	2	1
Stratified random	40	53	4	2	1	0
Systematic	40	52	7	1	0	0
Line						
Random	52	39	7	2	0	0
Systematic	34	56	8	2	0	0

samples, the land use found at each of the 100 points generated was recorded according to a pre-determined six category classification. You will notice that one of these categories is labelled 'other' which is a wise precaution in any exercise of this kind.

It is interesting to see the closeness of fit between the differing methods of point sampling in the two larger categories of arable and pasture, and how they differ from the line sample results. This variation is a sharp reminder that sampling can only provide a best estimate of the true answer.

EVALUATION OF THE SAMPLE

It is imperative to calculate the standard error of the sample so that a statement may be made about the population as a whole. This error in a point sample is calculated by using the formula:

$$\text{Standard error} = \sqrt{\frac{p \times q}{n}}$$

where p is the percentage of land in a particular category
   q is the percentage of land not in this category
   n is the number of points in the sample.

An example from Table 2.3 will clarify the method. The percentage of arable land indicated by the stratified random sample is 40. Thus the standard error is

$$\text{Standard error} = \sqrt{\frac{40 \times 60}{100}} \simeq 5$$

The standard error tells us the range within which the true answer falls; in this case 40% ± 5% or stated alternatively, it lies between 35% and 45%.

It will be recalled that the theory of sampling assumed that the data conform to the normal distribution as shown in Fig. 2.2. Referring back to this diagram you will see that one standard error merely accounts for 68% of the distribution. A more exact answer to the above problem is, therefore, that the percentage of arable land lying within the range 35–45% occurs 68 times out of 100, or, stated in statistical language, at the 68% *probability level*.

To obtain even greater precision (95% probability level) it is necessary to double the standard error indicating a range of 30–50% in the quoted example.

Using Table 2.3 calculate the standard error for pasture in this area. What do you notice about your result compared with that for arable land?

The limitations of sampling are evident when the standard error for market gardening is calculated. Using the value of 4% (Table 2.3) its standard error is 0·95 so that at the 68% probability level (1 Standard Deviation), the range of the estimate is from 3·05 to 4·95% whilst at the 95% level it enlarges to become 2·1 to 5·9%.

Whenever actual values as opposed to frequency of occurrence are obtained by sampling as in a line sample, then an alternative formula must be substituted:

$$\text{Standard error} = \sqrt{\left(\Sigma x^2 - \frac{(\Sigma x)^2}{n}\right) \times \frac{1}{n} \times \frac{1}{n-1}}$$

where x is a value, n is the number of values contained in the sample and Σ equals the sum of. Note Σx^2 is not the same as $(\Sigma x)^2$: refer to Table 2.4.

Table 2.4

Summary of results of line sampling

	x	x^2	Total length of line (cm)
Line 1	11	121	12
2	10	100	15
3	8	64	14
4	8	64	12
5	13	169	15
6	10	100	12
	$\Sigma x\,60$	$\Sigma x^2\,618$	80
$\bar{x} = 10$	$(\Sigma x)^2 = 60^2 = 3600.$		

Situations where this may apply include, for example, varying acreages of hops on 50 sample farms, or number of employees in 50 sample factories. In both cases the sample mean ($\bar{x}$) would be obtained and its standard error then calculated by substitution in the above formula. The answer would then provide a truer estimate of the range within which the mean of the total population would lie.

This procedure is necessary in line sampling, where, since the actual length of the line occupied by a category of land use is measured, numerical values are obtained. Suppose for example, one wished to find the area used for arable farming and decided to establish six random transects across the map study region. The results may be as in Table 2.4 where x is the number of cm per transect occupied by arable land. The sample mean $(\bar{x})$ is 10 cm and the standard error at the 68% probability level is 0·6 so that the true answer lies between 9·4 and 10·6 cm. It is probably more helpful to express this in percentage terms: the area of land occupied by arable farming is 75% ±6% at the 68% probability level.

It would be fair to conclude that the evaluation of line sampling is a more lengthy and tedious procedure and that point sampling is to be preferred wherever possible. This longer method of calculating the standard error cannot be avoided if actual values (*ie.* interval or ratio data) as opposed to classificatory or nominal data (*eg.* number of points assigned to land use categories) are used.

DESCRIPTION OF DATA

Table 2.5

Extract from agricultural statistics of England and Wales 1974.
Wheat, barley, oats: estimated yield in kilos per hectare
in each county

	Wheat	Barley	Oats
ENGLAND	4958	3967	3967
Avon	4481	3916	4029
Bedfordshire	5397	4117	3803
Berkshire	4544	3753	3753
Buckinghamshire	4519	3778	3854
Cambridgeshire	5222	3979	4092
Cheshire	4368	4117	3879
Cleveland	5234	4297	4297
Cornwall	4569	3038	2975
Cumbria	5372	4205	4167
Derbyshire	5397	4255	4657
Devon	3803	3339	3289
Dorset	4330	3452	3753

Frequently published data are in the form of numerical lists such as that shown in Table 2.5. This table is merely a brief extract from similar data for all the counties of England and Wales.

It is important to realise that lists of this kind organised in alphabetical order, may almost certainly need re-arranging on a *spatial* basis when used to answer geographical questions. For this reason these data were reorganised on a regional basis and the designated western counties of England are shown in Table 2.6.

Table 2.6

Estimated Yields (Kilos/hectare) for counties
reorganised on spatial basis

	Barley	Oats
Avon	3916	4029
Cheshire	4117	3879
Cornwall	3038	2975
Devon	3339	3289
Dorset	3452	3753
Gloucestershire	3916	4255
Hertfordshire and		
Worcestershire	3979	3954
Lancashire	4117	4255
Shropshire	4067	4029
Somerset	3753	4054
Mean	3496	3847
Standard deviation	378	

Source: Based on Agricultural Statistics of England and Wales, HMSO, 1974.

To extract information from numerical data it is usual to ask two preliminary, inter-related questions:

1. What is the central tendency of the data? This could very loosely be described as the 'norm' and is measured by the mean, the median and the mode.
2. How widely are the data spread about this norm? This is indicated by range and/or standard deviation.

When possible to do so, it can be most valuable to determine the variability of the data and to discover what trends are revealed by the data so that a valid prediction may be made about future expectations.

MEASURES OF CENTRAL TENDENCY

1. The Mean
Calculation of the arithmetic mean of a numerical array is very
simple and a task already familiar to you. The formula to use is:

$$\bar{x} = \frac{\Sigma x}{n}$$

Within a particular set of data the mean is useful for dividing those
which occur above from those which occur below the mean value.
Referring to Table 2.6, it is seen that four of the counties occur above
the mean yield in barley and five in oats. What may be more
geographically significant is that Cornwall and Devon are both shown
to fall below the mean for their sub-region in barley and oats. Hence
the mean value could indicate a potential geographical problem.
The mean is very useful too in comparing two sets of data. Look at
Table 2.7. The mean yield of oats in the wetter north west is the
same as that for the drier north east.

Table 2.7
Mean Crop Yields in Four Regions of England

	Barley		Oats	
	Mean	Standard deviation	Mean	Standard deviation
North West	4065	252	3723	101
South West	3662	175	3541	225
North East	3918	214	3725	240
South East	3816	366	3540	378

Caution, however, must be exercised when using the mean, since
the year for which it is given may be an eccentric one (see later in
this chapter) and the data may be skewed, rendering the mean of
little value. A skewed distribution is one in which the majority of the
values lie towards one extremity of the range. The closer the distribution of the data being considered to the normal distribution (Fig.
2.2) then the greater is the usefulness of the mean.

2. The Median
The median value is the one which divides the array exactly in half
so that an equal *number* of values occur above and below it. This is

indicated on Fig. 2.6. To establish this value it is first necessary to arrange the data in rank order.

The median is a helpful measure when the distribution is skewed and it should normally be employed in conjunction with the mean.

3. The Mode

The mode is merely the most frequently occurring value in a distribution. When two values occur with equal frequency the distribution is said to be bi-modal as in Fig. 2.6.

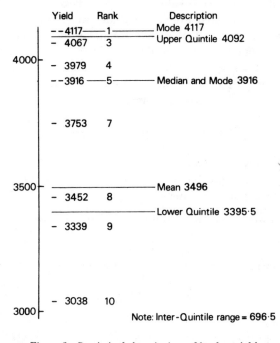

Fig. 2.6 Statistical description of barley yields
(based on Table 2.6)

In a normal distribution the mean, median and mode are all represented by the same value. (Look back at Fig. 2.2.)

MEASURES OF DISPERSION

In addition to identifying the central tendency of data, it is equally important to know how wide ranging such data may be. The worthlessness of the mean temperature of Verkhoyansk $(-17 \cdot 5°C)$ is renowned since the range extends from 15°C in July to −50°C in January.

Two ways are suggested of measuring dispersion: the standard deviation which indicates the spread or cluster of data about the mean, and the inter-percentile range which performs a similar function for the median value.

1. The Standard Deviation

This is the strongest measure of dispersion because it takes into account all the numerical values. If the standard deviation is small then values are clustered around the mean, but if it is large then wide differences are indicated. None of the standard deviations in Table 2.7 is large, but it is still possible to say that there is a greater fluctuation in oats yields in the south east than in the north west.

Determining the standard deviation with the help of an electronic calculator is easy. The formula to use is:

$$\text{Standard deviation} = \sqrt{\frac{\Sigma(x - \bar{x})^2}{n}}$$

where x is the value of an item

$\bar{x}$ is the mean value of all the items

n is the number of items.

It is expedient to tabulate this calculation as indicated below

Table 2.8
Pro-forma for the Calculation of the Standard Deviation

x	$x - \bar{x}$	$(x - \bar{x})^2$

Total

Calculate the mean and standard deviation for oats yields in Table 2.6.

2. The Inter-Percentile Range

This is a simple and quickly obtained measure of dispersion, but as may be expected it is a much coarser measure than the standard deviation. Normally an array is arranged in rank order and divided into four parts each containing an equal number of values. It is then said to be divided into quartiles. The one containing the highest values is called the upper quartile, the one with the lowest values is the lower quartile. To obtain the upper quartile value, calculate the mean of the lowest value in the upper quartile and the one below it. Similarly the lower quartile value is the mean of the highest value in the lower quartile and the value immediately above it.

The difference between the upper and lower quartiles is called the *inter-quartile range*. The lower its value, the less dispersed are the data.

The array may be divided into any number of equal parts each with the same percentage of the *number* of values. This is termed *percentile*. Look at Fig. 2.6. There are ten values here so that they may be divided into five equal parts to form quintiles. The procedure described in the preceding paragraph was employed to obtain the inter-quintile range of 696·5.

VARIABILITY OF DATA

A measure of variability for a particular set of data is provided by the standard deviation. Whilst standard deviations between data sets may be directly compared, a more sophisticated measure is to derive an index which reduces the two data sets to a comparable base. One such index is the coefficient of variation calculated by the formula

$$\text{coefficient of variation} = \frac{\text{standard deviation}}{\text{mean}} \times 100$$

For example, using the agricultural data in Table 2.6, the value for barley is:

$$\text{coefficient of variation} = \frac{378}{3496} \times 100 = 10·8$$

The lower this value the less variable are the data. Calculate the coefficient of variation for oats yields in Table 2.6. How does it compare with that for barley?

TRENDS IN DATA

One of the aims of contemporary geography is to predict what may happen in the future. If one can establish whether or not crop yields are improving, calculate the rate at which they are improving, then an estimate of future expectations may be made based upon valid evidence. This detection of trends is an important function of all statistical analysis and you may well be familiar with governmental forecasts from population census data. Such a trend may be difficult to identify unless running means are calculated.

Look at Table 2.9. Is it possible to detect a trend in potato yields from the data in column 3?

A simple way of drawing a trend line is to divide the time span into two halves and to determine the mean value for each half. This is shown in column 4 of Table 2.9. Assign each value to the middle year of its respective time span (1962, 1972) and plot them on a graph. Draw a straight line through the two points as shown in Fig. 2.7. Although this reveals an overall increase in yield in the twenty years since 1957, clearly there are marked fluctuations from time to time as shown in the continuous line in Fig. 2.7. Do these irregularities have a pattern? Counting the sequence of occurrences above and below the trend line indicates that short spells of two poor years are usually followed by three or four better ones.

Table 2.9
Potato Yields (tonnes/hectare) 1957–1977

	Yield	3 Year moving mean	
1957	19·3		
58	17·8	19·8	
59	22·3	20·9	
1960	22·8	23·2	
61	24·6	24·2	
62	25·1	24·6	Mean 1957–67:23·9
63	24·1	24·6	
64	24·6	25·8	
65	28·6	26·7	
66	26·8	27·4	
67	26·8	26·5	
68	25·8	26·2	
69	26·1	27·2	
1970	29·6	28·9	
71	30·9	30·1	Mean 1967–77: 29·7
72	29·9	31·1	
73	32·6	32·1	
74	33·9	32·9	
75	32·1	30·8	
76	26·3	30·3	
77	32·6		

A finer measure of any cyclical pattern may be achieved by using *moving means* which smooth out irregularities and stress only major fluctuations. Moving means are calculated by the mean of groups of successive and overlapping years. Usually groups of 3, 5 or 10 years are chosen. In the example here, a 3 year span was selected. Values for 1957, 1958 and 1959 were added and a mean of 19.8 obtained. This was allocated to the middle year, 1958, as shown in Table 2.9, column 3. Using the values for 1958, 1959 and 1960 as the second step, the procedure was repeated for each successive year throughout the table.

The comparison between the mean and moving mean is shown on Fig. 2.7. Does the finer measure indicate that one may reasonably

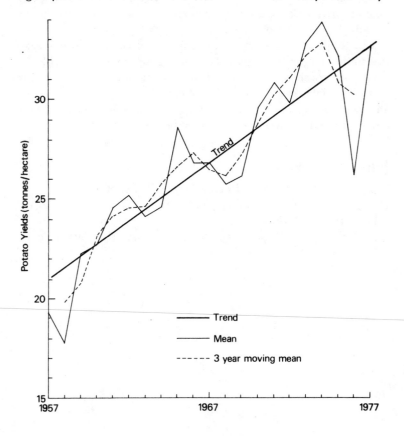

Fig. 2.7   Annual potato yields showing mean and moving mean

expect markedly longer periods of high and increasing yields inter-
rupted by only one or two poorer successive seasons? So a pattern
and a problem have been highlighted to which you may return after
reading Chapter 4.

In order to test the value of this technique for yourself, turn to
the data in Table 4.12 on page 68. Draw a graph similar to Fig. 2.7
for either precipitation or wheat yields.

Summary

It is hoped that the methods of data collection and processing which
you will frequently need to use have been explained in this chapter.
Should further elaboration be required, you are recommended to
consult the texts listed below.

The important guideline to remember is that **statistical
methods are subservient to your geographical problem.**
Your energies should be devoted to thinking about such problems
and not to laborious numerical calculation. Wherever possible use
an electronic calculating machine, or if you are fortunate, a computer terminal to minimise what soon become very dull routines.

Further Reading

Ebdon, David (1977) *Statistics in Geography.* Blackwell.
Hammond, R. and McCullagh, P. S. (1974) *Quantitative Techniques
in Geography.* OUP.
Siegel, S. (1956) *Nonparametric Statistics for the Behavioral Sciences.*
McGraw-Hill.

3. Farming I — System and Pattern

Variety of Farming Types

Farms vary in scale from the small peasant holding upon which food for the family is grown to the enormous collectives of the USSR providing food and raw materials for the nation, and in some cases for international trade.

Crops grown and animals kept vary with climatic type, physical terrain and cultural background. Methods used may depend upon technological know-how, experience of farmers and capital availability. This diversity of farming on the earth's surface is illustrated by the following two descriptions, one of which refers to conditions in India and the other in New Zealand:

> Ploughing, for example, was done with great labour using a three-inch point set in a wooden share. Irrigation required drawing up one bucket at a time: a week's labour by three men and two oxen was needed to irrigate a single acre of wheat. Sickles the size of a man's hand were used for harvesting all the grain, and the grain was threshed under the slow treading of the hooves of oxen.
>
> *Source:* McKim Marriott, 'Technological Change in Over-developed Rural Areas,' in Lyle W. Shannon, ed., *Underdeveloped Areas.*

> Many a New Zealand dairyman never sees the milk he handles. Machine milkers transfer it from the cow by pipe to a tank truck, which transports it to the factory where it is pasteurized, tested for butterfat, and pooled into a general supply received by a factory, which may produce 35 tons of butter a day. The farmer works with mechanical appliances – trucks, tractors, electric fences, hay mowers, tedders, stackers, and ditchdiggers. On broken country, aeroplanes are used for fertilization and seeding by air and even for dropping fencing materials in high country.
>
> *Source:* John B. Condliffe, 'New Zealand,' in Adamantics Pepelasis, Leon Mears and Irma Adelman, eds., *Economic Development.*

An early attempt to classify farming types was made by Derwent Whittlesey in 1936 and with minor modifications it persists today. You may recognise some of his terms as chapter headings in economic geography text books which you have used: nomadic herding, intensive subsistence tillage with rice dominant, commercial grain farming. Is it then possible to identify the elements and linkages of farming to form a system as outlined in Chapter 1? Such a system should be applicable to all types and scales of farming from shifting cultivation to commercial grain growing; from nomadic herding to commercial dairying.

The Farming System

Look at Fig. 3.1 which summarises the elements and linkages of a farming system which is applicable to any scale of operation in any given context. Some of the terms will be unfamiliar to you, but by referring back to this key diagram as you read the following section on farming, you should at the end recognise its value.

Possible uses of the land are limited to a greater or lesser extent by the three groups of elements: physical, economic and cultural. Selection from the choices available is a most complex decision-making process dependent in part upon *behavioural* elements which are really those factors conditioning how man behaves in given situations. Also important contributors to the decision-making are *stochastic* (or chance) elements and the *perception* level of the decision-maker. Decisions result in actions which are expressed in definite patterns of land use. Such patterns may prove rewarding and result in wealth or may be disastrous with accompanying poverty. These differing consequences of the farming pattern thus generate *feedback* into the system. Wealth normally creates an economic surplus which in turn may be channelled to responsible experiment which encourages such innovations as the introduction of barley beef and milking parlours. Poverty allows no such experimentation. It is this polarisation which was described in the two contrasting accounts at the beginning of this chapter.

If you are familiar with the elements and linkages within the farming system, you will understand the sequence and structure of the later chapters on agriculture, where the more important elements are elaborated and their roles discussed.

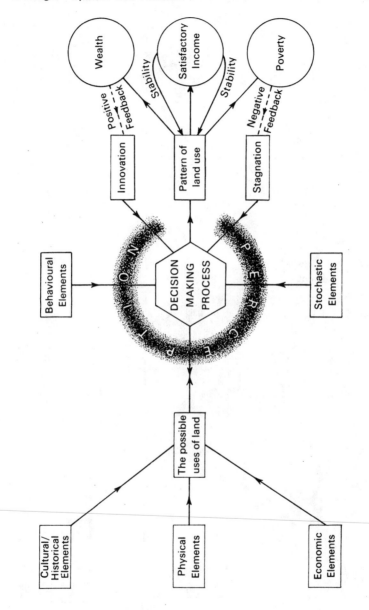

Fig. 3.1 The Farming System

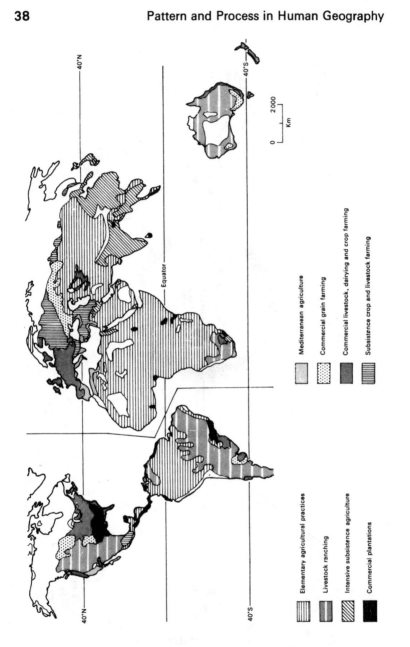

Fig. 3.2 Major agricultural regions of the world (*based on Whittlesey's classification*)

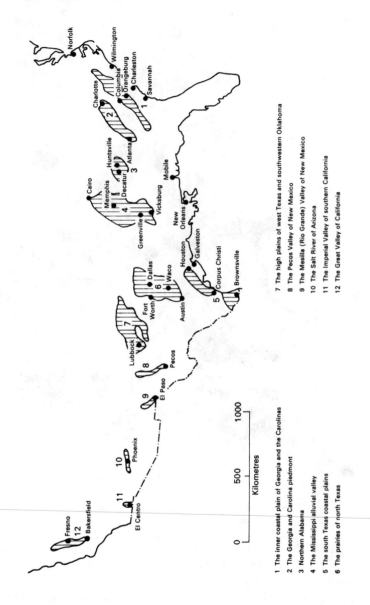

1 The inner coastal plain of Georgia and the Carolinas
2 The Georgia and Carolina piedmont
3 Northern Alabama
4 The Mississippi alluvial valley
5 The south Texas coastal plains
6 The prairies of north Texas
7 The high plains of west Texas and southwestern Oklahoma
8 The Pecos Valley of New Mexico
9 The Mesilla (Rio Grande) Valley of New Mexico
10 The Salt River of Arizona
11 The Imperial Valley of southern California
12 The Great Valley of California

Fig. 3.3 Major cotton growing areas in the U.S.A. (*Morgan, W. B. and Munton, R. J. C., Agricultural Geography*)

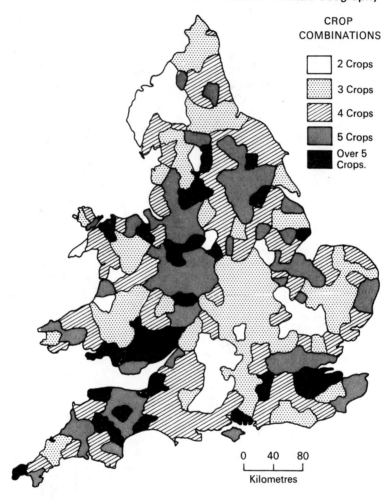

Fig. 3.4   Crop combinations in England and Wales (*Coppock, J. T., An Agricultural Atlas of Great Britain*)

PATTERNS OF LAND USE

The spatial distribution of farming activity is the starting point of any geographical enquiry. Thus the initial requirement is to identify patterns of farming which may be expressed in many differing ways on a variety of scales. Pattern is linked closely to classification and the selected criteria upon which such a classification is based. Its impact is related to both scale and style of presentation.

Examples of a variety of scales and styles are included in this section and you are asked to examine their merits and limitations carefully as you proceed.

As distribution maps are common in modern atlases you may already be familiar with world patterns of particular crops and animals. A generalised world pattern – that of Whittlesey referred to earlier — is shown in Fig. 3.2. The 'regional' divisions here are

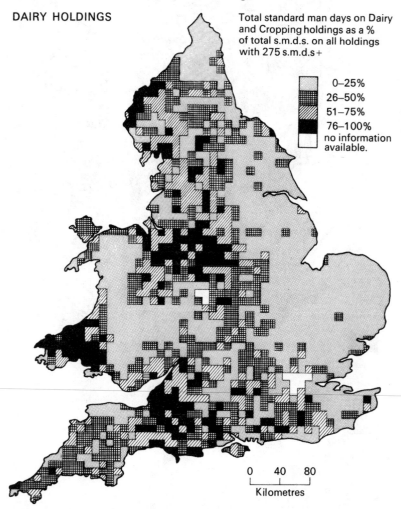

Fig. 3.5 Dairy holdings in England and Wales (*Ministry of Agriculture, Types of Farming in England and Wales*)

essentially based upon crop and livestock combinations, methods of farming used and whether or not the products are consumed by the grower or sold for cash.

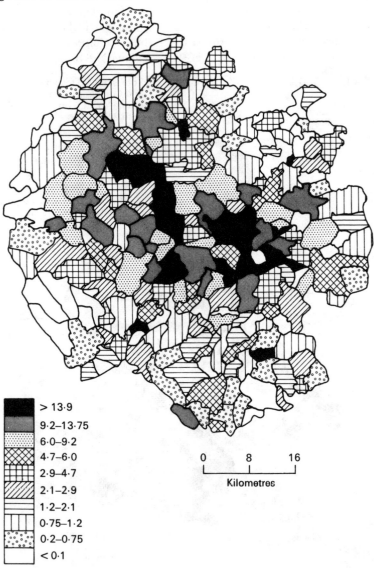

Fig. 3.6(A)   Density of cider apple production in Herefordshire (tonnes/ hundred hectares)

> 9·2 tonnes per 100 hectares
1·2–9·2
< 1·2

0   8   16
Kilometres

Fig. 3.6(B) Zones of decreasing intensity of cider apple production in Herefordshire

At national level, the pattern of a well-known crop is often depicted as in Fig. 3.3. This has been drawn subjectively from a number of regional texts and merely indicates where cotton growing is concentrated. It gives no information about the strength of this concentration, nor of the importance of cotton growing compared with other crops also grown within the shaded areas.

For England and Wales, Coppock has produced a whole series of maps many of which are *choropleth* maps indicating a measured value for a particular distribution. Examples from his *Agricultural Atlas* include: land tenure, size of holdings, proportions of crop acreages in different sized holdings, value of land, mechanisation and employment structure. Of particular interest are his maps of crop combinations, a simple example of which is shown in Fig. 3.4. Because of its generalised nature, this map can give only an indication of regional specialisation; other more sophisticated maps constructed by Coppock should be examined.

The Ministry of Agriculture has published a series of 'Type of Farming' maps for England and Wales such as the one shown in Fig. 3.5. This map was produced by quadrat sampling methods, 1/6th of the holdings in each 10 km grid square being investigated. The criteria used to determine the relative importance of dairying is the amount of time spent on the enterprise. Labour is measured by the term 'standard man day' a term which is explained in Chapter 5 on page 93. In the areas shaded black on Fig. 3.5, between 76% and 100% of the measured labour on the farm is devoted to dairying.

How does the level of information for the distribution of dairying in England and Wales compare with that for cotton growing in the USA in Fig. 3.3?

On a more localised scale, a single crop may be portrayed by dots or in a choropleth map such as Fig. 3.6 where the density of production is shown. This eradicates the problem of differing sizes of unit for which the information, upon which the map is based, was originally supplied – in this case the parish. What are the relative merits of a choropleth compared with a dot distribution map?

Occasionally a map may be so detailed as to defeat attempts to detect a general trend. Perhaps this is true in Fig. 3.6A which has been simplified into three zones in Fig. 3.6B by reducing the number of categories and regrouping them. The value of this exercise will be revealed in Chapter 5.

Patterns of farming in a region are sometimes available in reports from agricultural institutes such as that for the Eastern Counties produced by the Cambridge University School of Agriculture. A sample survey was carried out and farms subsequently classified according to type of enterprise such as grain and dairy. From the distribution of these farm types it was possible to delimit 'type of farm' areas as indicated in Fig. 3.7 where more than 50% or 70% of the farms belonged to a particular category.

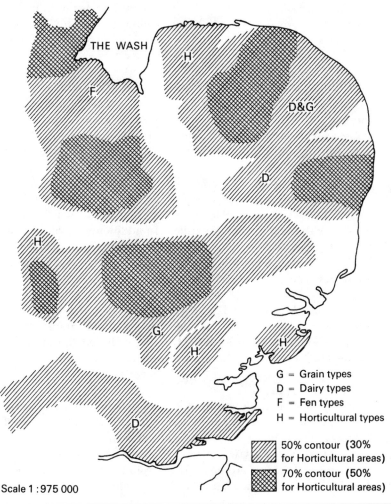

THE WASH

H

F

D&G

D

H

G

H

H

D

G = Grain types
D = Dairy types
F = Fen types
H = Horticultural types

50% contour (30%
for Horticultural areas)

70% contour (50%
for Horticultural areas)

Scale 1 : 975 000

Fig. 3.7 Type of farm areas in the Eastern Counties (*Cambridge University, School of Agriculture, Occasional Paper No. 8*)

Implicit in many of the pattern maps has been the idea of an agricultural region. Some ambiguity is associated with this term and its meaning in a context should be clarified. Region may be interpreted as an area in which the bulk of a particular activity is contained, for example, the cotton growing region in Fig. 3.3. Equally it may be interpreted as the area in which a particular activity is the dominant form of land use as implied in Fig. 3.7.

What is perhaps more significant is to identify an agglomerated or clustered pattern as in Fig. 3.6A. Such a homogeneous area presents a problem of explanation, and investigation may be profitably focused upon it, as is shown later in Chapter 5.

PATTERN BUILDING IN ENGLAND AND WALES

It is possible to construct your own pattern of farming either through original fieldwork within a small area – especially if transects or point samples are employed – or you may wish to use data which have already been collected either as statistics or as published maps.

If you are constructing your map through local fieldwork, then it is sensible to use the same classification as that employed in the Second Land Utilisation Survey so that your results will be comparable with maps already published. In addition you will be able to up-date an existing map, noting in particular any change in permanent crops and possibly inserting farm boundaries which were a sad omission in the official survey.

STATISTICAL SOURCES

Two major data sources are available: Agricultural Statistics and the June Annual Census Returns. Both are collected and compiled by the Ministry of Agriculture, Fisheries and Food.

Agricultural Statistics

This volume contains a wealth of information about crop acreages and numbers of livestock together with their yields and the sizes of holdings. There is a special horticultural section. It is from this volume that Table 2.5 was extracted. Unfortunately the smallest unit for which values are given is the county and therefore their usefulness in small scale enquiry is distinctly limited.

June Census Returns

In June of each year, farmers send details of their crops, livestock and labour force to the Ministry. These details are aggregated to form parish statistics although in some instances where very few farms are involved, two parishes may be joined together. Those for recent years are normally held in the local office of the Agricultural Development and Advisory Service (A.D.A.S.). It is usually possible for a serious student to gain access to these records. Alternatively you may apply to the central office at Guildford where a copy of a particular extract will be made for a nominal fee. From such returns it is possible to construct maps for a particular enterprise or relevant combination of enterprises. In no circumstances is it possible to obtain information about a specific farm.

Despite certain limitations of these statistics which arise from the time of year at which the returns are made and the basis upon which they are collected and aggregated, they are the only record available and for most purposes may be regarded as acceptably reliable.

The Second Land Utilisation Map
The mammoth task of mapping the land use of Great Britain on a scale of 1:25000 has been undertaken since 1960 by Dr. Alice Coleman aided by a vast army of volunteers. Many sheets of this inventory, containing more than 70 categories of usage, have now been published. It is a pity that farm boundaries were omitted from the survey and no indication of crop changes could be included. The ways in which these maps may be used for hypothesis testing are explained in the next chapter. How may they now be used to identify farming patterns?

Methods varying in complexity such as those already outlined may be applied to the maps which are conveniently divided into grid squares or quadrats. The following suggestions may be helpful:

To identify one category of land use, for example, grassland.
1. Cover that part of the map in which you are interested with tracing paper.
2. Examine each grid square in turn and label it 1 if grassland is present or 0 if absent.
   or using tracing graph paper, label with a suitable key those squares with > 50%, 25–50%, < 25% of grassland.
3. Delimit areas of differing intensity.

To identify combinations such as arable and market gardening repeat the procedures outlined above *or* for each square count the number of activities significantly present (say occupying 10% of the area of the square) within each square to produce a classification similar to that in Fig. 3.4. Other methods to recognise 'scapes' are explained by Dr. Coleman in her article in *Geography* as listed below.

It is at this point that you may wish to review the various methods illustrated in this chapter and to evaluate their usefulness and relevance to a scientific geographer. Several questions which may profitably be asked are:

1. How does the level of information presented in the maps contained in this chapter differ? Is this level related to scale or style or both?
2. How carefully and upon what basis are the criteria for classification selected? How helpful is this classification to a geographer?
3. What spatial problems do the patterns pose?

Remember that patterns are not an end product in themselves but form a basis from which to investigate the problems they inevitably generate.

Further Reading

Chisholm, M. (1962) *Rural Settlement and Land Use.* Hutchinson.

Coleman, A. (1969) 'A geographical model for land use analysis'. *Geography*, vol. 54, no. 242, pages 43–55.

Coppock, J. T. (1971) *An Agricultural Atlas of Great Britain.* Faber.

Morgan, W. B. and Munton, R. J. C. (1971) *Agricultural Geography.* Methuen.

Walker, Michael. (1977) *Agricultural Location.* Blackwell.

ACCESSIBLE SOURCES OF AGRICULTURAL DATA

British Maps

1″ Land Use Maps: remaining sheets of inter-war survey in reference libraries.

2½″ Land Use Maps. Although not all sheets are published, the survey has been completed and unpublished maps are held at the London School of Economics.

1″ Agricultural Land Classification Maps. Land grade 1–5 according to agricultural potential.

1″ Series of Soil Survey Maps – partial coverage only.

2½″ Series of Soil Survey Maps – partial coverage only.

Atlases

Oxford Economic Atlas.

Agricultural Atlas of England and Wales – J. T. Coppock.

National Atlases: for example, The United States, An Atlas of Saskatchewan.

Statistics

Great Britain

Agricultural Statistics compiled by Ministry of Agriculture, Fisheries and Food: county summaries of all aspects of agriculture.

Parish Statistics available at local A.D.A.S. office or from Ministry of Agriculture, Epsom Road, Guildford.

Generalised statistics are contained in *A Century of Agricultural Statistics 1866–1966*. H.M.S.O.

Detailed economic statistics are to be found in many management handbooks. For example, *Farm Management Handbook*. Economics Department, University of Bristol.

The World

World Food and Agricultural Organisation: Production Yearbook provides details of major crops for each country: area, production and yields. Also contains details of livestock numbers, farm machines and prices obtained for crops and animals.

F.A.O. Trade Yearbook itemises principal agricultural exports and imports for each country on a quantitative basis.

4. Farming II — Physical Elements

The search for explanation of landscape patterns has long been the task of the geographer. Once a pattern of crop or animal farming has been satisfactorily identified (as outlined in Chapter 3) then a scientific approach may be taken to help find reasons for this particular distribution which are in Harvey's terms both 'reasonable and satisfying'.

The interaction between man and his environment is perhaps the oldest principle upon which modern geography rests. Although it is less fashionable these days to study environmental influences, they remain dominant in regions of physical extremity and retain a role in any context. Work from the past suggests four significant elements which influence land use: altitude, slope, soil type and climate. Examples of methods for testing single hypotheses related to those forces will be outlined below, but before doing so, an important relationship between pattern and process must be introduced.

Optima and Limits Schema

Look at Fig. 4.1 which shows an adaptation of a model devised by McCarty and Lindberg. This 'optima and limits' model introduces an important concept in agriculture, namely that of optimum or best location as in industry. Within a circumscribed area, physical elements combine to provide optimum growing conditions for a particular crop, for example, wheat in the Prairies. As you move away from this optimum location, conditions begin to deteriorate – terrain becomes more broken, climate drier and/or colder and soil type changes – so that profitable pursuit of the particular activity diminishes. Eventually a point is reached where production is no longer possible because of the adversity of the physical elements. McCarty and Lindberg have shown how this structure may be applied to the cotton growing area of the USA (Fig. 4.1). Try to

50

THE MODEL

PROCESS

PATTERN

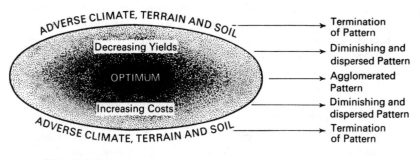

ADVERSE CLIMATE, TERRAIN AND SOIL ⟶ Termination of Pattern

Decreasing Yields ⟶ Diminishing and dispersed Pattern

OPTIMUM → Agglomerated Pattern

Increasing Costs ⟶ Diminishing and dispersed Pattern

ADVERSE CLIMATE, TERRAIN AND SOIL ⟶ Termination of Pattern

——— Limit of Cultivation

REALITY

COTTON GROWING IN THE SOUTH

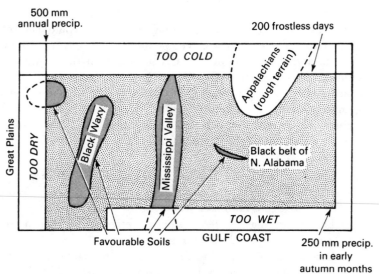

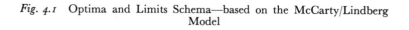

Fig. 4.1 Optima and Limits Schema—based on the McCarty/Lindberg Model

apply this yourself to spring wheat growing in the Prairies.

The implications of this model are important because they emphasise that although optimum conditions may be restricted to a smaller area, growing a particular crop in sub-optimal conditions will nonetheless take place, albeit with diminished intensity. This decrease of intensity with increasing distance, called the concept *gradient*, is one of the basic ideas in geography which we shall constantly meet. Gradient influences the level of acceptability of an hypothesis. You should not necessarily expect clear cut answers, but rather ones which reflect the wider permissiveness of physical elements than has hitherto been recognised in geography. In a recent study of Deeside, Davidson concluded that even in a physically diverse area, relief and soil exerted only minor limitations on farming. In the examples of hypothesis testing which follow, attention is confined to the evaluation of a single variable rather than the multi-variate approach in more advanced work, such as that of Hewes which is also included. However, in carrying out your own tests on single items, it is important to realise that the factor you are considering is not the only one to which land use problems are related.

Testing the hypothesis that land use is related to altitude
Within any climatic zone, height above sea level partially controls the severity of the elements. Temperature decreases as altitude increases and thus an upper limit is placed upon the growing of certain crops. In Britain such a limit for hay and potatoes is normally regarded as 330 m whereas in the Himalayas wheat and barley ripen at 3000 m.

Using the current 1:25000 Land Utilisation Maps the relationship between use and altitude may easily be tested by the following procedure:

1. Choose a map which has a marked variation in altitude.
2. Establish a 100 random point sample and for each point record its altitude and land use.
3. The results may be plotted on a scatter graph such as the partially completed one in Fig. 4.2.
4. Determine the mean altitude and the altitudinal range for each of your land use categories as shown in Tables 4.1 and 4.2.

Evaluating the evidence
1. Examine your scattergraph and note whether or not there seems to be an optimum altitude range for a specific type of use.

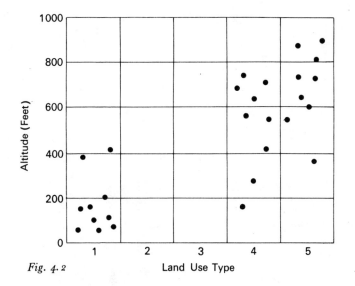

Fig. 4.2 Land Use Type

Can you detect a gradient effect from such an optimum? For example, in Fig. 4.2 most of the market gardening (1) is found between 100 and 200 feet yet the range is from 50–400 feet. The range indicates the limits of the McCarty model within the context of this investigation.

2. Compare your mean and range values with those in Tables 4.1 and 4.2. Examine these tables and your own results and attempt to make a general statement about the relationship of land use with altitude. In Wales the classical zonation of usage is revealed, although this is not so in other regions. Whilst woodland normally occurs at higher altitudes than market gardening, this is more true for some regions than others.

Clearly no firm conclusions can be drawn from limited evidence and minimal analysis, but even now it is possible to detect that forces other than altitude play a large part in determining land use.

Testing the hypothesis that land use is related to slope

Early attention of geographers focused on the degree of slope as being significant. However, with modern technology this importance is waning. Today a 6° slope represents few problems and even those of 11° (gradient 1 : 5) may be ploughed and cut. In Southern Europe

Table 4.1

Altitudinal range for categories of land use based on 100 point random sample in each of the named regions

Region	Market gardening	Arable	Pastoral	Woodland	Heath	Settlement	Other
			Land use				
N.E. England	150–400	75–575	50–700	75–700	25–400	25–200	20–450
Wales	425–550	250–700	50–1000	350–1700	50–2900	50–525	100–3300
N. Midlands	300–550	150–525	250–900	250–650	350–600	250–700	250–650
S. Midlands	50–250	25–950	25–850	50–900	350–650	100–700	50–900
Fen Margin	10–75	10–275	10–250	10–150	175–225	25–100	10–275

Table 4.2

Mean altitude of land use categories in each of the named regions

Region	Market gardening	Arable	Pastoral	Woodland	Heath	Settlement	Other
N.E. England	261	313	264	396	263	196	90
Wales	300	446	516	809	1262	375	1017
N. Midlands	509	324	416	447	461	404	441
S. Midlands	358	451	396	494	500	425	220
Fen Margin	19	85	70	58	212	72	18

Altitudes expressed in feet as on Land Utilisation Maps.

and Asia problems of very steep slopes are overcome by terracing.

It is more profitable to regard aspect of the slope as more significant, since micro-climate is critically affected by aspect. It is
customary to contrast the 'adret' or sunny slopes growing cereals
with the wooded 'ubac' or shady slopes of Alpine valleys. In view of
what has been said earlier, it is perhaps unrealistic to expect slopes
to be prohibitive in their usage. Instead, they should be regarded as
showing a tendency to favour some activities rather than others.
Once again the land utilisation map may be used as the basic data
upon which to test our hypothesis.

Procedure
1. Establish a specific hypothesis: land use patterns on north
   facing slopes differ markedly from those on south facing slopes.
2. Decide the detail of the enquiry and establish the classification
   to be employed – for example, that in Table 4.3.
3. Select maps containing north and south facing slopes and
   generate a stratified random point sample of 25 or 50 points for
   each of these two aspects.
4. Record the results and summarise them in a table such as
   shown in Table 4.3.
5. Analyse the results and decide upon the validity of the original
   hypothesis by answering such questions as:

   Which categories of land use definitely occur more frequently
   overall on south facing slopes?
   Are there any particular areas where the tendency is much
   stronger or weaker than others?
   What kinds of land use appear more tolerant of slope aspect?

Even this unsophisticated way of validating evidence may lead you
to challenge a generalised assumption you may formerly have held
and spur you on to collect more substantial evidence and subject it to
more rigorous statistical methods of analysis to which we now turn.

Testing the hypothesis that cropland is associated with lowland
The importance of a flat terrain for crop growing, especially with the
increasing use of mechanisation, has often been stressed. Hence by
implication we assume cropland to be concentrated in the lowland.
The data to test this hypothesis have been extracted from a proposed
advanced level question on agriculture in which you were asked to

Table 4.3

Land use and slope aspect based upon a 50 point stratified random sample for north and south facing slopes in each region

Region	Market gardening		Arable		Pastoral		Woodland		Heath		Settlement		Other	
Aspect of slope L.U. map	N.	S.	N.	S.	N.	S.	N.	S.	N.	S.	N.	S.	N.	S.
Yarmouth, I.O.W.	6	9	10	16	11	13	6	4	6	4	6	2	5	2
Coldstream	3	5	19	18	19	14	1	4	6	4	2	3	0	2
Durham	1	1	15	25	15	15	8	5	3	3	6	1	2	0
Monmouth	4	6	9	10	14	14	12	11	2	1	3	6	6	2
Caernarvon	0	1	4	3	24	24	7	6	11	5	2	5	2	6
Total	14	22	57	72	83	80	34	30	28	17	19	17	15	12

use *Spearman Rank Correlation* techniques. The aim of this procedure is to establish whether or not there is a significant *mathematical* relationship between two sets of data. The result will not tell us whether or not this is a *causal* one. The sequence of steps for applying this method are set out below together with a completed worksheet Table 4.4. Follow this step by step, checking in the table because you will be asked to use this method later.

Table 4.4

Column 1 Province	Column 2 % lowland	Column 3 % cropland	Column 4 rank lowland	Column 5 rank cropland	Column 6 d	Column 7 d^2
Sicily						
Trapani	83	86	1	4	−3	9
Palermo	40	76	11	7	+4	16
Messina	23	51	12	9	+3	9
Agrigento	73	87	5	3	+2	4
Caltanissetta	71	91	6	2	+4	16
Enna	52	80	8	6	+2	4
Catania	50	74	9	8	+1	1
Ragusa	74	93	4	1	+3	9
Siracusa	79	85	2·5	5	−2·5	6·25
Sardinia						
Sassari	64	38	7	11	−4	16
Nuoro	44	19	10	12	−2	4
Cagliari	79	47	2·5	10	−7·5	56·25
						150·5

Source: Annuario Statistico Italiana 1961, Rome 1962.

Step 1. It is statistically necessary to state the hypothesis in negative terms and call it the *null* hypothesis. (In this case: there is no relationship between lowland and cropland.) Our aim is to reject this null hypothesis upon the basis of the evidence and then we shall be able to accept the alternative hypothesis – viz. 'there is a relationship between lowland and cropland'.

Step 2. Place in rank order the percentages of lowland in column 2 and enter the rank order in column 4. *Note:* When two values are tied then the sum of the two ranks is divided equally between them. For example, Siracusa and Cagliari are 2nd equal and so their rank value is 2·5 each. Similarly, this procedure of using the average rank is also used when three or more values are tied.

Provided there are not too many tied rank values they may safely be ignored. Should your exercise contain many such values then the formula needs a corrective to be applied (see Siegel, *Non-Parametric Statistics*, pages 206–207). Normally the proportion of tied values is small enough to be ignored.

Step 3. Place in rank order the percentages of cropland and enter the values in column 5.

Step 4. Enter the difference in rank order between the two variables (*ie.* % lowland and % cropland) in column 6.

Step 5. Square the values in column 6 and enter in column 7.

Step 6. Apply the formula:

$$r_s = 1 - \frac{6\Sigma d^2}{(n^3 - n)}$$

where r_s = coefficient of correlation

d^2 = difference in ranking squared

n = number of items ranked

Σ (big sigma) = sum (add up) the items which follow it in the formula.

$$r_s = 1 - \frac{6 \times 150·5}{12^3 - 12} = 1 - \frac{903}{1716} = 0·474.$$

$$r_s = +0·474.$$

Step 7. The r_s value will range between +1 and −1 and the closeness of approximation to 1 is a measure of the strength of the relationship between the two variables. A value of +1 indicates a perfect positive correlation whilst that of −1 reveals a completely inverse relationship. In reality most values fall within the range rather than at its extremities and therefore it is necessary to see whether or not the value is statistically significant, *ie.* that the result has not arisen by chance. The r_s value is related to the number of items ranked (n) and a table indicating statistically valid results for differing values of n is given in Appendix II on page 322. Values are given for two confidence levels – 95% and 99%. You will recall from the work on sampling that 95% confidence level means that the answer is likely not to occur by chance 95 times out of 100 (page 24).

Step 8. If the result is a valid one then you can with confidence reject the null hypothesis and by corollary accept the hypothesis, namely that cropland is associated with lowland. In this particular example you will have discovered that the coefficient value of +0·474 is not statistically significant (the lowest value where $n = 12$ being 0·506) so that the null hypothesis cannot be rejected with confidence.

Step 9. Think out the *geographical* implications of your result and take appropriate action. Helpful suggestions for implementing this step are indicated below.

Consider the characteristics of the area being investigated. What is the nature of its terrain? What is the nature of its agriculture? How backward are the methods on undercapitalised small peasant holdings? In addition to information which you may find in your regional texts you may find the table of data on Canicatti on page 94 helpful. Are the data used in this exercise representative of the national situation in Italy? In Table 4.5 is listed similar statistical information for the 40 provinces of Northern Italy. Using these data and the same method re-test the hypothesis. What result do you find and what lessons about the nature of original data must be learned? Before re-testing the hypothesis you may be encouraged by ·the results obtained by Hidore in his investigation of the relationship between grain farming and the distribution of level land in the Mid-West. His coefficient value of +0·743 where $n = 72$ was significant at the 99% confidence level. What is your value for Northern Italy? Is it possible to make a general statement incorporating the findings of Hidore and yourself?

Testing the hypothesis that land use is related to soil type
Ultimately agricultural production depends upon the soil – its texture, depth and composition all having a part to play. The influence of soil is normally discussed in a broad context such as the terra roxa of the coffee lands in Brazil or the black earths of the USSR. An account of the agricultural productivity of the world's soils is contained in Thoman's *Geography of Economic Activity*. However, it is possible to test the hypothesis upon data collected within a small study area. Two differing examples are included for you to work through.

Fig. 3.6A showed the distribution of cider apple production in Herefordshire.

Table 4.5

Percentages of Lowland and Cropland in the Provinces
of Northern Italy

Province	Low-land	Crop-land	Province	Low-land	Crop-land
01 Torino	41	28	21 Bolzano	0	7
02 Vercelli	56	45	22 Trento	0	8
03 Novara	30	22	23 Verona	74	68
04 Cuneo	40	35	24 Vicenza	49	46
05 Asti	68	76	25 Belluno	0	5
06 Alessandria	70	66	26 Treviso	88	72
07 Aosta	0	3	27 Venezia	100	70
08 Imperia	27	25	28 Padova	97	85
09 Savona	25	21	29 Rovigo	100	79
10 Genova	11	22	30 Udine	52	30
11 La Spezia	41	25	31 Gorizia	96	44
12 Varese	53	26	32 Trieste	67	15
13 Como	23	17	33 Piacenza	52	62
14 Sondrio	0	3	34 Parma	46	51
15 Milano	99	70	35 Reggio E.	60	61
16 Bergamo	33	29	36 Modena	59	71
17 Brescia	39	36	37 Bologna	67	69
18 Pavia	85	72	38 Ferrara	100	78
19 Cremona	100	82	39 Ravenna	94	81
20 Mantova	97	84	40 Forli	63	67

Source: Annuario Statistico Italiana 1961

Whilst some crops are noted for being choosy about soil type –
especially those which prefer lime – others are remarkably tolerant.
The cider apple tree is in this latter category, and it may therefore
be expected that no preferences will be apparent. Within the former
county of Herefordshire, which is the premier producer in Britain of
such apples, there are eight soil types. These are indicated together
with their areas of tillable hectares and the number of hectares of
apple orchards contained within each soil type in Table 4.6.

If soil type had no influence upon the distribution of orchards then
one would expect these orchards to be shared between the soil types
in proportion to their area: for example, type 1 occupies 4·66% of
the tillable hectares and should therefore contain 4·66% or 110
hectares of the cider apple orchards. These values are known as the
expected values, while the actual values, for example 38, are called
the *observed* values.

Table 4.6

The Distribution of Cider Apple Orchards in Herefordshire

Soil type	Tillable (ha)	Percentage of total	Orchards (ha)	Percentage of total	Expected orchards (ha)
1	8 177	4·66	38·0	1·6	110
2	12 329	7·05	66·4	2·7	166·5
3	4 264	2·22	40·5	1·7	52·4
4	77 366	44·11	916·0	38·5	1041·4
5	116	0·05	—	0	1·2
6	850	0·48	0·2	0·01	11·3
7	52 492	29·91	686·5	29·13	706·2
8	20 176	11·50	613·75	26·11	271·5

(Soil types based on Burnham, 'The soils of Herefordshire', Wool-
hope Club Transactions, 38, 1964.)

Although by examining Table 4.6 it is possible to see the relative
attraction of certain soil types for orchards, often such relationships
are not so obvious and one may need to employ a ratio technique or
index of concentration. The simplest way of achieving such a measure is
to divide the observed value by the expected value. If the answer is
greater than 1 then the soil type has more than its share and can be
said to favour the crop. Conversely if the value is less than 1 then
there is no positive association, *eg.* such a value for soil type 1 in
Table 4.6 is:

$$\frac{\text{observed value}}{\text{expected value}} = \frac{38}{110} = 0·34.$$

Determine indices of concentration for each of the soil types in the
table. Does this enable you to make more precise statements than
previously about the association between soil type and the distribution of cider apple orchards?

The Chi-Square test
Whilst differences between the observed and expected values have
been identified, such differences could have occurred by chance. To
see whether or not this is so the *Chi-Square* (χ^2) *test* may be applied.
This method is simply a comparison to see if the relationship is
statistically significant, *ie.* there is a high probability that the
association is not a chance happening.

    The formula for the test is:

$$\chi^2 = \Sigma\frac{(O-E)^2}{E}$$

where O is the observed frequency and E the expected frequency.

As in the case of the Spearman Rank Correlation exercise it is necessary to establish the *null hypothesis* written as H_0: there is no association between land use and soil type.

Before proceeding, because of the nature of the Chi-Square distribution, there are a number of precautions to be taken:

1. The Chi-Square test is concerned with frequencies and therefore *percentage values* cannot be used.
2. The total of all the observed frequencies must be at least 20.
3. As a rough guide the expected frequency in any category should not be less than 5. So that in the example provided, soil categories 5 and 6 cannot stand alone. Furthermore there should not be such a marked discrepancy between the observed frequencies between categories, namely from 38–916. It will therefore be necessary to reduce the number of categories if this is geographically feasible. In this case the number of categories has been reduced to the three most important ones as set out in Table 4.7.

Table 4.7

Chi-Square Test

	Soil type		
	4	7	8
observed frequency	916	686	614
expected frequency	1041	706	272
observed – expected	−125	−20	342
(observed – expected)^2	15 625	400	116 964
$\dfrac{\text{(observed – expected)}^2}{E}$	15	0·7	430

$$\Sigma \frac{(O-E)^2}{E} = 446.$$

Procedure: It is useful to tabulate the information as indicated above as you proceed:

Step 1: Allocate the observed frequencies to the categories of soil type (these are controlled by the geographical situation).

Step 2: From the null hypothesis determine the expected frequency for each category.

Step 3: Re-arrange the number of categories if necessary as in Table 4.7.

Step 4: Complete the table and compute the value of Chi-Square.

Step 5: This numerical value alone is not informative until its significance is ascertained from statistical tables or the graph in Appendix III, page 322, for a given confidence level.

Step 6: Consult graph or table – remembering the degrees of freedom (df) are the number of categories minus 1; (2 df in this case).

Step 7: Either accept or reject the null hypothesis and interpret the result geographically as illustrated below.

The result of this test enables the null hypothesis to be rejected and clearly confirms that the marked association of apple growing and soil type is not a chance happening. As we shall see in the next chapter, this is only one aspect of investigating a particular problem.

It is often difficult to obtain data similar to those used for the above test, so the second example using a simple stratified random point sample could serve as a model for initiating a similar test in your own locality based on your own fieldwork. In this case rock types have been substituted for soil, but their nature is such that the soils would reflect very directly the characteristics of their parent rock.

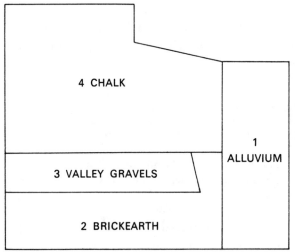

Fig. 4.3 Schematic arrangement of rock types along part of the Sussex coast

Fig. 4.3 shows in diagrammatical form the rock types of part of the

Sussex coast around Littlehampton. A 200 point stratified random survey was undertaken to test the hypothesis. A simple 4 category land use classification was employed, viz. barley, wheat, pasture and other uses. Because this was a stratified survey points were allocated to each soil type in proportion to its area. From Table 4.8 you will see Chalk occupied 50% of the total study area and hence was allocated 100 points.

Table 4.8

Distribution of Sampling Points

	% of area	No. of random points
Chalk	50	100
Brickearth	25	50
Valley gravels	15	30
Alluvium	10	20
	100	200

The results of the survey were as shown in Table 4.9.

Table 4.9

Observed Values of Land Use in Differing Rock Types

Soil type / Land use	Chalk	Brickearth	Gravel	Alluvium	Total
Barley	38	6	3	0	47
Wheat	42	32	7	2	83
Pasture	20	5	20	18	63
Others	0	7	0	0	7
Total	100	50	30	20	200

Because of the nature of Chi-Square as indicated earlier a certain amount of combining of categories will become necessary.

Table 4.10

Reclassified Observed Values

Soil type / Land use	Chalk	Brickearth	Gravel	Alluvium	Total
Cereals	80	38	10	2	130
Pasture	20	5	20	18	63
Total	100	43	30	20	193

The geographical nature of the problem immediately suggests that a two-fold land-use division be made between soils favouring cereal production and those favouring pasture: it is upon this basis that the data have been reorganised in Table 4.10.

The expected frequency of occurrence is derived from the null hypothesis H_0: that land use is not associated with soil type.

Since chalk occupies 50% of the area it is expected that 50% of each of the types of land use will be contained within it, *ie.* 50% of 130 in the case of cereals and 50% of 63 in the case of pasture. All the expected values are contained in Table 4.11.

Table 4.11

Expected Values of Land Use in each Rock Type

Soil type Land use	Chalk	Brickearth	Gravel	Alluvium	Total
Cereals	65	32·5	19·5	13·0	130
Pasture	31·5	15·75	9·45	6·3	63
Total	96·5	48·25	28·95	19·3	193

To determine the value of Chi-Square, proceed as before. On this occasion you will notice there are 4 columns and 2 rows and so there will be 3 degrees of freedom $(c-1)$ $(r-1)$. The value is 67·3 which once again is highly significant statistically.

It would seem therefore that there is sufficient evidence to reject the null hypothesis and state that the attraction of chalk and brickearth for cereal growing and gravels and alluvium for pasture is no chance happening.

The Influence of Climate upon Farming

Of all the physical elements so far considered, perhaps climate is the most important. Its impact however is difficult to measure in quantitative terms, and it may be for this reason that geographers on the whole content themselves with establishing broad limits such as those indicated for cotton growing in Fig. 4.1. One great problem is the lack of local statistics in sufficient detail or degree of sophistication. Raw climatic data are of limited value in assessing the agricultural potential of an area. For example, amount, reliability and seasonality of rainfall, although helpful, are not comprehensive enough since this rainfall must be related to evaporation rates and even more importantly, to infiltration rates since plants derive their moisture intake from the soil.

The McCarty and Lindberg model implied that the climatic range for the survival of crops is wide, but that the zone of maximum yield is much more restricted. Attention may more profitably be focused therefore upon the relationship between yields and climate, rather than re-examining the broadly defined distribution patterns found throughout the countries of the world.

Sheep are frequently grazed on pastures in the drier margins – for example, in Australia – yet their yield of meat may well be low. Symons records that in Utah experiments revealed that sheep gained 1·5 kilos when watered regularly but lost 2·8 kilos when watered every third day during a forty day period. In Chapter 2 on page 28 brief reference was made to the yield of oats in the north west compared with the north east of England. This assumed relationship between precipitation and yield is now examined for a more relevant problem, that of wheat growing in the Prairies. It should be remembered, however, that the data used suffer the limitations already outlined.

Testing the hypothesis that wheat yields in Saskatchewan are related to annual precipitation

Swift Current is a location in Saskatchewan in the great 'wheat belt' of North America. Details of the precipitation wheat yields and annual precipitation are given in Table 4.12 for a twenty year period. There are a number of ways in which these data may be used to see whether or not the hypothesis is valid.

The simplest method is shown in Fig. 4.4 where the two variables are graphed. Since yield is dependent upon precipitation, it is known as the *dependent variable* and plotted on the vertical or y axis.

Precipitation is known as the *independent variable* and is plotted on the horizontal or x axis.

On the graph it is possible to draw in by eye an overall trend line indicating that a relationship does exist. A very rough guide to help you draw in such a line is that it should pass through the mean of the x values and the mean of the y values and leave the same number of points above and below the line. More precise instructions are given in the next chapter where you are introduced to regression analysis, page 90.

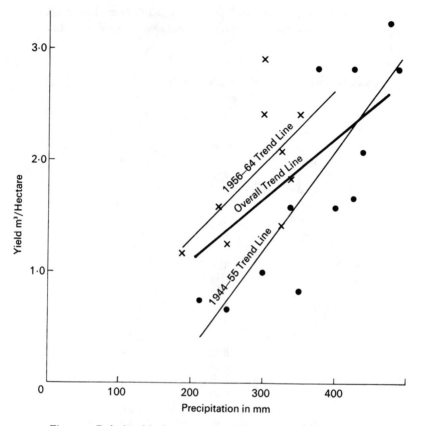

Fig. 4.4 Relationship between wheat yield and precipitation in Saskatchewan

Because of the wide scatter of points about this line it is evident that the problem must be investigated more closely. For example, when there are 305 mm of precipitation, yields vary from 1·08–3·15 m³. Inspect the data in Table 4.12 and you will find that yields are higher in relationship to precipitation after 1955 than before this date. Does this indicate that drought resistant strains are now being planted? It will be helpful to consult Dunlop's paper, listed as further reading, to discover other reasons for recently improved yields.

If these values for the years 1944–55 and 1956–64 are plotted separately, using different symbols as in Fig. 4.4, and individual trend lines drawn for the two categories, it will be seen that the scatter of points about the two lines is less in each case, thus indicating a stronger trend. However, no definite statement can yet be made on subjective evidence.

Table 4.12

Saskatchewan: Wheat Yield and Precipitation, 1944–1964, at Swift Current, Saskatchewan

Year	Precipitation in mm x values	Yields in m³ per hectare y values
1944	432	3·06
1945	254	0·72
1946	356	0·90
1947	305	1·08
1948	343	1·76
1949	216	0·81
1950	406	1·71
1951	432	1·80
1952	483	3·51
1953	381	3·06
1954	495	3·06
1955	445	2·25
1956	305	3·15
1957	305	2·61
1958	254	1·35
1959	318	2·25
1960	356	2·61
1961	191	1·26
1962	330	1·53
1963	343	1·98
1964	241	1·71

Source: Canada – A Geographical Interpretation, ed. Warkentin.

One method of analysis introduced earlier is the Spearman Rank Correlation and application of this could provide you with a statistical measure of the *strength* of the relationship between yield and precipitation and whether or not such a relationship had occurred by chance. It may well be expedient to subdivide the data into the two time periods suggested to discover whether or not the association is becoming stronger or weaker. What conclusions are you able to draw from your results?

An alternative method is to use regression analysis, full instructions for which are found in the next chapter page 90.

The influence of climatic hazard

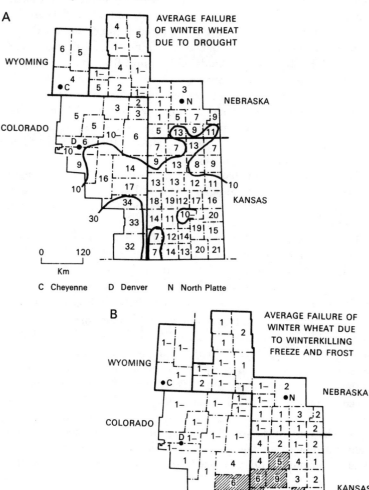

Fig. 4.5(A) and (B)   Causes of wheat failure on the Great Plains (*Hewes, L.*, *'Causes of wheat failure in the dry farming region, Central Great Plains, 1939–57'*)

The failure of the monsoon to arrive on time makes a dramatic impact upon those people dependent upon it, and through the media upon us. Equally disastrous are unexpected cyclones and floods.

On a more limited scale but very significant and dramatic are climatic hazards of several kinds on farming: frost, hail, wind and drought. Unfortunately a strong stochastic (chance) element is present in the occurrence of these hazards. Since they do not conform to a recognisable seasonal rhythm, they defy prediction. Whilst it is possible to assess the number of frost-free days for successful growing of a particular crop – 200 for cotton – the incidence of late frost may be more crucial in the final analysis.

The effects of climatic hazards is examined by Hewes who sought causes of wheat failure in the Central Great Plains between 1939 and 1957. It is suggested you read this important paper because it illustrates the concept of multiple causation.

The Central Great Plains is a region of high climatic risk in which dry farming methods are used to combat hazard. Hewes was able not only to deduce the degree of failure but proportion the percentage of failure to a number of factors. The results he presented as isopleth maps, two examples of which are shown in Fig. 4.5A and B.

It is curious to note that failure due to frost is more prevalent in the south of the region than in the north. Is this because farmers fail to perceive frost as a hazard in the warmer south? Failure due to drought is widespread throughout the region but is more significant in the central and southern parts. This theme of how man perceives his environment is pursued in Chapter 6 when further reference will be made to this area and the drought hazard in particular.

To what extent do you think the pattern of variation in potato yields introduced on page 32 may be explained by climatic hazard? What information do you need to collect in order to test this hypothesis?

Summary and Concluding Exercise

An attempt has been made in this chapter to help you identify and evaluate the effects of physical elements upon farming patterns by applying the methodology of scientific enquiry as outlined in Chapter 1. Sound guidelines for this approach are also to be found in the work undertaken by A-level students and summarised by Daugherty. Relationships between land use and terrain in part of Northumberland were examined by testing relevant hypotheses.

Although attention has focused upon the testing of single or isolated hypotheses such as may be undertaken by yourself, do not underestimate the problems or exaggerate the results. Even within the realm of terrain alone, detailed evaluation of its capacity for agriculture is complex. The methods used by the post-graduate research worker are outlined by Davidson who devised a capability index for farms in Lower Deeside. One example—that of slope—will indicate the kinds of problem involved in resource evaluation. Slope is not merely a matter of degree but also of regularity. How does the researcher overcome the problem of classifying a field with a regular 10° slope compared with one containing hummocks of 10° slopes? This is indicative of the difficulties faced by Hewes in applying multiple hypotheses to solve an advanced problem.

Most investigations reveal unexpected anomalies and isolate further problems to be solved. Therein lies the intellectual challenge of our work as geographers rather than in finding neat and tidy answers. Is this true of the concluding exercise below, based upon a recent A-level question?

Hypothesis testing in geography need not be confined to fieldwork but may be undertaken using published maps.

Look at Fig. 4.6A which shows the land use of the area west of Sevenoaks. This 60 sq.km. extract has been derived from the Second Land Utilisation map. Figs. 4.6B, C and D show the distribution of terrain elements likely to influence farming activities. Test your understanding of the scientific method of enquiry as exemplified so far in this book by applying it to examine the extent to which land use is related to the terrain around Sevenoaks.

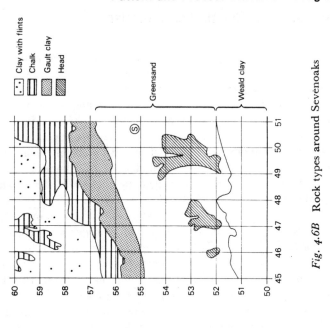

Clay with flints
Chalk
Gault clay
Head

Greensand

Weald clay

Fig. 4.6B   Rock types around Sevenoaks

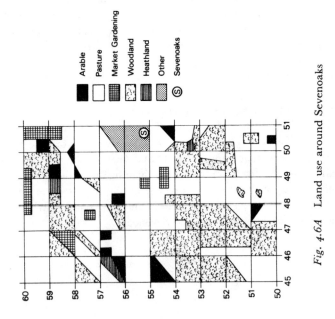

Arable
Pasture
Market Gardening
Woodland
Heathland
Other
Ⓢ Sevenoaks

Fig. 4.6A   Land use around Sevenoaks

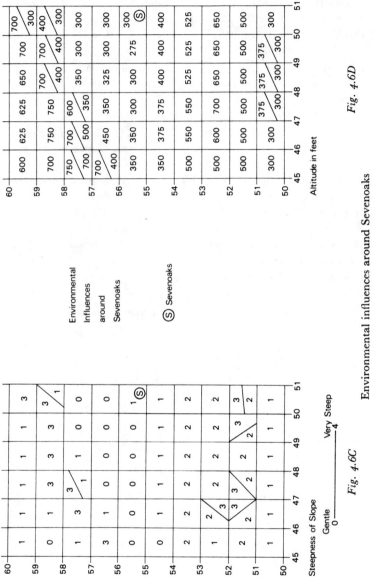

Fig. 4.6D

Fig. 4.6C

Environmental influences around Sevenoaks

Further Reading

Daugherty, R. (1976) 'Analysis of Land Use Data' *Teaching Geography*, no. 27. Geographical Association.

Davidson, Donald A. (1976) 'Terrain evaluation: a testing technique in Lower Deeside'.

Dunlop, J. S. (1970) 'Changes in the Canadian Wheat Belt 1931–69'. *Geography*, 55, pages 156–168.

Gregor, H. F. (1970) *Geography of Agriculture: Themes in Research*, Chapter 3. Prentice-Hall.

Hewes, L. (1965) 'Causes of wheat failure in the dry farming region, Central Great Plains, 1939–1957'. *Economic Geography*, 41, pages 313–30.

Hidore, J. J. (1963) 'Relationship between cash grain farming and landforms' *Economic Geography*, 39, pages 84–89.

McCarty, H. H. and Lindberg, J. B. (1966) *A Preface to Economic Geography*, Chapters 3 and 11. Prentice-Hall.

Morgan, W. B. and Munton, R. J. C. (1971) *Agricultural Geography*, Chapter 4. Methuen.

Scottish Geographical Magazine, vol. 93, no. 2, pages 108–119.

Symons, L. (1967) *Agricultural Geography*, Chapter 2. Bell.

Thoman, R. S. (1962) *Geography of Economic Activity*, Chapter 5. McGraw-Hill.

5. Farming III — Economic Elements : The Von Thünen Model

However favourable the physical environment may be to farming, it will remain unused until human resources are applied to it. Thus the farming system is as much an economic one as it is an ecological one.

The farm, like an industrial firm, is a risk-taking business and a number of economic elements apply to both. You may wish to challenge many of the assumptions which follow and indeed some of their limitations are discussed in the next chapter. Nevertheless they remain important economic ideas which must be introduced at this stage.

An overall supporting concept is that of '*Economic Man*'. He possesses full knowledge about a given situation; he is entirely rational in his behaviour and his main objective is to make as much profit as he can. The ways in which resources of land, labour and capital are allocated to achieve this goal of *profit maximisation* will have a profound effect upon the scale, style and spatial pattern of farming in the developed, western world.

How should resources be used to achieve this goal? The solution to the problem is related to *economies of scale* and three so-called '*laws*' of economics: supply and demand, comparative advantage and diminishing returns.

It is essential to think of selling products as well as producing them. When demand is constant and supply large, then the price of goods tends to be low and vice versa. Such a situation clearly has locational implications in terms of the area occupied by a crop and/or intensity of production. Can you think of examples of each situation in the world today?

In farming there is uncertainty of supply because of climatic variations and the incidence of disease. Additionally there is uncertainty of demand, and in the more perishable market gardening and fruit crops, the farmer must accept whatever price he can obtain.

Hence prices may range widely between seasons and rational planning to maximise profits becomes almost impossible. The *behavioural* consequences of this are examined in the next chapter. The acuteness of the problem of large fluctuations in price and an inability to adjust farming production routines to meet changes of supply and demand in the short term, have led to a system of guaranteed prices and contract selling. Examples in the UK include blackcurrants grown for 'Ribena', a blackcurrant health drink, peas for frozen food firms and sugar beet. Thus stability of a pattern once established can be prolonged.

Profits must be related to costs of production which in turn are affected by scale economies, diminishing returns and the concept of comparative advantage.

A saving in costs can be made if labour or capital is efficiently and fully employed. To achieve this a minimum size of enterprise may be necessary. Such savings are known as *scale economies* because they arise from an optimum size of unit. For example, the ideal size for a dairy herd to be managed by one man in a modern parlour is 100 cows. Similarly a 3·5 m combine harvester in a normal season will cope with 100 hectares of grain and the capacity of a sugar beet lifter is 32 hectares. If scale economies of this kind are made, then individual farmers will necessarily limit the variety of their enterprises and thus affect the overall pattern of farming in the area. Harvey partially attributed the concentration of hops in Kent to local scale economies such as availability of skilled labour together with marketing facilities. The net effect of economies of scale would be to develop a tendency towards regional specialisation of specific farming activities and thus strengthen a similar tendency suggested by the physical environment.

The degree of specialisation is further enhanced by the concept of *comparative advantage*. This identifies the advantage of growing one crop and/or livestock combination in preference to another in order to gain maximum profit.

The gains from scale economies and comparative advantage are circumscribed by the concept of *diminishing returns* which determines the boundary where the returns from production no longer justify an increased input of resources. There is a limit to which fertiliser can usefully be added to improve a soil and to the level of irrigation water to combat drought. This idea is illustrated in Fig. 5.1. The same amount of fertiliser, A and B, is added but the return at point

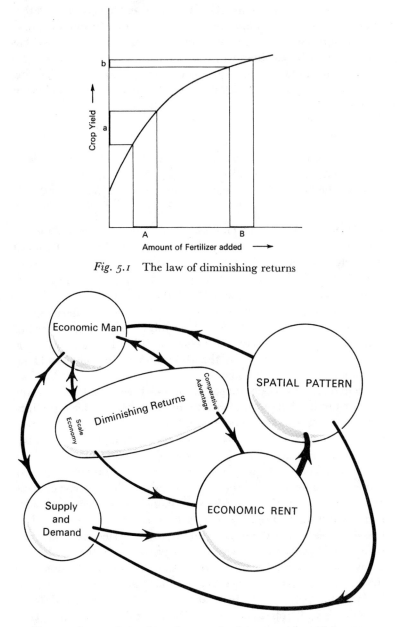

Fig. 5.1　The law of diminishing returns

Fig. 5.2　Inter-relationship of economic elements and spatial pattern

b is far lower than at point a. Less obviously and in economic, rather than physical terms, diminishing returns may be expressed by over-production and a consequent lowering of prices such as has happened with Canadian wheat in the past.

The contribution of these elements to spatial patterns of farming is shown in Fig. 5.2 in which the key role played by a new element *economic rent* is introduced.

Economic Rent

"The controlling factor in the determination of land use is land rent. That form of land use which provides the greatest rent will make the highest bid for the land and hence displace all others'. *Dunn*.

Land rent or *economic rent* as it is more usually known differs from the idea of rent for a house or.flat. Effectively it is the surplus return resulting from using the land for growing one crop rather than another. This is shown graphically in Fig. 5.3A where the greater return of growing crop A rather than B is indicated.

The importance of economic rent has long been understood by agricultural economists. In 1805 Duncomb's report for the Board of Agriculture on the county of Hereford describes how an orchard is worth £3 per acre 'whereas the same land for pasture would be worth less than 12 shillings per acre'.

Economic rent really depends upon those elements already discussed in this chapter which subsume such items as fixed produc-tion costs per hectare (labour, seed and fertiliser, for example), yields, market price, transport costs (particularly in the case of bulky crops) and distance from the market. These variables have been given different emphasis by different writers but it is the last element – distance from the market – which has received most attention. Fig. 5.3B shows how economic rent decreases with increasing distance from the market until it is absorbed at X. The line RX is known as the R slope and its angle of steepness will vary with the elements listed above in this paragraph. Hence different crops and crop combinations will result in differing R slopes as shown in Figs. 5.3C and D. It is particularly advantageous to grow bulky and/or perishable crops near to the market. Theoretical slopes for a number of crops as devised by Dunn are shown in Fig. 5.3D.

This idea of distance from the market as a key factor in determining

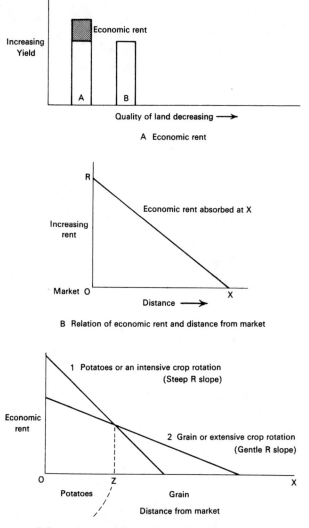

A Economic rent

B Relation of economic rent and distance from market

C Economic rent and distance from market: two competing land uses

Fig. 5.3(A–C)   Economic rent and distance

rent was postulated as long ago as 1776 by the economist Adam
Smith who recognised that land near a town yielded a higher rent
than equally fertile land further away. Indeed he produced a zonation
of land use not dissimilar to that of von Thünen.

The effect of distance from the market upon prices received for wheat by U.S. farmers is well illustrated in Fig. 5.4. Since much of the wheat is exported from the eastern seaboard, there is a general decline in the net return to farmers with increasing distance inland. What other differences do you notice in this pattern? How would you try to explain them?

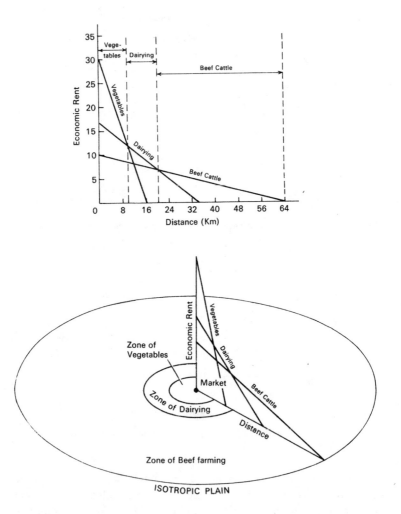

Fig. 5.3(D)   Economic rent and farming patterns

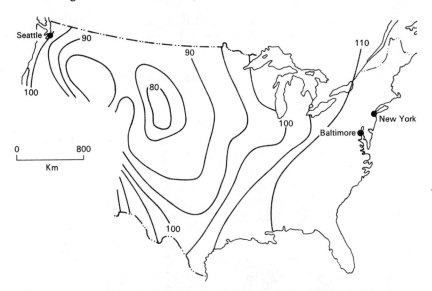

Fig. 5.4 Regional variations in prices for wheat received by farmers in the
U.S.A. (1925-34) (*Open University—Spatial Aspects of Society Unit 19*)

The von Thünen model
Von Thünen was a practical farmer working near Rostock in the
early part of the nineteenth century. Although his published work
'The Isolated State' appeared in 1826, it received little attention
until the last decade.

The key to the understanding of von Thünen's idea is economic
rent for he was concerned with the net return from a unit of land.
One great attribute of his model is that it links economic concepts
with spatial location (see Fig. 5.5) and it remains a pioneer work in
this field.

To develop his ideas about land use patterns within an area, von
Thünen in common with many other model builders made simplifying assumptions about the real world. These are:

1. The area was an 'isolated state'. By this he meant there was
    no external trading. Indeed the market for the state's agri-
    cultural produce was confined to one large, centrally placed
    city.
2. The area was conceived as a featureless plain or *isotropic
    surface*: equal ease of movement in every direction and no
    variation in soil fertility, topography or climate existed.

3. The farmer himself was regarded as an entirely rational 'Economic Man' who, with perfect knowledge, maximised his profit.

Only transport costs were allowed to vary and they were considered to be directly proportional to distance from the market. Such a model where all the variables except one are neutralised is known as a *partial equilibrium model*.

The resultant pattern of land use around such a city is that of rings as shown in the top half of Fig. 5.5. Chisholm's more helpful

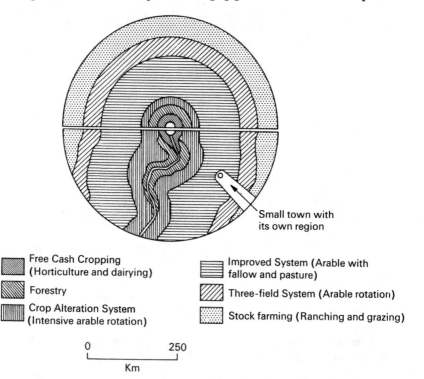

Free Cash Cropping
(Horticulture and dairying)

Forestry

Crop Alteration System
(Intensive arable rotation)

Improved System (Arable with
fallow and pasture)

Three-field System (Arable rotation)

Stock farming (Ranching and grazing)

Small town with
its own region

0   250
Km

Fig. 5.5 Land use in von Thünen's 'Isolated State' (*Based on Morgan, W.B., 'The doctrine of the rings'*)

elaboration of each zone is indicated in brackets after the original. The term 'free cash cropping' meant that crops did not have to rotate in a fixed order, largely because manure from the city could re-fertilise the soil. Hence the farmer had greater freedom of choice of enterprise in this zone. Ring 2 contained the timber for fuel – very bulky to transport and frequently required. Rings 3, 4 and 5 strongly imply a declining intensity of usage with increasing distance since Ring 3 has no period of fallow, Ring 4 one fallow year in every seven and Ring 5 is fallow every third year. Ring 6 is regarded as an even more extensive form of land use, yet butter was a significant product being capable of withstanding higher transport costs.

The unreality of the model was recognised by von Thünen himself who introduced modifications such as a navigable river which reduced the traditional ox-cart transport costs by 90%. As a consequence the circular rings became longitudinal zones along the line of the river (see the lower half of Fig. 5.5). Also recognised was the presence of a smaller market generating a similar zoning, but on a diminished scale. Although dating back 150 years, this model has not really been superseded. With so many obvious limitations why does it remain significant?

The von Thünen treatise is not so much a theory as a method of analysis, but since it is claimed to have general applicability then it may correctly be regarded as a model. Some confusion of interpretation arises because the model is a mixture of observation in the case of zone 1 and deductive reasoning of what the pattern of land use would be in the other zones on the basis of the various assumptions made. You are advised further about this problem in the works of Chisholm and Morgan listed at the end of the chapter.

In reality it is probable that the land use in rings 2–6 did not rigidly conform to that indicated in Fig. 5.4 even in von Thünen's day and therefore it is futile to expect them to do so in the industrial and highly urbanised society in which we live today.

Of particular significance is von Thünen's method of analysis – the partial equilibrium approach – which represents an early example of the scientific method of enquiry. In this case he postulated a *normative* pattern of land use to be tested against reality. A normative pattern is one which may reasonably be expected on the basis of a number of stated premises. Remind yourself of the most significant of von Thünen's premises, namely that land use would be related to distance from the market and it is upon this fundamental concept that our attention should be focused. A number of case studies on differing scales and in differing kinds of environment where this relationship is examined will now be introduced together with data for you to test the hypothesis yourself. In some cases only brief outlines of the more salient points are included and you are advised to follow up those examples which particularly interest you in the prescribed reading at the end of the chapter.

The Relationship of Land Use and Distance

LARGE SCALE EXAMPLES

Case I The concept of the world or continental 'metropolis'
The idea that the developed world forms a city with similar effects on a world scale as von Thünen's central city is the essence of a thesis advanced by Peet in 1969. This world city he identified as Western Europe and North-eastern United States. He argues the case for the von Thünen zones being expressed on a world scale through the

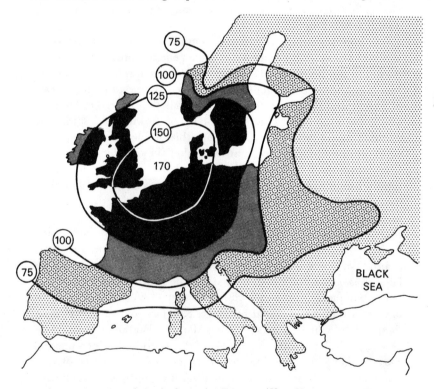

Fig. 5.6 Intensity of Agriculture in Europe (*Van Valkenburg, S. V. and Held, C. C., Regional Geography of Europe*)

sequence of the outward movement of cultivation boundaries, first to the interior of the USA and then to the Southern Continents as the demands of this world city increased. In fact this idea was not a new one since Jonasson had applied the von Thünen model on a continental scale in 1925. North-west Europe was regarded as one vast conurbation which caused a decrease in the amount of land devoted to cereal growing. This vacated land was then used for market gardening and dairying, Denmark and Holland being prime examples of this change. Zones of decreasing intensity of farming encircling South East England and the Low Countries are illustrated in Fig. 5.6. The intensity has been measured by yields of eight crops and you can see the regularity with which intensity decreases as you move from the centre of highest yields.

Case II Zones in the New World: New South Wales
An interesting variation and adaptation of the von Thünen model has been developed by Rutherford, Logan and Missen for New South Wales in general and Sydney in particular. The 'R' slopes appropriate to the Australian context are shown in Fig. 5.7. The

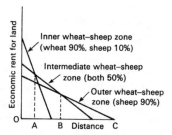

Fig. 5.7 'R' slopes in Australia

transition from an inner zone of predominantly wheat growing changes to an outer one of predominantly sheep farming. The spatial patterns predicted by these 'R' slopes are shown in Fig. 5.8A where a modification of the zones into a series of north–south belts caused by terrain, has been incorporated. Fig. 5.8B elaborates further this distortion because of the varied relief found along the coast. Thus one of the simplifying assumptions of the original von Thünen model has been overcome. Later in their book, *New Viewpoints in Economic Geography*, empirical evidence for this projected land use pattern is examined.

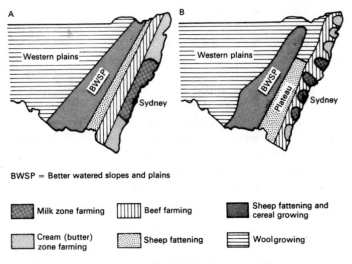

BWSP = Better watered slopes and plains

▦ Milk zone farming   ‖‖‖ Beef farming   ◼ Sheep fattening and cereal growing

▦ Cream (butter) zone farming   ▦ Sheep fattening   ≡ Wool growing

Fig. 5.8(A) and *(B)*   Types of farming regions in New South Wales
(*Rutherford, J., Logan, M. I. and Missen, G. J., New Viewpoints in Economic Geography*)

SMALL SCALE EXAMPLES

Case I   Multiple land use around Addis Ababa

The land use pattern around Addis Ababa was analysed by Horvath in 1969. A generalised map of his findings is shown in Fig. 5.9.

This area is certainly not an isotropic plain since it contains two distinct physical relief regions, two differing climates and two especially important soil types. Furthermore, four groups of people each with differing taboos and attitudes to work are found here. Is it then reasonable to expect land use to be related to distance?

Look at Fig. 5.9. The eucalyptus forests were first planted towards the end of the last century to satisfy the building and fuel needs of the city. The location of this forest is in keeping with von Thünen's thesis.

Vegetables are grown in an elongated zone along the rivers because of their need for irrigation, but they are located as close to the town as environmental conditions permit. Vegetables grown further out are adjacent to the main road so that on a transportation time basis they could be regarded as in the inner zone. The area of milk production appears as the major stumbling block in accepting this land use pattern as evidence in support of the von Thünen thesis. Milk is produced where the cooler climate ceases to favour crop growth. The handling of the milk is restricted to a particular ethnic group, yet it is concentrated along the road for speedy access to the city and so in no way negates the underlying principle of land use and distance to the city – measured on a time rather than a linear basis.

The work of Horvath has been commented upon in detail because it provides the field evidence with which to evaluate the hypothesis that land use varies with distance in the complex real world. Such an evaluation can only be verbal and subjective, but the next case quoted enables statistical evaluation of the evidence to take place.

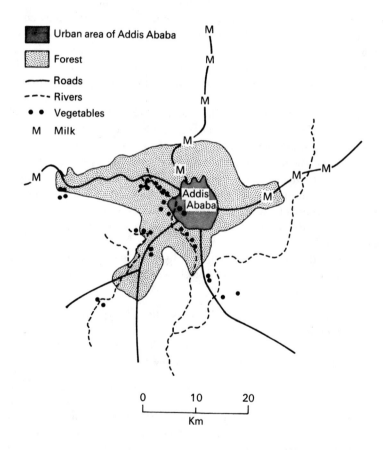

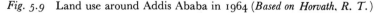

Fig. 5.9 Land use around Addis Ababa in 1964 (*Based on Horvath, R. T.*)

Case II A single crop around Hereford

From Chapter 3 you will be familiar with the pattern of cider apple growing around Hereford and the generalisation of this pattern in Fig. 3.6B suggested a zonation revealing decreasing intensity of production with increasing distance. How could this hypothesis be tested more rigorously?

You will have noticed in Fig. 3.6A that the density of production for each parish has been plotted. With these data it is possible to test statistically the *distance-decay* (or gradient) hypothesis by *regression analysis.*

Before proceeding to do this, however, it is helpful to state a number of significant similarities of premise between this particular pattern and the von Thünen model. First the area may truly be regarded as an 'isolated state' since all the apples are sold in the county town. Secondly, the scale of the area is similar to that in which von Thünen worked. Since the region was largely by-passed by the industrial revolution, the time difference of a century is not really significant. Effectively there is equal ease of transport from all parts of the county to the market and differences in climate are not such as would affect the pattern of a tolerant crop.

However, the area cannot be regarded as an isotropic surface since you have already noted the attraction of a particular soil for apple growing in Chapter 4, page 61, and Fig. 5.10 shows the distribution of topographical features adverse to orchards.

Is it possible to simulate an isotropic surface and so neutralise these two variables?

Such a surface may be achieved by a simple yet useful process known as *sieving.* This term will be clarified by the example; proceed as follows:

1. Consider all the values for only one soil type so that the soil variable is neutralised.
2. Within that soil type remove all parishes which contain adverse topography; this will neutralise the terrain.

Effectively you have now achieved an isotropic surface upon which to test the hypothesis which has its basis in the von Thünen model where without doubt the declining intensity of any one activity from Ring 1 to Ring 6 is postulated. If successful, one may then begin to feed in the isolated variables to see if the relationship holds in the real world, as will be indicated later.

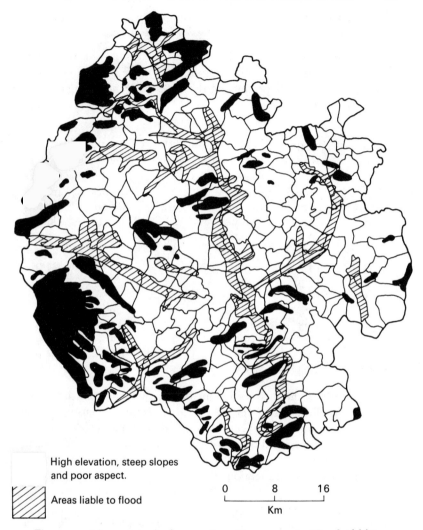

High elevation, steep slopes
and poor aspect.

Areas liable to flood

0   8   16

Km

Fig. 5.10   Adverse terrain for growing cider apples in Herefordshire

Earlier the Spearman Rank Correlation method was used to
establish whether or not a significant association existed between
two sets of variables (page 57). When a correlation coefficient is
calculated for the relationship between density of apple production
and distance from market, a value of −0·71 is obtained. This
is statistically significant at the 99% confidence level.

Provided that the values of r_s are statistically significant it is possible to plot a 'best fit' or *regression line* in order:

1. To *establish* in graphical form what the association is between the two variables. For example, in the case of Table 5.1, that density of apple production decreases with increasing distance from the market.

Table 5.1

Density of apple production and distance from market for twenty parishes on an isotropic surface

Parish no.	Density (tonnes per oo hectares)	Distance from market (km)	Parish no.	Density (tonnes per oo hectares)	Distance from market (km)
1	48·1	3·2	11	10·7	19·2
2	13·0	7·2	12	7·3	22·0
3	14·6	9·5	13	3·9	24·9
4	17·9	9·5	14	10·5	24·9
5	14·9	9·7	15	7·9	25·3
6	7·4	14·5	16	8·8	27·5
7	15·3	15·3	17	10·2	29·8
8	22·7	16·1	18	4·5	29·9
9	7·1	17·5	19	0·5	34·8
10	12·4	18·8	20	3·7	36·2

2. To *predict* the unknown value of one variable from the known value of the other – for example, to forecast the density of apple production for a given distance from the market.
3. To *isolate* marked deviations from the generalised relationship as depicted in the regression line and hence isolate a problem for further investigation.

Procedure for plotting the regression line

The data contained in Table 5.1 have been plotted in Fig. 5.11 using the steps outlined below. The values in Table 5.2, derived from production figures from some 300 parishes subsequently allocated to one of 9 distance zones, so that you may plot a regression line for yourself.

1. Determine which variable is dependent upon the other. This is achieved by using geographical expertise. In this example, density is dependent upon distance and hence distance is called the *independent* variable and density the *dependent* variable.

2. Plot the independent variable along the horizontal or X axis and the dependent variable along the vertical or Y axis. It is essential to number the points so that later identification is facilitated.
3. Examine the array of points to see if a trend can be identified visually by inspection.

Table 5.2

Density of apple production and distance from market.
Parishes aggregated into distance zones

Zone	Density (tonnes per oo hectares)	Distance from market (km)	Zone	Density (tonnes per oo hectares)	Distance from market (km)
1	20·0	3·2	6	5·7	20·9
2	14·5	8·0	7	4·8	24·1
3	11·9	11·3	8	2·4	27·4
4	7·4	14·5	9	1·2	30·6
5	7·4	17·7			

4. Plot with an asterisk the mean point of the array. This is determined by the mean of the x values (distance from market) and the mean of the y values (density). In the case of the attached tables, these values are:

	Table 5.1	Table 5.2
mean value of x ($\bar{x}$)	19·8	17·5
mean value of y ($\bar{y}$)	12·1	8·3

However you draw this regression line, it must pass through this mean point.

Increasingly sophisticated ways of drawing the regression line are:

1. Drawing the line by eye, ensuring as far as possible that an equal number of points lie above and below the line.
2. A more accurate regression line may be constructed by calculating two further means:

(a) Through the mean of the array already marked by an asterisk, draw a vertical line to divide the array into two parts.
(b) Find the mean value of x and the mean value of y for those points which lie to the right and the left of this dividing line:

		L.H.S.	R.H.S.
Table 5.1		$\bar{x} = 12.7$	$\bar{x} = 28.3$
		$\bar{y} = 16.8$	$\bar{y} = 6.3$
Table 5.2		$\bar{x} = 9.2$	$\bar{x} = 24.1$
		$\bar{y} = 13.3$	$\bar{y} = 4.3$

(c) Plot these mean values by asterisks. You now have three
fixing points for the regression line which must pass through
the mean of the total array and as close as possible to the
other two mean values as calculated for the L.H.S. and
R.H.S. of the array. Erase the asterisks after drawing the
line. This is shown in Fig. 5.11 as the unlabelled line.

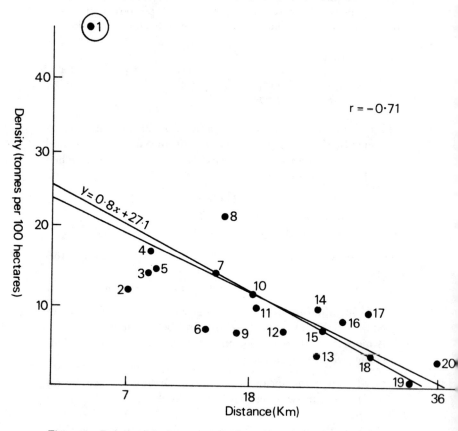

Fig. 5.11 Relationship between density of cider apple production and
distance from the market

3. To calculate a regression line accurately is simple but very tedious without the use of a calculating machine.

To do this you use the formula:

$$y = mx + c \quad or \quad y = a + bx$$

in order to obtain the point of origin of the line and the slope of the line. *a* or *c* represent the point on the *y* axis where the line begins when $x = 0$ and is calculated by the formula:

$$a = \frac{(\Sigma x^2 . \Sigma y) - (\Sigma x . \Sigma xy)}{(N . \Sigma x^2) - (\Sigma x)^2}$$

where N is the number of items.

To compute *b*, which indicates the average change in *y* with a given change in *x* use the formula:

$$b = \frac{(N . \Sigma xy) - (\Sigma x . \Sigma y)}{(N . \Sigma x^2) - (\Sigma x)^2}$$

Although these values are indicated on the accurately computed line in Fig. 5.11 it is seldom worth all this effort – and certainly not if you have no calculating machine available.

It is much more important to *interpret* the regression line you have drawn.

Interpretation of the regression line

With a correlation coefficient of -0.71 which is statistically significant at the 99% confidence level, there is abundant evidence to reject the null hypothesis that no relationship between distance and land use exists and hence to accept the original hypothesis. The relatively close fit of the points to the line also indicates the strength of the relationship. You may now safely conclude that you have found valid and substantive empirical evidence to support the *theoretical* predictions of the von Thünen model.

You will notice that some points are further away from the line than others. Those at the extremities, such as the ringed number 1 in Fig. 5.11, are sometimes known as *residuals* but are more correctly designated *outliers*. They do not fit into the generalisation and hence require further investigation to discover the reasons for this. Thus as in any scientific investigation, whilst one problem is solved others are revealed. A further enquiry which may be profitably undertaken is to investigate the attributes of those parishes with values above the line from those with values below it to see if further, refined generalisation is possible. As indicated earlier, if you knew only one value, for example distance, you could predict with confidence the expected production of cider apples at that distance.

You have been presented here with a shortened version of the full investigation which revealed the fact that distance was a far stronger determinant of density than either soil type or topography. This was achieved by feeding in these variables as suggested earlier, the validity of the regression analysis remaining significant.

Case III   A single crop in Lincolnshire : peas for freezing
To test the hypothesis that density of peas grown for freezing is related to distance from the freezer plant
The rigid time-limits of less than 1 hour imposed upon growers by pea processors together with the economic ideas already discussed would suggest that the distance–decay hypothesis should be tested in this context.

Look at Fig. 5.12A which shows the distribution of pea growing in Lincolnshire together with the processing locations. This map is based upon those contained in an important paper by Dalton, which should be read. You now have the basic data for testing the hypothesis and should be familiar with the methodology used in Case II above. In the absence of parish boundaries and with a number of processing locations the method will require some modification.

To overcome the problem of parishes, a network of 100 sq km quadrats was constructed and the number of hectares of peas grown within each determined. The direct distance from the centre of each quadrat to its nearest processing plant was measured. These values are shown in Fig. 5.12B. Despite weaknesses in this method – especially the size and placing of the quadrats – a statistically significant coefficient of correlation of -0.22 resulted from relating distance and density of production. Proceed to plot the two variables on a graph as in Fig. 5.11 and draw a regression line. To what extent does the exercise reveal a number of interesting residual areas which it would be profitable to compare with either a topographical or simple soil or geological map? By now you should be able to interpret your answer geographically and in the light of the context of the whole section on farming which you have read.

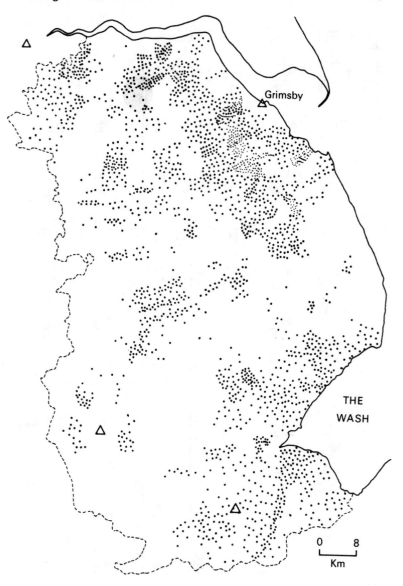

One dot represents 20 acres (8·1 hectares) of peas

Fig. 5.12(A)   Distribution of peas grown for freezing in relation to processing plants (*Dalton, R., T. 'Peas for freezing: a recent development in Lincolnshire agriculture'*)

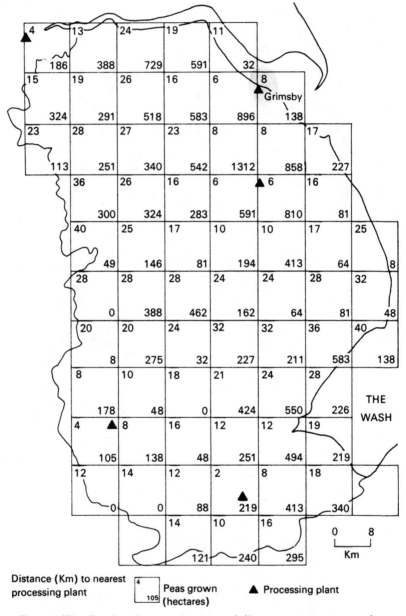

Fig. 5.12(B)   Density of pea production and distance to nearest processing plant (*Based on Dalton, R.T., 'Peas for freezing: a recent development in Lincolnshire agriculture'*)

Case IV A single crop in Kent: hops in the nineteenth century
In his study of locational change in the pattern of hop growing in
Kent, Harvey identified a core area of high density production
centred upon Wateringbury and Yalding. Furthermore, he found
that the density declined with increasing distance from this core area
as shown in Fig. 5.13. As in the case of the Herefordshire orchards,

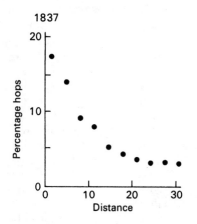

Fig. 5.13 Decline in density of hop cultivation with distance (km) from
Wateringbury in 1837 (*Harvey, D. W., 'Locational change in the Kentish hop
industry and the analysis of land use patterns'*)

although the core area was concentrated upon a highly favourable
soil type, outside this area the decreasing density was independent
of physical constraints illustrating once again the significance of the
distance decay process.

The relationship between distance and labour input on the farm
In all the examples considered the relationship of land use to distance
has been related to density of production. In less developed parts of
the world, an hypothesis relating distance and labour input at
individual farm level has been advanced by Chisholm. He shows
that in Finland net output decreases as distance from the plot
increases; this is particularly true when holdings are fragmented.
Chisholm asserts that fall in yields is attributable to distance alone.
This has clear implications for patterns of land use around small
settlements in less developed areas.
    Labour inputs are calculated by a uniform measure known as the

standard man day (*smd*). In the developed world the commonly accepted numbers of man days for specific activities are shown in Table 5.3. As you can see they vary widely from crop to crop and animal to animal.

Table 5.3

Standard man days (based on Farm Management handbooks)
Man-days per hectare or per head of animal

Wheat, barley, rye	8·6	Bare fallow	1·2
Oats, mixed corn	11·1	Grass for mowing	4·9
Pulses for stock	9·8	Grass for grazing	0·6
Potatoes	49·4	Dairy cows	15
Sugar beet	41·9	Dairy heifers	9
Turnips, swedes	29·6	Beef cows	4·5
Mangolds, fodder beet	51·8	Bulls	7
Other crops	17·2	Other cattle	3
Vegetables, brassicas	49·4	Sows and boars	4
Vegetables, root	51·8	Other pigs	1·2
Vegetables, pulses	30·8	Upland sheep, one	
Other vegetables	98·8	year old and over	0·5
Hops	247·0	Lowland sheep, one	
Small fruit	111·1	year old and over	1
Orchards with small		Other sheep	0·25
fruit	135·8	Poultry, six months	
Other orchards	61·7	old and over	0·3
Flowers, nursery stock		Poultry, under six	
	123·5	months old	0·1

Where agriculture is not mechanised, the relationship between distance and land use is likely to be accentuated because it is estimated that between 10% and 25% of production time is spent in walking to the fields. In addition cartage of produce from the fields is 8·6 times per tonne/km more costly when motorised vehicles are not used.

A particular case study of the relationship between distance and labour input was undertaken by Chisholm for Canicatti, a settlement in central Sicily. You should already be familiar with the general background to this area from your work in Chapter 4.

Since Canicatti is a hill top settlement its immediate environs are particularly poor. Using an Italian land use map and official data, Chisholm compiled the zonation of land use and calculated the labour input for each zone as contained in Table 5.4. The relation-

Table 5.4

Canicatti, Sicily: percentage of land area in various uses and labour requirements per hectare in man-days

Percentage of land area

Distance in kms from Canicatti	Urban	Irrigated arable and vegetables	Citrus fruits	Vines	Arable-with-trees	Olive	Trees*	Arable un-irrigated	Pasture and productive waste†	Coppice	Average number of man-days per hectare in each distance zone
0–1	44·7	—	—	15·8	—	—	19·7	19·7	—	—	52
1–2	—	—	—	18·0	16·7	8·4	41·0	15·9	—	—	50
2–3	—	—	2·6	2·3	21·8	14·4	35·4	23·6	—	—	46
3–4	—	—	2·1	13·3	18·7	0·6	47·2	18·1	—	—	50
4–5	—	—	—	5·1	19·2	2·4	28·4	43·4	1·4	—	42
5–6	—	1·0	—	6·3	4·7	1·6	17·6	64·1	4·7	—	41
6–7	1·3	0·7	—	3·3	6·7	—	18·3	68·7	0·9	—	40
7–8	—	0·3	—	4·0	7·7	—	23·6	62·4	0·8	1·6	39
Total	1·0	0·3	0·4	6·1	11·1	2·2	26·3	50·8	1·4	0·4	—
Average number of man-days per hectare		300	150	90	50	45	40	35	5	5	42

* Mainly almond, hazel, carob and pistacchio.   † Sometimes sown.

Source: Chisholm, M., Rural Settlement and Land Use.

ship to distance is self-evident without statistical analysis and 4 km
seems to mark a significant breaking point beyond which open
arable land predominates. The net effect of this decreasing labour
input upon the farming pattern can be deduced from Table 5.4,
namely a reduction in the importance of labour intensive vines and
olives as distance increases.

The distance–intensity relationship inverted
A characteristic of the contemporary scene is the phenomenal
growth of cities. As a result of this expansion, Sinclair has hypothesised that the von Thünen zonation should be inverted so the
intensity of agricultural activity *increases* with increasing distance
from the city. Sinclair replaces the 'R' slope with what he termed
the 'V' slope, as shown in Fig. 5.14, indicating the value of land for
agriculture.

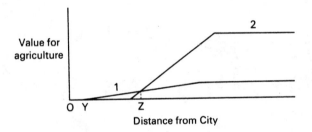

Fig. 5.14 Inverse relationships around expanding urban areas (*Sinclair, R.,*
'Von Thünen and urban sprawl')

The steepness of this slope varies with the intensity of agricultural
investment which in turn is related to the degree of anticipation of
urban growth. Because of this anticipated expansion of the city, very
little or no investment is made on land close to it. The slope levels off
beyond a certain point beyond which the effects of town growth
cease to be felt. Slopes for two differing kinds of land use are shown
in Fig. 5.14. Can you suggest what each might represent?
    The spatial pattern generated by this model is shown in Fig. 5.15.
Zone 1 tends to be held by land speculators awaiting urban development, whilst in Zone 2 farmers are reluctant to invest money because
they intend to sell at the most profitable moment. In Zone 3 farming
is extensive in character; it is not until Zone 4 is reached that dairying appears. Whilst the underlying cause of this inversion is **antici-**

pated expansion, it would not have been possible without modern technology favouring large scale production and mass transport.

Whilst there seems to be some field evidence for this type of zonation around a number of mid-western cities of the USA, this is certainly not true for the inner zone adjacent to the city of Hamburg shown in Fig. 5.16.

This map was constructed in 1952 by Stamer who regarded distance from the city being responsible for the zonation. The idealised pattern which might be expected as a result of ideas introduced in this chapter has been modified by soil conditions. This last study emphasises that no one set of elements is entirely responsible for a land use pattern.

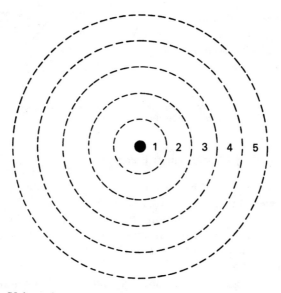

KEY 1. Urban farming.
　　　 2. Vacant grazing.
　　　 3. Field crop and grazing.
　　　 4. Dairying and field crop.
　　　 5. Specialised field grain and livestock.

Fig. 5.15 Zones around expanding urban areas (*Sinclair, R.*, '*Von Thünen and urban sprawl*')

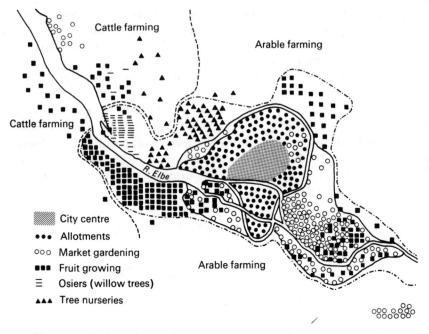

Fig. 5.16 Agricultural land use zones around Hamburg in 1950 (*Open University Spatial Aspects of Society Unit 19*)

Summary and Concluding Exercise

This chapter has attempted to identify the more significant economic elements and to show how they affect spatial patterns. Many examples have been introduced to illustrate the *primate concept* in geography known as distance–decay which you will meet again in later chapters. Methods and data for you to test this all-important idea for yourself have been deliberately included.

Equally it is right that you should appreciate the limitations of a model and have met the controversial viewpoint of Sinclair, though it is still based on distance as the principal component. It is possible for you to test this idea of Sinclair by using the 1 :25 000 Second Land Utilisation Maps or by fieldwork in the rural–urban fringe of larger cities, especially in parts of the country where the population is growing, and see whether or not usage of the inner zone conforms more to the Sinclair or von Thünen model.

As at the end of the last chapter a revision exercise is again included so you may attempt to answer a problem based on a recent A-level question.

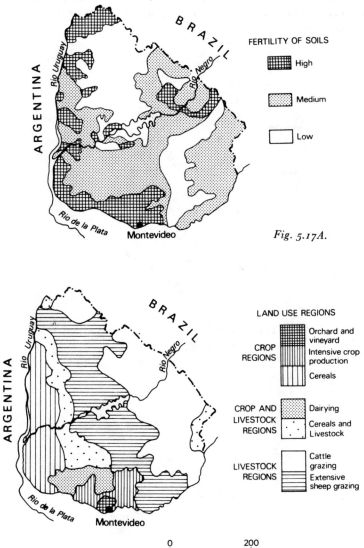

FERTILITY OF SOILS

▦ High

░ Medium

☐ Low

Fig. 5.17A.

LAND USE REGIONS

CROP REGIONS
- Orchard and vineyard
- Intensive crop production
- Cereals

CROP AND LIVESTOCK REGIONS
- Dairying
- Cereals and Livestock

LIVESTOCK REGIONS
- Cattle grazing
- Extensive sheep grazing

Fig. 5.17B.

Look at Figs. 5.17 (A,B,C) which show the distribution of soil fertility, land use and major towns in Uruguay. To what extent does the pattern of land use reflect the principles of the von Thünen model? How far does type of soil influence the strength of this relationship? How far does the presence or absence of a major town affect the pattern?

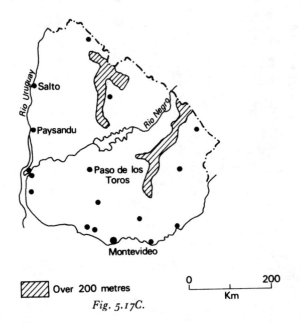

Over 200 metres

0   200
Km

Fig. 5.17C.

Further Reading

Bradford M. G. and Kent W. A. (1977) *Human Geography: Theories and their Applications.* Chapter 2. O.U.P.

Chisholm, M. (1962) *Rural Settlement and Land Use.* Hutchinson.

Dalton, R. T. (1971) 'Peas for freezing: a recent development in Lincolnshire Agriculture'. *East Midland Geographer,* 35, pages 133–141.

Dunn, E. S. (1954) *The Location of Agricultural Production.* University of Florida Press.

Found, W. C. (1971) *A Theoretical Approach to Land Use Patterns.* Arnold.

Harvey, D. W. (1963) 'Locational change in the Kentish hop industry and the analysis of land use patterns'. *I.B.G.*†, 33, pages 123–144.

Horvath, R. J. (1969) 'Von Thünen's isolated state and the area around Addis Ababa'. *A.A.A.G.**, 59, pages 308–323.

Morgan, W. B. (1973) 'The doctrine of the rings'. *Geography,* 58, pages 301–312.

Peet, J. R. (1969) 'The spatial expansion of commercial agriculture in the nineteenth century: a von Thünen interpretation'. *Economic Geography,* 45, pages 283–301.

Rutherford, J., Logan, M. I. and Missen, G. J. (1966) *New Viewpoints in Economic Geography,* Chapters 2 and 12. Harrap.

Sinclair, R. (1967) 'Von Thünen and urban spawl'. *A.A.A.G.,* 57, pages 72–87.

†Transactions of the Institute of British Geographers.
*Annals of the Association of American Geographers.

6 . Farming IV — Behavioural Elements

The pattern of farming in an area results ultimately from the decisions made by a large number of individual farmers who live there. The physical and economic elements may be common to them all, but the farmer's perception of and reaction to such elements will vary according to his personality. It is for this reason that an understanding of how, and upon what basis, decisions are made is elusive. Little work has yet been done on this topic to help our understanding.

Many people now challenge the concept of 'Economic Man' as outlined in the last chapter. They are trying to develop a body of theory based upon more realistic human behaviour which recognises that man's knowledge is imperfect and that he has many goals other than just profit making. This new concept is called '*bounded rationality*'.

There is no doubt that the farmer has imperfect knowledge, if only because he cannot predict the weather. Some psychologists argue that in any event the decision-maker cannot handle all the data needed for solving a problem. He also desires to avoid 'effort-requiring' work!

What of goals other than profit making? Found introduces the idea of *utility* in place of price in order to make comparisons. Utility is wider in concept than price since it takes into account non-market factors. In a subsistence economy it is important to ensure regular food supplies throughout the year. In the commercial world it is less important for a farmer earning £20,000 per annum than for one earning a mere £2,000. In the former case the farmer may be just as happy to grow wheat as sugar beet in a particular field because he intuitively feels the net result on his farm overall would be the same. Harvey indicates that a farmer might be interested as much in leisure as in profit, once a *satisfactory* level of income has been achieved.

One major problem in trying to identify the basis upon which decisions are taken is that man is often inconsistent. He may well make a different decision on the basis of the same data on two different occasions. Furthermore, decisions are often conditioned by the extent to which a farmer thinks events will happen and thus he tries to estimate the outcomes of such events. His estimate will vary with the degree of optimism or pessimism which is in turn related to personality traits such as temperament and ambition. Also contributing to this are age, experience and level of general education. The strength and duration of such events themselves will also affect man's awareness of them. Thus emerges the concept of the *decision-making environment* as opposed to the real environment as introduced in Chapter 1.

Perception of Farmers

The major environmental problem facing the farmer is the uncertainty of climatic elements. This is especially so in marginal areas such as the Great Plains of the USA, where Saarinen attempted to assess how aware the farmers are of the drought hazard. This awareness is called *perception level* and as you will see this varies from place to place and person to person.

The area known as the Great Plains is shown in Fig. 6.1. On this map are also indicated six counties which Saarinen used in his investigation. Permanent settlement in this area took place as recently as the late nineteenth century and an initial failure to distinguish between its climate and that of the Midwest resulted in severe soil erosion. Saarinen's aim was to discover whether or not present day farmers are fully aware of the vagaries of the climate and especially to measure the farmer's perception level of the drought hazard. To achieve these aims he carried out a questionnaire survey on a sample of farmers in the six counties shown in Fig. 6.1.

The measured or real environment
To form an objective assessment of the climatic characteristics in general, and aridity in particular, look at the data contained in Table 6.1 and the maps of raindays, hours of sunshine and evaporation rates during the critical growing period as shown in Figs. 6.2 and 6.3. The Palmer Drought Index is a comparative measure combining both the length and severity of drought and in column 8 of

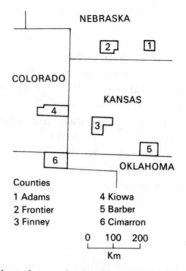

Fig. 6.1   Saarinen's study area in the Great Plains (*Based on the Atlas of the U.S.A.*)

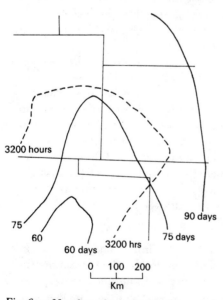

Fig. 6.2   Number of rain days and hours of sunshine (*Based on the Atlas of the U.S.A.*)

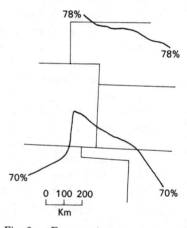

Fig. 6.3   Evaporation rates between May and October (*Based on the Atlas of the U.S.A.*)

Table 6.1
The reality

County	1 Average annual precipitation in mm	2 Average size of farms (hectares)	3 Population density per sq. km	4 Average number of years lived in area by farmer	5 Average age of farmer	6 % time drought	7 % time severe and extreme drought	8 Severity of most recent drought
Adams	609	130	133	24	47	42	16	1
Barber	635	468	20	26	53	47	14	4
Frontier	482	557	13	22	42	42	11	2
Finney	482	580	32	34	50	47	15	5
Cimmaron	431	794	8	23	44	49	18	4
Kiowa	356	1736	2	21	48	47	13	4

Source: based on Ambrose, 'Analytical Human Geography'.

Table 6.2

The perception of the farmers

| | 1 | 2 | 3 4
% expectation of
drought next year | | 5 | 6
Summary findings of
perception level
of drought risk | |
County	% farmers mentioning dryness as disadvantage	% farmers remembering most recent drought	Most experienced farmers	Least experienced farmers	Farmers' estimate of drought years/100	% more perceptive	% less perceptive
Adams	71	69	24	33	17	25	75
Barber	87	81	35	22	16	27	73
Frontier	67	53	50	37	20	50	60
Finney	94	77	40	55	29	62	38
Cimmaron	86	100	40	54	35	69	31
Kiowa	100	94	57	60	35	82	18

Source: as for Table 6.1.

Table 6.1 it has been simplified into a five point scale where 1 indicates incipient drought, and 5 extreme drought.

Using the tabulated and map data, summarise the main characteristics of the climate of the region paying special attention to the *spatial distribution* of aridity. Next attempt to evaluate aridity as a hazard for the wheat farmer. Do some areas appear more hazardous than others?

The perceived environment
The results of Saarinen's survey are summarised in Table 6.2, the columns of which are self-explanatory. Of particular interest is column 6 which differentiates between the less and more perceptive farmers.

Examine carefully the data contained in Tables 6.1 and 6.2 and try to answer the following questions:

1. To what extent are farmers' estimates of the frequency of drought accurate? Do you consider these farmers to be optimists or pessimists?
2. Is there any spatial variation in this accuracy? If so, how may you account for it?
3. Are there significant differences between the perception of the least and most experienced farmers? Are such differences related to the average age of the farmers?
4. Is the recall of the most recent hazard related to its severity?
5. What influence on perception level has the most recent drought?

Attempt to summarise your answers to the above questions in a series of general statements concerning perception of the drought hazard. How are these related to your own evaluation carried out earlier in this chapter?

From the work which you have just completed you will have become aware of some of the major findings of Saarinen. All the farmers were conscious of dryness as a disadvantage but they overestimated the number of very good years. As aridity increases so the perception of it is more acute: their expectation of very good years decreases and they become more cautious in forecasting.

There can be little doubt that perception level is an important component in the decision-making environment. However, the key question to be answered is: what actions result from differences in this level? It is reasonable to expect differences in perception of the drought hazard to be reflected in the land use pattern of the Great Plains.

A greater awareness of the drought hazard would normally limit the number of farming choices perceived as available. Look at Fig. 6.4 which shows the distribution of three grades of farming enterprise. Is there any evidence to suggest the pattern results from

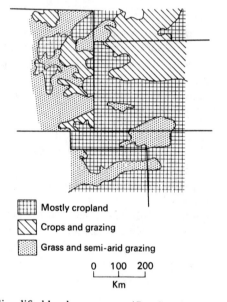

⊞ Mostly cropland

⊠ Crops and grazing

⊡ Grass and semi-arid grazing

```
0   100  200
└────┴────┘
     Km
```

Fig. 6.4   Simplified land use pattern (*Based on the Atlas of the U.S.A.*)

differences in perception level? Are there marked differences between the wetter east and the drier west? In answering this, refer to Fig. 6.1 to locate the counties studied by Saarinen. Remember, too, the work of Hewes which was discussed in Chapter 4 on page 70. He discovered that frost damage in the south of the region was more severe than in the north and a question was then posed about perception level.

When you consider these two results together do they now suggest an interesting hypothesis? In perceiving environmental hazards, there is a critical level beyond which human sensitivity is particularly alerted, and beyond which there is little room for human error of judgment if disaster is to be avoided.

In Chapter 4 you were introduced to Davidson's attempt to devise a capability index for farm land. His study also tried to ascertain the extent to which farmers perceived the limitations of their land. Similar methods to those of Saarinen were employed and revealed similar optimistic attitudes. Farmers with land objectively classified as poor tended to over-estimate its capability. Davidson suggests two hypotheses to explain this mis-match. The farmer's priority is with security: he wishes to minimise his risks rather than make the maximum profit. This idea is elaborated later in the chapter. Alternatively some types of farming, such as extensive cattle rearing, may not alert farmers to limitations imposed by relief and soil: climatic hazard may be more operative in this context.

Whatever the explanation, it is clear that some Deeside farmers take decisions in the belief that their land is reasonable in quality whereas it may be quite marginal. To what extent this is a general practice is a question of fundamental importance requiring further post-graduate research.

Strategies of Farmers

To combat environmental uncertainty, the farmer must develop a strategy to succeed or even to survive in marginal areas. Gould introduced in 1963 through the 'Theory of Games' a possible method of outwitting the environment. This theory of games rests upon making rational decisions despite many uncertainties – such as the weather – and the development of a winning strategy. This may be achieved by trial and error or it may be achieved more scientifically through the application of games theory. Gould exemplifies this by using simplified data and climatic seasons in the difficult environment of central Ghana. The staple crops grown and their return in wet and dry years is shown in Table 6.3. The problem posed is which

Table 6.3

Crop yields in Ghana

	Wet year	Dry year
Yams	82	11
Maize	61	49
Cassava	12	38
Millet	43	32
Hill rice	30	71

Source: Ambrose, P. Analytical Human Geography.

combination of crops should be grown. The first step in solving this problem is to use *linear programming* methods which may be familiar to you from your mathematics. Steps to follow are:

1. Draw two vertical scales approximately 10 cm long and separated by 2 cm, and divide them 0–100 as in Fig. 6.5.
2. Label one scale wet and the other dry.
3. Plot the returns for each crop as shown in Table 6.3 on the appropriate wet or dry scale and join the points as shown in Fig. 6.5.

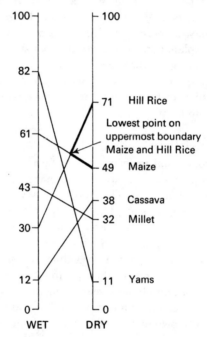

Fig. 6.5 Graphical solution to determine optimum crop combination (*Ambrose, P., Analytical Human Geography*)

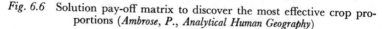

	Wet Years	Dry Years	Col. 1	Col. 2	Col. 3
Maize	61	49	$61-49 = 12$	$\dfrac{41}{12+41}$	$= 77.4\%$
Hill Rice	30	71	$30-71 = 41$	$\dfrac{12}{12+41}$	$= 22.6\%$

Fig. 6.6 Solution pay-off matrix to discover the most effective crop proportions (*Ambrose, P., Analytical Human Geography*)

4. Look at the lowest point on the uppermost boundary for an indication of which crops will prove the most profitable in these uncertain conditions. The two crops meeting at this point are hill rice and maize, and it is these two crops which will make the most efficient use of the land. In what proportions should they be grown?

5. To answer this question insert the returns for maize and hill rice in a '*pay-off matrix*' as shown in Fig. 6.6 and proceed as follows:

   (a) subtract the dry year value from the wet year (column 1)

   (b) disregard any minus sign and apportion the difference to the alternate crop and divide by the sum of the two differences (column 2)

   (c) the answer in column 3 indicates the proportion in which the two crops should be planted to minimise the risk of famine, namely, maize 77·4% and hill rice 22·6%.

Two small problems will help you reinforce this method.

In Madhya Pradesh province in India, the subsistence farmer has a choice of growing either rice or sorghum. The calorific value of these crops in wet and dry years is shown in Table 6.4. Construct a pay-off matrix to discover in which proportions the subsistence farmer should grow these crops to minimise his risks.

Table 6.4

Calorific values of crops in Madhya Pradesh, India

	Wet year	Dry year
Rice	63	43
Sorghum	28	58

Source: Yeates, M. H. *An Introduction to Quantitative Analysis in Economic Geography.*

Table 6.5

Crop returns on a West Country farm

	'Wet warm' year	'Dry cool' year
Pasture	8	2
Cereals	6	8
Legumes	10	4
Fruit	16	24
Roots	15	6

Table 6.5 shows the returns for a variety of crops on a West Country farm in years loosely designated 'wet warm' and 'dry cool'. Use linear programming methods to determine which crop combination will yield the highest profit.

You will have noticed that the aims of the two farmers differ and thus it is necessary to consider in more detail the idea of *optimiser* and *satisficer*.

Optimiser and satisficer concept

Whatever opportunities may present themselves for rational planning, employing research data from agricultural institutes and sophisticated computer programs in the future, Harvey argues in a convincing way that present-day patterns have evolved through trial and error until a *satisfactory* one emerged and became established so reaching a state of equilibrium.

Fundamental to this hypothesis of Harvey is the concept that man is a *satisficer* rather than an *optimiser*. In other words, instead of being concerned with striving for maximum productivity and profit (optimiser), once a satisfactory level has been achieved then a pattern and routine of activity will stabilise (satisficer). This equilibrium leads to uniformity and hence the agglomeration of particular kinds of agricultural activity such as cotton growing or dairying as noted in the earlier chapters. The tendency towards regional specialisation is further reinforced by group psychology manifested in the desire of individuals to conform to the norm for the area. If several neighbours of a farmer are growing hops then it is only natural that he feels that he too should do so. The force of this group behaviour is especially important too in the spread of innovation which will be examined later.

To date, little empirical work has been undertaken to test the optimiser/satisficer hypothesis. However, a study in Central Sweden undertaken by Wolpert showed that the average farmer only attains two-thirds of the potential which his resources would allow were they harnessed to maximise production. Furthermore, he found it was possible to sub-divide the area into five zones of productivity indicating that the forces of group psychology were at work in the region as a whole. This is important when considered in conjunction with Hagerstrand's work within the same area and which is to be introduced a little later in this chapter.

Table 6.6

Analysis of farmers' decisions: frequency of occurrence

Farmers' priority	1	2	3	4	5	6	7	8	9	10
Factor A	5		1							
Factor B		1		1	1	3				
Factor C		1	1	1	3					
Factor D	1	1	1	1	1					
Factor E		1				1	1			
Factor F		1	1		1					
Factor G		1			1				1	
Factor H		2		1		1	1		1	
Factor I							1			1
Factor J								1	1	

The routes by which the individual farmer reaches a decision are complex and varied. Nevertheless the problem is one to be pursued if satisfactory explanations of farming patterns are to be attempted. It is possible for you to begin by including relevant questions when undertaking fieldwork on farms. One method suggested by Ambrose is to construct a series of significant factors and ask for these to be placed in order of priority by individual farmers. The results of such an experiment in Cambridgeshire are summarised in Table 6.6.

Before undertaking fieldwork, ten factors were suggested as being especially important in contributing to decision-making on the farm. These are listed below and are found on the left-hand side of Table 6.6.

Factor A   Market value of crops...government policy.
Factor B   Soil type.
Factor C   Utilisation of machinery to minimise waste of capacity.
Factor D   Utilisation of labour to keep occupied during the year.
Factor E   Slope and aspect.
Factor F   Seasonal distribution of net rainfall.
Factor G   Incidence of early and late frosts.
Factor H   Availability of a gross market (food freezer/super market).
Factor I   Fashion.
Factor J   Tradition.

Farmers were asked to rank these 1–10 in order of priority. The response of farmers was recorded in Table 6.6 from which you can read that five farmers placed factor A – the market value of crops – as being of the highest priority.

Although the evidence is insubstantial and inconclusive this idea could be further developed and tested in your own fieldwork. Suggestions for such development may be derived from the work of

Table 6.7.

Ranking of Decision-Making Factors in order of importance

Rank	Factor	Total Score
1.	Market demand	642
2.	Income	524
3.	Profits	523
4.	Experience	490
5.	Personal risk	479
6.	Free time	385
7.	Personal preference	365
8.	Labour	332
9.	Proven type of farming in area	314
10.	Capital	213
11.	Enterprise previously established	176
12.	Buildings/machinery	164
13.	Transport costs	138
14.	Trained staff	106
15.	Agricultural training	82
16.	Government policy	74
17.	Prior knowledge	59
18.	Under-used land	56
19.	Co-operatives	33

Source: Ilbery

Ilbery who found that in the physically homogeneous area of North-East Oxfordshire land use varied considerably from farm to farm. To test the hypothesis that such differences could only result from economic and behavioural forces, he compiled a list of these and farmers were asked to grade the importance of each on a five point scale where *0* signified irrelevant and *4* essential. Farmers were asked to award points in this way for each of their two principal activities. Thus the overall importance for each factor could be estimated from the total points awarded to it by all the farmers. The results are summarised in Table 6.7.

Arranged in rank order, the first three factors are economic ones but thereafter behavioural ones predominate. What can you deduce from the five at the bottom of the list? Do you think this evidence supports the earlier satisficer concept and the idea that the farmer prefers security, stability and low risk rather than high profits?

The equilibrium state of agriculture as outlined is not a static but a dynamic one because of new technological developments in society as a whole. Long ago a major breakthrough in farming was the 'Norfolk Rotation'. Less dramatic in nature but still significant are developments in the last 25 years: modern milking parlours, barley beef, broiler chickens in this country, new strains of rice in South East Asia and growing mechanisation throughout the world serve as examples of such innovation. It was suggested in the systems diagram in Chapter 3 that innovation has its origins in wealth. How do innovations spread to become common practice and so improve farming methods and productivity?

The Diffusion of Innovation

When you hear a new 'pop' record what is your reaction to it? Do you accept it immediately? Are you cautious and only accept it when the majority of your group say they approve? Or do you belong to the minority who cling to their old collection and only accept the new after a long period of time? If the reaction of all your group to a new record were to be plotted it would probably conform to the pattern shown in Fig. 6.7A. At first acceptance is slow and then it reaches 'take-off' point, after which it is accepted by the bulk of people. However, there always remain a few stubborn people who are reluctant to accept change. The 'S' shape of the curve in Fig. 6.7A summarises what is regarded as normal group reaction to any innovation. The steepness of the curve in the middle results in part from *geometrical* progression. If two people accept they each influence another one and so the total becomes four. If these four people then each spread this idea to another person then eight people adopt the idea and so the snowball effect grows.

Is there any evidence for such a pattern? Look at Fig. 6.7B. This shows the rate of adoption of some new machines in the USA between 1940 and 1960. Although there are minor differences between the graphs they all conform to the basic 'S' curve. The same pattern is also revealed in a study of the distribution of hybrid corn in a number of the states of the USA as shown in Fig. 6.7C. Details of this study are to be found in Yeates' book listed in the suggested reading.

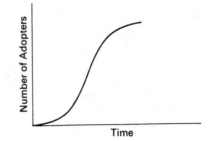

Fig. 6.7(A)   Group reactions to innovation

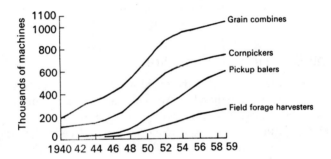

Fig. 6.7(B)   Adoption of machines in the U.S.A. (*Tarrant, J. R., Agricultural Geography*)

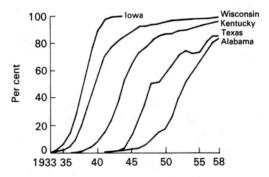

Fig. 6.7(C)   The diffusion rate of hybrid corn seed in five American states (*Tarrant, J. R., Agricultural Geography*)

So far the discussion has been confined to how an innovation is adopted in relation to the time from which it is introduced. As geographers we are particularly interested in how diffusion patterns spread over space from an initial location. A number of such diffusion patterns in Sweden have been studied by Hagerstrand who also developed *simulation models* of how an idea would spread, given certain assumptions. The most important of these assumptions was that the amount of contact between farmers and hence the possibility of adoption would be related to distance. Hence the process of distance–decay, which played such a vital part in the last chapter, would again operate from the location of the first adoption.

We are not to be concerned here with the simulation model but the actual pattern. The map shown in Fig. 6.8 indicates how a subsidy to help farmers improve their pastures spread in the district of Asby, in Central Sweden, between 1928 and 1932. The distribution shown is that for 1932. The area is divided into cells of 25 sq km and the numbers represent the numbers of adopters contained in each of these cells. The isopleths indicate the percentage of actual adopters compared with the potential if all adopted the new idea.

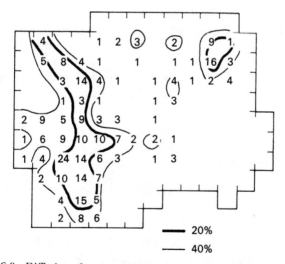

—— 20%

—— 40%

Fig. 6.8 Diffusion of pasture subsidies in Central Sweden (*Abler, R., Adams, J. S., Gould, P., Spatial Organisation*)

There is an inner core in the southwest of the area with a high acceptance and two zones where the rate diminishes as the distance from the core area increases. The fact that it is not an even fall-off may be because of the broken topography and especially the presence of lakes which inhibit social contacts. In any event, when you think of your own circle of friends, social contacts must contain a random element, and this may well help explain the smaller area of higher acceptance in the east.

The net result of the diffusion process would seem to reinforce the spatial agglomeration of a pattern noted earlier.

Summary

How far would you agree that the most significant conclusion to be drawn from our various farming studies in the last four chapters is that an agglomerated pattern – or agricultural region – seems to be dominant and repetitive and that it results from physical and economic elements and is reinforced and perpetuated by behavioural ones? Equally significant is the process of distance decay which permeates and transcends all the groups of elements considered.

Further Reading

Found, W. C. (1971). *A Theoretical Approach to Land Use Patterns*, Chapters 6, 7, 8, 9. Arnold.

*Gould, P. R. (1963) 'Man against the environment: a game theoretical framework'. *A.A.A.G.*, 53, pages 290–7.

Harvey, D. W. (1966) 'Theoretical concepts and the analysis of agricultural land use patterns in geography'. *A.A.A.G.*, 56, pages 361–74.

Ilbery B. W. (1977) 'Point score analysis: a methodological framework for analysing the decision-making process in agriculture'. *Tijdschrift voor economische en sociale geografie.* vol. 68, no. 2, pages 66–71.

*Saarinen, F. (1966) 'Perception of the drought hazard on the Great Plains'. Research Paper 106, Dept. of Geography, Chicago University.

Tarrant, J. R. (1974) *Agricultural Geography*. David and Charles.

Wolpert, J. (1964) 'The decision process in a spatial context'. *A.A.A.G.*, 54, pages 537–58.

Yeates, M. H. (1968) *An Introduction to Quantitative Analysis in Economic Geography*, Chapter 4. McGraw-Hill.

*Reproduced in Ambrose, P. (1966) *Analytical Human Geography*. Longman.

7. Industry I — Patterns of Industry

Just as a wide variety of farming types and scales were identified in Chapter 3, so there is equal diversity in patterns of industry. Ways in which this variety is shown in maps each using different criteria are introduced here and an explanation for patterns sought in Chapter 8.

It is usual in the first instance to differentiate between primary, secondary and tertiary industries. Primary industries are extractive ones and supply raw materials – such as iron ore – to be used in secondary or manufacturing industries. Tertiary industries, known as service ones, are non-productive but provide a service to society, for example, banking. This classification is a very broad one and to some extent subjective. A more detailed and commonly accepted classification is the official *Standard Industrial Classification*, published by HMSO. The major divisions – called orders – together with an example of the subdivisions for one order – called minimum list headings – are contained in Table 7.1 at the end of this chapter, p. 138.

Examples of Industrial Patterns

The simplest description of an industrial pattern is a dot distribution map for a single industry as shown in Fig. 7.1. The level of information in such a map is low: there is no indication of the scale of production measured in terms of actual output, number of factories located or people employed in each town. Despite these limitations it is, however, possible to describe the industry as widely distributed especially when compared with the concentration of woollen towns in West Yorkshire or cotton towns in Lancashire. The pattern of these latter two industries will already be very familiar. Nearest neighbour analysis introduced later in Chapter 11 on page 203 will enable you to describe more precisely such dot distributions.

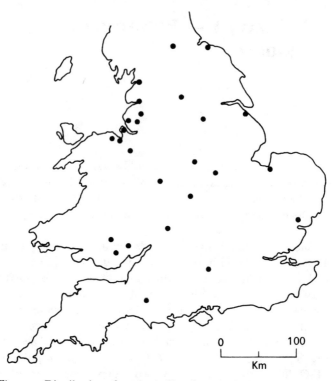

Fig. 7.1   Distribution of synthetic fibre factories in England and Wales

Using the same principle, but substituting circles proportional to
the number of people employed in place of dots, some idea of the
scale of industry may be presented as in Fig. 7.2. The detail for
Bristol itself is further displayed in Fig. 7.3, but without an explana-
tory text, the map alone is of little further help. When Britton's text
– cited at the end of Chapter 8 – is read then one is able to form a
picture not only of the scale but of the type of industry. For example,
in zone 5 the majority of people work in the paper and board
industries whilst those in zone 8 for the most part are employed in
metal goods manufacture and to a lesser extent in mechanical
engineering. How could Fig. 7.3 be improved to provide a more
accurate description of the industrial pattern? To convert the circles
into piegraphs indicating diversity is one obvious suggestion. What
further data are required to facilitate this? The more readily

accessible sources of industrial data are listed at the end of this chapter.

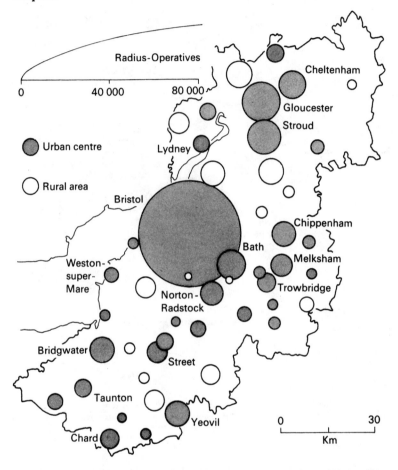

Fig. 7.2 Bristol Region: total manufacturing operatives 1963 (*Britton, J. N. H., Regional Analysis and Economic Geography: A Case Study of Manufacturing in the Bristol Region*)

Two contrasting ways of describing patterns in maps are seen in Figs 7.4 and 7.5. The pattern of Taranto in the Mezzogiorno area of Italy is portrayed in a simple non-quantified map showing the distribution of differing types of industries whereas the London map shows the intensity of industrial activity using the number of

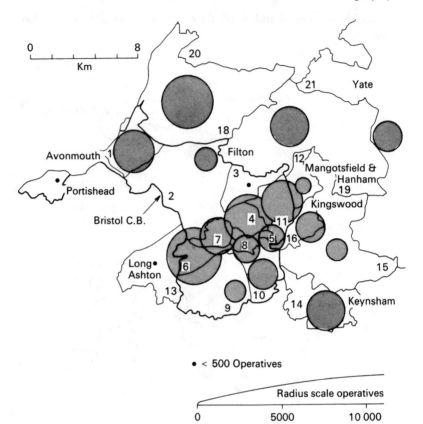

Fig. 7.3 Bristol Sub-region: manufacturing operatives 1963 (*Britton, J. N. H., Regional Analysis and Economic Geography: A Case Study of Manufacturing in the Bristol Region*)

employees as its criterion. How do these differ from Fig. 7.2? Study the two distribution maps, Figs 7.4 and 7.5, carefully and decide which you find the more informative. Your answer will really depend upon the purpose for which you wish to use the map.

Look at Fig. 7.6. Again taken from Martin's study of London, the distribution of one industry for which a *location quotient* has been calculated, is shown on a grid square basis. Such a quotient enables the degree of concentration to be ascertained and is calculated by the formula:

$$\text{Location quotient} = \frac{\% \text{ of area's employees in Industry A in quadrat R}}{\% \text{ of area's employees in all industries in quadrat R}}$$

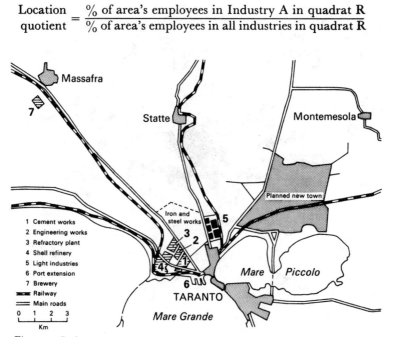

Fig. 7.4 Industry around Taranto (*Mountjoy, Alan B., The Mezzogiorno.*
Problem Regions of Europe Series)

There is a growing tendency in recent studies to use quadrat maps
such as the one in Fig. 7.6. As in sampling (Chapter 2) the size of
the quadrat will depend upon the scale of the problem and the
amount of detail required in order to achieve greater accuracy. Such
maps lend themselves to detailed analysis, the calculation of centres
of gravity and changes in such centres over time. This format is also
very suitable for computer programming thus facilitating computer
drawn maps and prediction of future trends. A simple example
employing a computer is found in Chapter 9.

This brief introduction to the variety of ways in which industries
may be mapped is by no means comprehensive and additional
reading is suggested. What is important in geography is to identify
the salient features of any pattern and realise their value in helping
solve spatial problems, such as agglomeration and over-specialisation
on too narrow a range of industries. The simplest form of location
quotients has just been introduced and attention is now turned to
descriptions of statistical data.

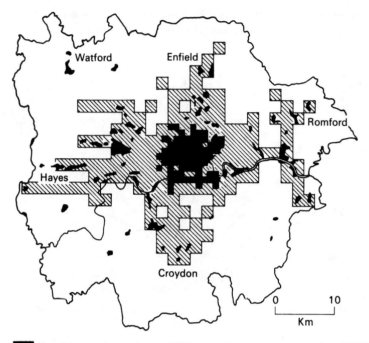

■ Densities continuously over 1500 operatives per square Kilometre (1954)

▨ Densities continuously over 300 operatives per square Kilometre (1954)

Fig. 7.5 Principal Industrial Areas of London (*Martin, J. E., Greater London: An Industrial Geography*)

Methods of measuring concentration and specialisation of industries within and between regions

Generalised assumptions are often made about the regional concentration of a particular industry, for example, the footwear industry in the East Midlands. It is valuable to test these assumptions against the statistical evidence. This may be achieved in one of three ways: by calculating the percentage of the nation's footwear employees in the East Midlands, by calculating the location quotient similar to that used by Martin in London or by determining the degree of specialisation.

The percentage figure is the one most easily obtained but is of limited value because it is only looking at one particular industry, whereas the other two indices reflect the general industrial structure of an area. Raw percentages will only reveal the more extreme forms of specialisation such as the paper, printing and publishing in the South East where 45% of that industry's labour force is located.

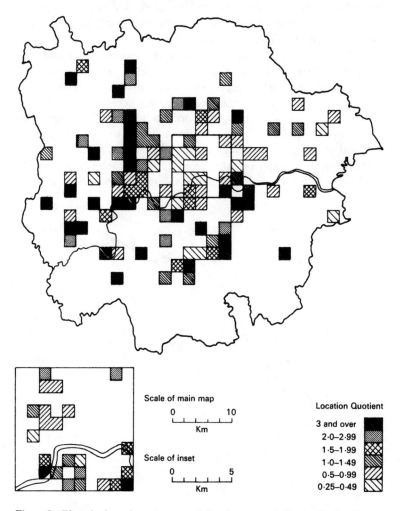

Fig. 7.6 Electrical engineering: specialisation map (*Martin, J. E., Greater London: An Industrial Geography*)

Using Table 7.2 calculate what percentage of workers in the making of vehicles is contained in the West Midlands together with the South East.

Percentage figures may also be used to construct a *Lorenz curve* which enables visual comparisons between industrial structures to be made. Look at Fig. 7.7 which is based upon data in Table 7.2. For each region in which you are interested, first it is necessary to find the percentage employed in each industrial category. For Yorkshire and Humberside these range from 20·2% (textiles) to 1·2% (shipbuilding). Arrange the categories in rank order and plot the percentages in this sequence as *cumulative percentages*. In this example textiles (20·2%) employ the most people, followed by mechanical engineering (15·9%), so together they account for 36·1% as shown by the asterisk in Fig. 7.7. Continue to plot all the industries in this way until all have been accounted for and of course you reach the total of 100% of the people employed.

How may this graph be interpreted? If each category of employment contained the same percentage, the graph would be a straight

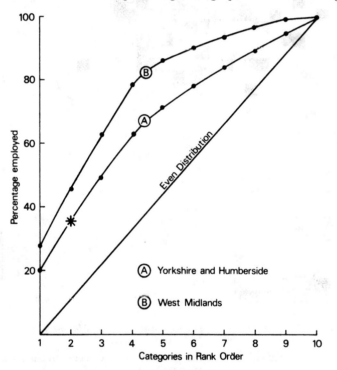

Fig. 7.7 Lorenz curve comparing the distribution of employment by occupation between Yorkshire and Humberside and the West Midlands.

line (even distribution). The less steep the Lorenz curve therefore, the more diversified is the industrial structure of a region. Using the data contained in Table 7.2 and your knowledge of Great Britain, construct a Lorenz curve for two regions which you think should have two very different structures.

A location quotient may be obtained by using the formula below:

$$LQ = \frac{\dfrac{\text{Number of people employed in industry A in area X}}{\text{Number of people employed in all maufacturing industries in area X}}}{\dfrac{\text{Number employed nationally in industry A}}{\text{Number employed nationally in all manufacturing industries}}}$$

The greater the index, the greater is the degree of concentration. In any event a value of more than 1 reveals that the region has more than its share of that particular industry. Conversely a value of less than 1 indicates that it has less than its share. Calculations are quick and easy with modern pocket calculators and direct comparisons of indices can do much to correct assessments made upon a visual inspection of the raw statistics.

An example of this method is to determine the degree of concentration of shipbuilding in Scotland which yields a location quotient of 4·4. This indicates not only the high concentration of shipbuilding in Scotland (it has more than four times its share) but since the index takes into account the overall employment structure, that there is a marked degree of specialisation and dependence upon shipbuilding. This is developed in the index of specialisation introduced below.

Using the data in Table 7.2, calculate location quotients for vehicle manufacture in the West Midlands and the South East. What additional information do these indices provide beyond the percentages obtained earlier?

A final way is to measure the degree of specialisation within a study area using the formula:

$$\text{Index of specialisation} = \sqrt{p_1{}^2 + p_2{}^2 \ldots p_n{}^2}$$

where p_1 is the percentage of people employed in industry 1, p_2 in industry 2, and so on.

Table 7.3 is an analysis of employees within the catchment area of Hull. On the basis of these data the index of specialisation has been calculated as 29·4. How can this be interpreted? The lower the index, the more diversified is the industrial structure of the area. Available literature gives no guidance concerning what may be

Table 7.2

Employees (thousands) in selected manufacturing industries analysed by regions, June 1974

| | South East | | | East Anglia | South West | West Mid-lands | East Mid-lands | Yorks and H'side | North West | North | Wales | Scot-land | Great Britain |
	Greater London	Rest of SE	Total SE										
Food, drink and tobacco	99·5	73·0	172·5	41·7	64·1	59·8	50·6	84·4	114·3	34·3	19·4	98·7	739·7
Chemicals and allied industries	56·6	72·4	129·0	9·9	16·5	21·0	28·2	35·5	96·6	50·9	16·7	27·9	432·1
Metal manufacture	19·1	19·0	38·1	2·1	7·3	126·1	39·9	92·3	25·3	48·9	83·1	43·4	506·6
Mechanical engineering	88·2	157·3	245·5	29·8	62·7	132·1	89·2	94·0	124·8	65·2	27·2	94·3	964·7
Electrical engineering	149·6	165·9	315·6	24·1	47·8	112·0	41·3	31·1	107·2	56·0	35·3	59·6	830·0
Shipbuilding and marine engineering	4·6	34·9	39·5	3·5	19·5	*	1·5	7·3	10·0	48·3	1·6	43·0	175·1
Vehicles	55·2	149·6	204·8	18·0	60·7	203·1	51·6	44·9	122·2	12·4	26·4	39·6	783·4
Textiles	11·2	11·7	22·9	2·9	13·1	27·5	114·2	119·5	133·4	26·2	16·7	69·4	545·9
Clothing and footwear	61·1	27·8	88·9	11·3	21·9	19·8	62·4	45·4	70·2	33·9	16·4	34·1	404·3
Paper, printing and publishing	138·7	122·4	261·1	19·6	40·1	32·4	29·3	36·0	79·3	21·8	12·8	49·8	582·2
Totals	683·8	834·0	1517·8	162·9	353·7	733·8	508·2	590·4	883·3	397·9	255·6	559·8	5964·0

Source: Department of Employment Gazette, July 1975, pages 643–646.

Table 7.3

Industrial analysis of employees in employment
Hull travel to work area—1973

	Males	Females	Total	%	(%)²
I. Agriculture, forestry, fishing, mining and quarrying (primary industries)	5255	801	6056	3·6	12·9
II. Food, drink and tobacco	6467	4234	10,701	6·3	39·69
III. Coal and petroleum products, chemicals and allied products	5135	3439	8574	5·0	25·0
IV. Metal manufacture and mechanical engineering	9706	2409	12,115	7·1	50·41
V. Instrument and electrical engineering	375	220	595	0·3	0·09
VI. Shipbuilding and marine engineering and vehicles	11,407	2047	13,454	7·9	62·41
VII. Metal goods not elsewhere specified	1641	1535	3176	1·9	3·61
VIII. Textiles, leather goods and fur, clothing and footwear	1610	792	2402	1·4	1·96
IX. Bricks, pottery, glass, cement, timber, furniture	4517	1002	5519	3·2	10·24
X. Paper, printing, publishing	1739	1169	2908	1·7	2·89
XI. Other manufacturing	688	403	1091	0·6	0·36
Total manufacturing	43,285	17,250	60,535		
XII. Construction	9387	587	9974	5·9	34·81
XIII. Gas, electricity and water	1762	193	1955	1·1	1·21
XIV. Transport and communications	13,118	1856	14,974	8·8	77·44
XV. Distributive industries	10,128	13,260	23,388	13·8	190·40
XVI. Insurance, banking, finance and business services	1971	2629	4600	2·7	7·29
XVII. Professional and scientific services	9931	16,948	26,879	15·8	249·64
XVIII. Miscellaneous services	5881	8366	14,247	8·4	70·56
XIX. Public administration	5184	2592	7776	4·5	20·25
Unclassified by industry	6	9	15		
Grand total	105,908	64,491	170,399		$\Sigma(\% \text{ Total})^2$ = 861·25

Source: Unpublished local Department of Employment and Productivity records.

% = percentage of Grand Total

considered high or low and at the moment one must rely upon regional comparisons. Britton has calculated indices for sub-regions of the Bristol area, a selection of which are: Bristol 31·4, Bridgwater 37·1, Bath 46·5, Chippenham 56·8. It is interesting to note the similarity of Hull and Bristol which are both traditionally concerned with port industries. Used in conjunction with the location quotient, the index of specialisation is a fair indicator of the vulnerability of a region to any fluctuations in the economy as a whole – for example, a recession in the car making industry and its effect upon employment in the West Midlands.

Changes in Industrial Patterns

Patterns are not static and it is important that significant trends are identified. Two examples using differing criteria are included below. Look at Table 7.4 where the net flow of new and branch factories

Table 7.4
Net flow of new and branch factories (in thousands)

	1952–59	1960–66
North	+1·5	+2·5
Yorkshire and Humberside	+0·7	−0·8
North West	+2·3	+7·4
East Midlands	+0·7	−0·1
West Midlands	−1·5	−6·3
East Anglia	+0·2	+1·6
South East	−3·0	−14·3
South West	+1·0	+2·5
Wales	+0·5	+2·6
Scotland	+2·2	+6·0

Source: Board of Trade.

between 1952 and 1966 is summarised. The most marked trend is the outmigration from the South East and to a lesser extent from the West Midlands. Conversely the North West and Scotland have witnessed a growth in their number of factories. After reading the next chapter which contains a case study of re-located industry, you should return to this table and try to offer an explanation for the apparent trend and also assess the limitations of this data set.

A more detailed analysis of changes in the regional pattern of

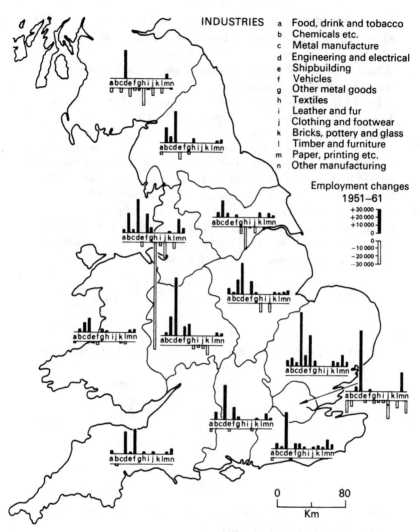

Fig. 7.8 Regional employment trends in manufacturing industries 1951–61
(*Smith, D. M., 'Recent changes in the regional pattern of British industry'*)

British industry was undertaken by D. M. Smith. One summary of
his work is shown in Fig. 7.8. To what extent does this reveal a
continuing contrast between those areas located north of the Wash–
Severn line and those to the south? Does this help explain the

distribution of designated areas shown in Fig. 8.3 on page 146? Study Table 7.4 in conjunction with Fig. 7.8 and ask yourself whether or not there is a conflicting picture of industrial change. Which do you feel is the more valid one? What lessons must be learned about data limitations?

From Fig. 7.8 a marked decline in textiles in Lancashire is evident. In a case study of Bolton, Bale has shown that 23 former cotton mills are now varied in use from engineering to yarn processing.

Since stress is now placed upon predicting trends, it is right to ask whether or not it is possible to anticipate changes. A figure frequently quoted in the regional plans of the Department of Economic Affairs, for example, the West Midlands Study, is the *activity rate* which expresses the relationship between the number of people of working age and the number of people actually employed. Thus the activity rate in theory reveals the employment potential of an area. The activity rate is determined by the formula:

$$\text{Activity rate} = \frac{\text{number of people employed}}{\text{total population of working age}} \times 100$$

Table 7.5

Population data (1971) and employment structure (1973) for Herefordshire

	Population of working age 000	Population actually employed 000
Males	41·8	28·0
Females	37·1	18·8
Total	78·9	46·8

Source: County Census Report 1971 and local records of Department of Employment and Productivity.

Thus, for Herefordshire, the activity rate would be 59·3. Calculate how the male activity rate differs from that of the female rate. Would the difference be as great in a Yorkshire textile town? How may these indices be interpreted?

A low activity rate indicates that a potential labour force exists within an area, but does not of course offer any guarantee that such a potential will be realised. It may also be complicated by the sociological and industrial structure within the area. Perhaps a more satisfactory guide is the number of people registered as unemployed. However, in the days of full employment, the activity rate is the only viable alternative indicator of a potential labour force. When you have read the next chapter you will realise the influence of a potential labour force in an area when deciding upon new locations for industry.

How can one assess whether or not an activity rate is low? Again the same problem arises as with location quotients. The only guidelines which can presently be offered are comparative values for other regions. Such values quoted by Britton include Bristol 57·6, Chippenham 47·3, Bridgwater 52·0, Bath 42·8, and Taunton 45·8. The figures for Herefordshire would seem to be comparatively high and the question may be asked why it is not of the same order as that for Taunton with which it has other common features.

Pattern identification in industry as in agriculture is merely the first stage of geographical investigation. Once recognised, an explanation must be sought for the pattern and approaches to this problem are discussed in the next chapter. Before passing on to this, however, a list of data sources which you may wish to consult in your own studies is provided below.

SELECTED DATA SOURCES

In attempting to build up the pattern of industry within a study area many practical difficulties arise because data sources tend to use different boundaries from the ones you may require and indeed change their own boundaries over time. Some sources too are not published and may be difficult of access. Only those readily available are quoted.

For Great Britain consult:

1. Advanced regional texts such as Smith, D. M. (1969) *Industrial Britain: the North West*, published by David and Charles. This is one example from a series on regions in Britain.
2. *Annual Abstract of Statistics* published by HMSO provides a wide variety of information at differing scales: national, county and regions. The *Monthly Digest of Statistics* gives similar information on a monthly basis.
3. *The Department of Employment and Productivity Gazette* published

monthly gives very helpful information including employment figures and wage rates.

4. Publications of the Regional Economic Planning Councils. For example, by the South West: *Region with a Future*, and on a smaller scale by Yorkshire and Humberside: *Halifax and the Calder Valley*.
5. *The Census of Production* gives generalised figures for England and Wales.
6. At local level several commercial directories are available and two particularly useful ones are *Kompass* and *Kelly's*, usually obtainable in reference sections of libraries.

For areas outside Great Britain consult:

1. *The United Nations Statistical Year Book.*
2. *The Annual Year Book of the E.E.C.*
3. Regional Atlases such as *National Atlas of the U.S.A.*

Table 7.1

Standard Industrial Classification

Order
      I. Agriculture, Forestry, Fishing
     II. Mining and Quarrying
    III. Food, Drink and Tobacco
     IV. Coal and Petroleum Products
      V. Chemicals and Allied Industries
     VI. Metal Manufacture
    VII. Mechanical Engineering
   VIII. Instrument Engineering
     IX. Electrical Engineering
      X. Shipbuilding and Marine Engineering
     XI. Vehicles
    XII. Metal Goods (not elsewhere specified)
   XIII. Textiles
    XIV. Leather, Leather Goods and Fur.
     XV. Clothing and Footwear
    XVI. Bricks, Pottery, Glass, Cement etc.
   XVII. Timber, Furniture etc.
  XVIII. Paper, Printing and Publishing
    XIX. Other Manufacturing Industries

XX. Construction
XXI. Gas, Electricity and Water
XXII. Transport and Communication
XXIII. Distributive Trades
XXIV. Insurance, Banking, Finance and Business Services
XXV. Professional and Scientific Services
XXVI. Miscellaneous Services
XXVII. Public Administration and Defence

Note: Only the orders are given. Each order is broken down into minimum list headings, *eg*.

Order
VIII. Instrument Engineering
  351 Photographic and document copying equipment
  352 Watches and clocks
  353 Surgical instruments and appliances
  354 Scientific and industrial instruments and systems

Source: The Standard Industrial Classification. HMSO 1968.

Further Reading

Bale, John (1976) *The Location of Manufacturing Industry*, Chapters 2 and 3, Oliver and Boyd.

Guest, Arthur (1970) *Advanced Practical Geography*. Heinemann.

Monkhouse, F. J. and Wilkinson, H. R. (1968) *Maps and Diagrams*. Methuen.

Smith D. M. (1965) 'Recent changes in the regional pattern of British industry'. *T.E.S.G.** July/August 1965, vol. 56, pages 133–44.

*Tijdschrift voor economische en sociale geografie.

8 . Industry II — The Search for Order and Explanation

COMPLEXITY OF THE PROBLEM

All real world patterns are complex but perhaps none is more puzzling or defiant of rational explanation than that of industry. The problem is posed by Cairncross when he writes: 'Suppose, for example, that we ask why some industry – say shipbuilding – has become localised on the Clyde. We really have two questions to answer, not one. First, why the Clyde rather than some other place – the Thames or the Severn? Second, why shipbuilding rather than some other industry – steel or textiles? We have to show, not only that there is a pull on shipbuilding to the Clyde, but that the pull is *relatively* greater than the pull on other industries'. The frustrations of geographers in attempting to answer such fundamental questions are well summarised by the late Professor Wilfred Smith: 'Distribution patterns (of industry) have been developed by trial and error, by conscious experiment and by spontaneous variation, on the part of a host of individual entrepreneurs in order to facilitate the practice of a particular economic activity'.

There are clear parallels between the forces which influence decision-making in industry with those already introduced in the chapters concerned with agriculture. Why then is the problem more complex?

The scale of enterprise in both farming and manufacturing may vary from the small single unit to large multiple units. In industry however the factory may be part of a large international combine exerting very different kinds of pressures on decision makers. For example, the Ford and Chrysler motor groups are not based solely in the UK and their decision-making may be subjected to wishes of the American based parent company.

The factory, like the farm, may produce one or several products and as in farming there is an optimum size of unit. However, the end product of one factory (sparking plugs) may be the raw material of another (car manufacture) so that the location of one factory may be affected by the location of other factories. This inter-dependence of units of industry is a complicating force.

Industrial patterns have evolved throughout two centuries of decision-making by individualists who may or may not have chosen a *minimax* location in the first instance. A minimax location is one where production costs are minimised and returns or profits maximised. This concept of minimax location needs modification. Since decisions are taken on the basis of imperfect knowledge at any moment in time, it is highly unlikely that the minimax location can be known. Perhaps a more helpful framework is one similar to the optima and limits schema suggested for agriculture in Chapter 4, page 50. An adaptation for the industrial context is shown in Fig, 8.1 where profitability decreases outwards from the hypothetical optimum location until the operation ceases to yield any return and therefore it is no longer viable.

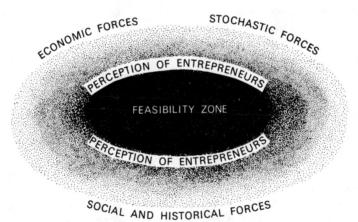

Fig. 8.1   Locating industry

Even if a minimax location is achieved initially, it is unlikely to remain so because of changes in the variables. Many examples may be chosen from the present century to illustrate that a minimax location in 1900 is not the same as that for 1970 if only because of the advent of road transport and a motorway network, the electricity grid making power supplies ubiquitous and technological advances affecting both the scale and type of labour required. Contrast the distribution of the man-made fibre industry in England and Wales (Fig. 7.1) with that of the traditional textile industries established in the nineteenth century. Although farming patterns are affected by such changes they are neither so marked nor so permanent, since with few exceptions the operations are less capital intensive than industry and are able to adapt more readily to changed circumstances. Industries are more circumscribed and you will be aware of this force of *inertia* which may be regarded as almost omnipresent in the Western World and nowhere is more clearly illustrated than on the coalfields of Britain.

One last complicating factor is the role of governments. Subsidies in agriculture tend to retain the status quo, but in the sphere of industry they have provided a planned and deliberate attempt to redistribute industry from the wealthier and more affluent parts to those in need. Thus the social factor may run contrary to the essential premise of classical economic theory that free competition exists. Governmental or social forces are not confined to any one country or political ideology. From your studies in regional geography can you think of examples from various parts of the world?

Despite the complexity of the industrial scene if one examines the distribution of industry it would seem to occur in agglomerated patterns suggesting the existence of common forces influencing the location choice by many firms. What then are these forces?

Factors Contributing to Locational Patterns of Industry

A brief summary of the forces which help promote a satisfactory environment within which industry may flourish will be followed later in the chapter by case studies in which their influence is assessed. After reading pages 151–164 you may need to return to this section and review the effectiveness of these forces in a more specific context than they are presented here.

RAW MATERIALS
Traditionally great emphasis is placed upon proximity to raw materials. This arose from the relative immobility of materials prior to advanced forms of transport but even today some industries are more tied to their raw materials than others. This dependence is related to the *material index* of the industry or the weight of raw

materials used in proportion to the weight of the finished product. Examples of industries with a high material index are metal refining, lumbering and sugar beet processing. Perishable materials also attract appropriate processing industries, for example, the frozen pea industry considered in Chapter 5.

Even when industries do pay particular attention to the location of their raw materials it is essential to remember these ties may be substantially weakened over time, not only by a changing freight rate structure, but also through improved technology as in the iron and steel industry which consumes far less coal than hitherto.

POWER

In the early stages of the industrial revolution power proved itself to be as important as the easy availability of raw materials: hence the agglomeration of industry upon the coalfields areas of the world which has remained there through the force of inertia. Since the advent of the high voltage national grid for electricity, industry in general has been freed from power as a locating factor. The dispersed pattern of industry in Switzerland where H.E.P. provided power in an easily transported form contrasts with the centralised patterns based on coalfields such as the Ruhr. Whilst in the nineteenth century the effect of power was to concentrate industry into a few areas, its most significant contribution in the twentieth century has been to facilitate decentralisation. There are exceptions to this general principle, for example, aluminium smelting which seems attracted to sources of cheap power as at Kitimat in British Columbia.

LABOUR

Historically the regional distribution of skills has been reflected in the type of industry found within regions. The textile industries of New England and the concentration of engineering in the Midlands of the UK are two examples of this. Labour and plant are alternatives and increasing automation has not only decreased the number of people required, but also changed the structure of employment. Today much of the work force in manufacturing consists of semi-skilled machine minders with very few really skilled people. The former may be trained relatively quickly whilst the latter are so few that they may be considered mobile. So once again industry has been freed from a firm bond to a particular type of labour but not from availability of labour. Hence the need to measure the potential pool of labour by activity rates as shown in Chapter 7. Look back at Fig. 7.1. Does this pattern support the hypothesis that regional skills are no longer relevant?

MARKETS

Proximity to market is yet another factor which is diminishing in significance except perhaps in the case of weight gaining industries such as baking and brewing. Even in these two activities, the pull of the local market compared with the scale economies effected when producing for a much larger regional or national market, has resulted in the emergence of fewer, larger multiple bakers and brewers. Perhaps in the past geographers have been mistaken in regarding the market as a fixed point whereas most markets are at least national in size. Clearly, other factors being equal, it is obviously advantageous to locate so that the bulk of the market is near at hand.

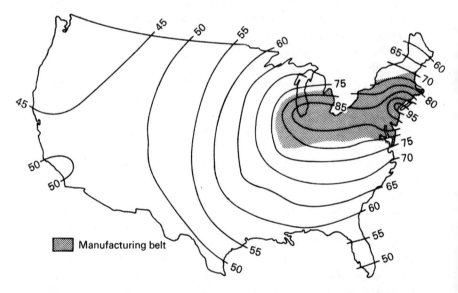

Fig. 8.2 United States market potential map—isolines express per cent values of the New York City market potential for 1948 (*Harris, Chauney D., 'The market as a factor in the localisation of industry in the United States'*)

Look at Fig. 8.2 which shows a marked relationship between the so-called manufacturing belt of the USA and isolines of market potential. Is the attraction of market forces responsible for the pronounced development of industry in the Midlands and South-East England? It should be remembered that the market itself may well vary over time and the market potential calculated by Harris in 1954 (Fig. 8.2) does not reflect the significant population changes along the West Coast. For example, the population of California rose from 15 to 20 million between 1960 and 1970 whilst the population of the New England States remained virtually static. Indeed, should California be regarded as a separate nation, it would be the sixth greatest in the world using income per capita as the criterion.

TRANSPORT

The weakening hold of the forces so far outlined has always resulted from improved transport facilities. With constant improvements in both networks and means of transport, raw materials may be carried more economically for longer distances and markets become increasingly more accessible. Although freight rate structures are complex, there is an overall tendency for costs per tonne/km to decrease as distance over land increases. Increased transport costs must be balanced against the advantages which accrue from scale economies. It would seem that the latter tend to be favoured by the entrepreneurs.

The emergence of freight traffic on the roads during the inter-war years and its greatly expanded volume since World War II has facilitated the decentralisation of light industries in particular. These are often located on industrial estates of the periphery of cities. The growing motorway networks and coming of containerisation may enhance this trend, despite increased fuel costs since the Middle East War.

GOVERNMENT POLICY

In society there may arise a conflict between what is socially desirable and what is economically feasible. Sometimes this may result in what Wreford Watson describes as 'uneconomic geography'.

With a policy of nationalisation the government of the UK became one of the major employers of industrial labour, yet direct intervention had begun nearly forty years ago with the Distribution of Industries Act which created special areas such as the North East, Clydeside and South Wales. These regions had become depressed areas with a large percentage of the work force unemployed largely as a result of the world economic recession coupled with their dependence upon a single heavy industry such as iron and steel. The government aimed to diversify the industrial structure in these areas by attempting to attract newer light industries into these regions by offering loans to set up factories, reducing taxation and industrial rates and by providing buildings and services in advance of demand. From this intervention arose the concept of the 'trading estate' where all industrial services were provided on an advantageous site. Examples of such estates are Team Valley near Newcastle and Treforest in South Wales. By 1975 there were some 157 estates in

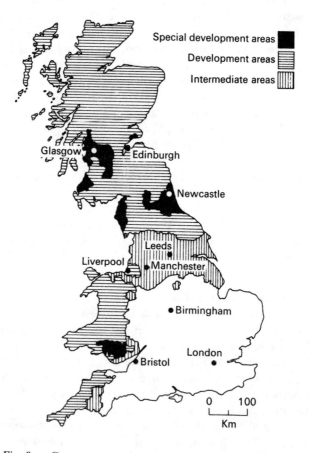

Fig. 8.3 Government assisted areas in Great Britain, 1973

existence of which 51 were located in Scotland, 49 in the North East and 20 in the North West.

This policy of making peripheral areas more attractive to private industry has been vigorously pursued by successive governments. The current distribution of designated 'development areas' is shown in Fig. 8.3. How does this reflect the persistence of regional inequality between areas of Great Britain? At regional level planners are concerned to relieve congestion in the conurbations and at the same time to control the sprawl of industry into the surrounding countryside. Therefore it is common to find – as in the West Midlands which forms the focus of the next chapter – areas designated as new towns or overspill towns to form growth points, whilst others are protected as green belts.

Governmental intervention is a world wide phenomenon. Examples may be found in the *Problem Regions of Europe Series* referred to in Chapter 7, whilst overt planning of the eastward movement of industry in Russia is well known. Japan imposes higher taxes on industries entering the city of Tokyo in order to slow down its growth rate. What examples can you recall from your regional studies of government influence on patterns of industrial location?

STOCHASTIC FORCES AND PERCEPTION
Wilfred Smith long ago hinted at the chance element contributing to the location of industry. Industries were begun by individuals often in their own home town and provided this was located within the zone of profitability indicated in Fig. 8.1, the industry would succeed and grow. The oft quoted classical case is that of William Morris. By chance he lived in Oxford and hence the siting of the Cowley works which today forms part of the British Leyland Motor Corporation. Is Cowley any more or less satisfactory than Coventry or Dagenham? Could he have succeeded in Penzance or Aberdeen?

Much stress on perception of agricultural forces was laid in Chapter 6. Perception equally plays its part in industry but is more difficult to identify because decisions are taken by a group of people (the board) rather than an individual, and there are few empirical investigations of it.

One attempt to discover how entrepreneurs perceived locational advantages was made by Bruce Bechtol who personally interviewed 1076 of the largest manufacturers in Guatemala. Bechtol was concerned with discovering the locational advantages *perceived* by the entrepreneurs and posed the question: 'Why did you locate your plant here in Guatemala?'

The responses to this question are summarized in Table 8.1.

Table 8.1

Perceived locational considerations of industrialists in Guatemala

| | First response | |
Factor	Number	%
Market	699	65
Labour	118	11
Raw materials	96	9
Communications and transport	76	7
Special incentives	76	7
Others	11	1
	1076	100

Source: Bechtol, Bruce E., 'A matter of perception'.

From this table market forces are perceived as easily the most significant. Although the domestic market is at present small, a large expansion and potential is anticipated within the Central American Common Market (CACM) as a whole. Labour, ranking second, is unskilled but is cheap and may be trained fairly easily as machine operatives. Managers and key technicians tend to be brought in from outside as suggested earlier.

Those industries citing raw materials as the most significant factor (9%) included manufacturers of cement, wood products and the processing of cotton and sugar.

The special incentives in Table 8.1 really refer to the kinds of government aid being offered in the UK. In addition the CACM has established a high tariff to protect its industries and 7% of the respondents regarded this facility as of over-riding importance.

This brief empirical study not only succeeds in identifying the reasons for industrialists establishing factories in Guatemala but provides some evidence of the forces of classical economics at work. Read back over the last few pages and summarise the field evidence for the theoretical considerations outlined. Later you should return to Table 8.1 and compare the responses of the Guatemalan industrialists with those in New Zealand (Fig. 8.4) and those in Bristol (Tables 8.3 and 8.4).

Bechtol advocates the collecting of more field evidence by interviewing industrialists but care must be taken in doing so. Such people are busy and should not be troubled by trivial enquiry. Even Bechtol evoked this response which may serve as a warning!

'None of your bloody business. All you bleeding heart idealists think we're here to screw the damn people regardless of how much good we do. Forget it...we don't answer any questions we don't have to'.

A second study by Taylor and McDermott investigated the perception level of industrialists in New Zealand. Look at Fig. 8.4. Sixteen items considered as important in evaluating the efficiency of a location are listed. These consist of both resources and services. Some 249 managers from Auckland and 279 from five secondary centres (Whangarei, Napier, Wanganui, Nelson and Timaru) were asked to assess their own location relative to the total economy of the nation. Each item was scored on a 7 point scale where 1 = excellent, 4 = average and 7 = very poor. Study Fig. 8.4 and identify differences in attitude of people living in Auckland, from those in the secondary centres.

For 8 of the 16 items – those marked with an asterisk in Fig. 8.4 – the authors developed objective measures from published data. When perception level and objective reality for these items were compared, curious results emerged. Whilst attitudes to transport and market access closely reflected reality, evaluation of labour availability was the converse. Assessment of other local provision such as technical services was also poor. This mismatch can only be described as curious since managers seemed to have a greater awareness of national phenomena rather than local ones.

Two further questions were investigated: does perception level vary with the type of product and with the way in which the industry is organised? The industries of Auckland were classified in seven categories and only one statistically significant variation emerged, that for labour costs. It would seem then that type of industry has little influence upon attitudes to the 16 factors.

On the other hand differences emerged from different types of organisation. Managers of older, larger, multi-plant firms regarded the professional services in the secondary towns as unsatisfactory whilst those of smaller, more recent, single plant firms were satisfied. The market potential of Auckland was more fully appreciated by the

larger, long-established and professionally managed producers than
by the smaller ones. Do the latter lack perspectives from outside by
which to judge the local advantages? Yet a function of size was ex-
posed by a lack of true assessment of labour relations, costs and
availability. Sufficient has been said to reinforce the idea of 'bounded
rationality' and to alert you to bias and lack of objectivity in the
decision-making process. Reading of the full text of this important
paper is recommended to you.

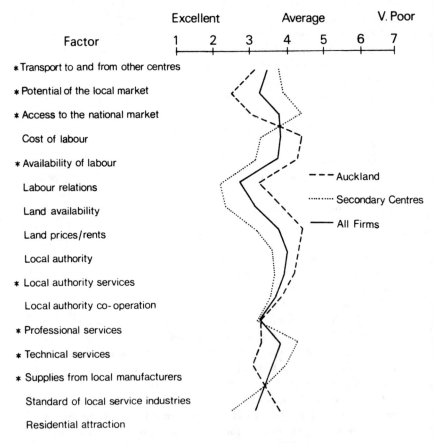

Fig. 8.4 Mean scale responses for Auckland and Secondary centre manufacturers. (*Source: Taylor and McDermott*)

Models of Industrial Location

Despite the complexities of the real world an attempt has been made to identify the forces contributing to locational patterns. How these individual forces interact has been postulated in models of industrial location.

1. ALFRED WEBER'S MODEL

In many ways the Weber model is used in industrial studies as that of von Thünen is used in agriculture. The common bond between the two models is distance minimisation. Formulated in 1909, Weber's model contained a number of initial premises some of which will now be familiar to you:

The area was regarded as homogeneous in terms of climate and topography.

He assumed a framework of perfect economic competition.

Some raw materials – water and sand – were regarded as present throughout the study area, or ubiquitous, whilst others – coal and iron – were confined to fixed locations.

Labour was available in fixed locations.

Transport was considered a direct function of weight and distance.

What weaknesses or major simplifications are you able to identify in the model at this stage?

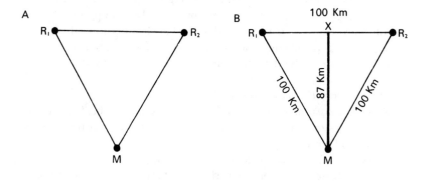

Fig. 8.5 Locating a factory

Let us consider some simple hypothetical illustrations of the theory involving two raw materials (R_1 and R_2) and a single market, M. In considering these illustrations you should look at Fig. 8.5A.

Case I   If both raw materials are ubiquitous then the industry will be located at the market.

Case II   Suppose R_1 is ubiquitous but R_2 is fixed to one location. Both raw materials are pure: *ie.* they lose no weight as a consequence of being manufactured. The factory will be located at the market. Why?

Case III   When both raw materials are pure and fixed in location, then the factory will again be located at the market since this solution involves the least movement.

Case IV   What happens when both raw materials are fixed and gross, *ie.* they lose weight during their processing? Suppose R_1 and R_2 lose 50% of their weight and 2000 tonnes of each are required. Where is the least cost location, or as it is sometimes termed, the minimum transport point (M.T.P.)? Look at Fig. 8.5B. The solution to this problem is achieved by Weber's locational triangle. If the factory were to be located at either R_1, R_2 or M then assembly and delivery costs would total 400,000 tonne/km but 374,000 at X. Work through the figures and assure yourself of this solution.

The latter case illustrates how an optimum solution to a simple problem may be reached within the limitations of the model. More complex problems involving several raw materials with differing weight losses – beyond our scope here – may be solved by using Varignon's frame or applying algebra or graphically. Although appearing complex, with the help of a suitable computer program solutions may quickly be reached. However elegant the mathematical solution to problems, one must assess its geographical validity especially in the light of the weaknesses of the basic model.

Weaknesses of the Weber Model

1. Weber assumed raw materials and markets to be fixed points whereas they are more accurately areas. Each area represents a zone of feasibility (Fig. 8.1).

2. Weber adopted a classical economist's approach. He assumed the unrealistic framework of perfect competition and he discounted the complexities of the human decision-making process.

3. The model is a static one taking no account of spatial changes in the supply of raw materials or demands of markets. Remember, however, it was developed as a result of Weber's experience at the end of the nineteenth century. How many of Britain's iron masters could have foreseen importing ores from Sweden, Canada, South America and West Africa?

4. Industries today are not merely processing industries. As we have seen earlier, the finished products of one industry may form the raw materials of another.

5. Although Weber later made allowances for differing labour costs and agglomeration tendencies, his model is essentially dominated by transport costs which are totally unrealistic. Such costs are not directly proportional to distance and the concept of the tonne/km is really a misconception.

6. Labour is not fixed in location but is mobile.

Despite these weaknesses this important model has validity and significance for geographers today if we concentrate upon the underlying concept of least cost location which Weber makes synonymous with minimum transport point.

2. MYRDAL'S MODEL OF CUMULATIVE CAUSATION

This model has been chosen to contrast with that of Weber and to illustrate the changed ideas concerned with industrial location. Myrdal evolved his model during the mid-1950s with special reference to the developing countries although it could well claim to operate within a wider context.

Recognising that inequalities exist between regions, Myrdal suggested the hypothesis that economic forces would tend to increase such differences rather than equalise them. Once an industry is established in a region it will generate a demand for better communications and public services which in turn make the area more attractive to new industries. Hence agglomeration or concentration of industries will result in a consequent migration of people to the more affluent parts. This happened to some extent in the West Midlands and the South East of England. Hence a polarisation between industry-rich and industry-poor regions will result from growth poles and growth points. (This has similarities to city-rich and city-poor hypothesised by Lösch and introduced later in Chapter 10, on page 191).

Such a model presupposes a free economy and one in which there is no government intervention. As we already know, such intervention is becoming more widespread throughout the world. Eventually the agglomeration of industries will create its own problems such as the inability of services to meet the demands of a vast industrial complex, the overcrowding of such regions and consequent transport problems. When this stage is reached then planned decentralisation of industry will commence such as is currently taking place in the British Isles and is illustrated by a case study in this chapter.

These two models have been selected to show different attitudes and ideas prevailing at two points in time. Weber was concerned with the initial building of a single plant in a minimum cost location, whereas Myrdal sought to offer an explanation for differences in the overall pattern of industries within a region. Both models are helpful to our thinking and together provide a useful framework within which to approach problems of industrial location.

EMPIRICAL CASE STUDIES OF INDUSTRIAL LOCATION
The following case studies have been chosen to illustrate the contrasting forces which help explain industrial patterns. Whilst the iron and steel industries remain tied to raw materials, lighter industries have greater freedom of choice in their location. What criteria are used by entrepreneurs in taking these locational decisions?

Case I. The Iron and Steel Industry of the Eastern U.S.A.
The distribution pattern shown in Fig. 8.6 will already be familiar to you. How does this pattern compare with that of Mexico in Fig. 8.6?

In both cases the industry is a very concentrated one: the U.S. Steel and Bethlehem Steel Companies together produce more than 40% of the national total. Notice the 85 market potential isoline which has been transposed from Fig. 8.2 to Fig. 8.6.

Until 1948 when the basing point system of freight rates was abolished, the Pittsburgh area enjoyed a privileged position. Now with an unrestricted freight rate system, this traditional area finds itself increasingly more distant from its market.

The predominance of the 'steel triangle' of Pittsburgh, Cleveland and Buffalo is being challenged by the growth of the Chicago area, which during the 1960s expanded at twice the rate of the Pittsburgh region. This growth rate is partially a response to the growing market of the Mid-West. Chicago is not only better located for this expanding market of the Mid-West, but also enjoys an advantageous water transport system for the assembly of raw materials.

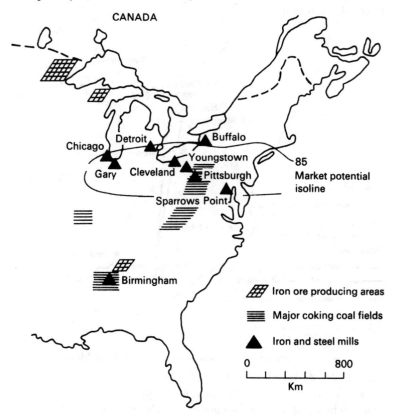

Fig. 8.6 Location of the iron and steel industry in Eastern U.S.A. (*Based on Rutherford, J., Logan, M. I. and Missen, G. J., New Viewpoints in Economic Geography*)

How does the Weber model help in the search for an explanation of the pattern in Fig. 8.6?

The Chicago–Gary complex is located between the iron ore in the west and coal in the east, and as indicated is now closer to the growing market. It is the latter which is especially significant when actual assembly and delivery costs are taken into account. Expressed as a percentage of total transport costs the breakdown is: coal 25%, iron ore 22%, finished product to the market 53%.

Perhaps it is reasonable to hypothesise that the overall pattern reflects the Weberian principle of minimising transport costs and the Chicago area is located within the feasibility zone of Weber's triangular solution.

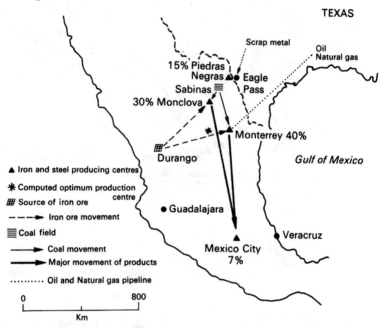

Fig. 8.7 Location of the iron and steel industry in Mexico

Case II. The Mexican Iron and Steel Industry

Mexico is rarely studied in regional geography and it is unlikely that you will be familiar with the country. Study atlas maps of the region and then look at Fig. 8.7 which contains the data relevant to the iron and steel industry. The percentages of iron and steel produced in each of four major centres are indicated together with the sources of coal and iron ore. The ore at Durango is high grade with a 60% content of iron. Scrap metal, which today is an important supplement, is imported from Texas via Eagle Pass and also obtained in Mexico City and Veracruz.

Unfortunately, coking coal is poor in quality and the only satisfactory source is Sabinas. However, both Monterrey and Monclova use oil and natural gas from Texas as sources of power. Labour may be regarded as ubiquitous since there is an abundance of unskilled labour and wages everywhere are low. The skilled labour force required is very small.

The national market is also small – the only consumers being located in Mexico City (3·4 million), Guadalajara (1·3 million) and Monterrey (0.9 million). In fact Mexico City itself constitutes 70% of the market. Freight rates are closely related to distances in Mexico and the cost per tonne of transporting steel from Monclova to Mexico City is 30% greater than from Monterrey.

To what extent does the distribution of iron and steel plants reflect the location factors earlier in this chapter? In particular has the Weber model any relevance? Do you think the percentage of production in each centre is indicative of its relative advantage within the country?

It is interesting to note that both the two large producers are situated between their supplies of coal and iron, but are a long way from their main market in Mexico City. This classical Weberian situation has been analysed by Kennelly and the optimum site is located 160 km west of Monterrey, which is already the largest of the producing centres. Does the close correspondence in location of both Monterrey and Monclova to the idealised mathematical solution support both the underlying principle of the model and lend credibility to the idea of feasibility zones rather than optimised fixed points?

This study of Mexico which may appear to be insignificant in scale and remote in location is significant because its simplicity matches that of the Weber model. The time span at which the industry developed too is appropriate. The Fundidora works at Monterrey were established in 1903 and are a nearer approximation to the Weber solution than those of Altos Hornos built at Monclova in 1944. Does this suggest that as time evolves so location factors become more complex?

Case III. Industry in the Bristol Region
The pattern of industry has already been introduced in Chapter 7 and Figs 7.2 and 7.3. In marked contrast to the two heavy industry case studies, the types of industry found around Bristol include the manufacture of aircraft, paper, footwear, furniture and processing of tobacco and foods.

In the 1960s John Britton attempted to discover through fieldwork what factors *actually* contributed to the decision of entrepreneurs to locate their factories in the Bristol region. Although he approached 217 companies some 62% or 134 responded: this represents a high response rate. (See the earlier comment on a similar study in Guatemala on page 147). It is recommended that you read this important study by Britton since only brief outlines of his methodology and conclusions are incorporated here.

Table 8.2
Locational factors: industrial survey

Labour:	Good labour relations in the area.
	Availability of labour in the area.
Market:	Access to markets.
	Anticipation of market growth.
	Low freight costs to market.
Site:	Scope for expansion on site.
	Attractive price of land or building.
	Presence of suitable building.
	Adequate supply and satisfactory type of water.
	Flat land.
Materials:	Low purchase price of raw materials and components.
	Low freight cost on raw materials and components.
	Availability of raw materials and components (apart from previous two factors).
	Low cost of fuel and power.
Personal:	Personal – with economic advantages.
	Personal – without economic advantages.
	Availability of local capital.
	Regional location of firm's headquarters.
War:	War dispersal.

Table 8.3
Ranked location factors: industrial survey
Frequency response for pre-war factories

Location factor	Frequency
Availability of labour in the area	58
Scope for expansion on site	35
Good labour relations in the area	29
Access to markets	29
Personal – with economic advantages	22
Availability of raw materials and components	19
Adequate supply and satisfactory type of water	17

Attractive price of land or building	12
Regional location of firm's headquarters	11
Low freight cost on raw materials and components	9
Presence of suitable building	7
Low freight cost to markets	7
Personal – without economic advantages	6
Availability of local capital	5
Flat land	2
Anticipation of market growth	2
Low purchase price of raw materials	1
War dispersal	1
Low cost of fuel and power	0
All factors	272

Source: Britton, J. N. H. (1967). *Regional Analysis and Economic Geography: A Case Study of Manufacturing in the Bristol Region.*

Table 8.4

Ranked location factors: industrial survey

Frequency response for post-war factories

Location factor	Frequency
Availability of labour in the area	22
Scope for expansion on site	14
Attractive price of land or building	13
Presence of suitable building	11
Adequate supply and satisfactory type of water	6
Access to markets	5
Regional location of firm's headquarters	5
Good labour relations in the area	4
Availability of raw materials and components	4
Personal – with economic advantages	3
Anticipation of market growth	3
Low freight cost on raw materials and components	2
Flat land	2
Personal – without economic advantages	2
Low freight cost to markets	1
Low cost of fuel and power	1
Availability of local capital	1
War dispersal	1
Low purchase price of raw materials and components	0
All factors	100

Source: Britton, J. N. H. (1967). *Regional Analysis and Economic Geography: A Case Study of Manufacturing in the Bristol Region.*

Each industrialist was asked to consider the factors listed in Table 8.2 and then to put them in rank order for his particular factory. Study carefully the list in Table 8.2; what other factors would you want to add in an investigation conducted by yourself?

The results of the survey are summarised in Tables 8.3 and 8.4 for factories established before and after the Second World War. Study these two tables and try to deduce some important general location factors. How does the order of priority discovered by Britton comply with or differ from the factors regarded as traditionally important?

Britton himself stressed the availability of labour and good labour relations were regarded as very significant, together with a site which facilitated expansion of production in response to the anticipated growth of markets in Southern England.

Case IV. De-centralisation of Industry from North-west London
Keeble's work on the post-war de-centralisation of industry would repay reading for again only a brief summary is included here. He aimed to assess the pattern of and the reasons for the re-location of industry from Greater London's most important industrial zone between 1940 and 1964. This he designated as the north-west and included within his study area: Hendon, Wembley, Willesden, Ealing and Acton. More than one-third of the industries were involved with re-location during this period.

The reasons for moving from the area are presented in Table 8.5. Restriction of site and labour problems loom large as reasons and correspond to the responses of industrialists in Bristol cited in Case III.

Table 8.5
Reasons for emigration from north-west London given by migrant firms

Reasons given for migration (arranged in rank order)	Frequency of responses	
	No.	%
Shortage of space	23	43
Shortage of labour	9	17
Termination of lease and increase in rental	5	9
Displacement through planning redevelopment	3	6
Age, layout, separation of factories	2	4
Cost of existing premises	2	4
Government embargo on extension*	2	4

Cost of labour	2	4
Restrictive labour attitudes, militant unions	1	2
High value of factory or land	1	2
Other	4	7
Total respondents	54	†

* By Board of Trade or Middlesex County Planning Authority.

† Figures do not add up to 100 because of rounding.

Note: The sixteen strategic dispersal and regional market branch plants were excluded from the above figures, since restrictive local conditions played very little part in their establishment. Two other branches did not provide information.

Source: Adapted from *Industrial Decentralisation and the Metropolis: the North-west London Case. I.B.G.*, no. 44.

Before examining where the factories re-located, look at the industrial structure of the area as portrayed in Table 7.2. The predominance of engineering would suggest that entrepreneurs would have considerable freedom in choosing a new location. Why? Two further questions need to be posed: where did the entrepreneurs choose to re-locate and upon what criteria were their decisions based?

Table 8.6

Reasons for re-locating within 100 km of London

Factors specified by firms (arranged in rank order)	Main factor frequency
Proximity to London	13·5
Availability of modern factory, or site, with ample room for expansion	9·5
Proximity to directors', or managerial staffs', homes	5
Possibilities of retention of existing labour force (new or expanded town case)	4·83
Existence of associated company	4·5
Availability of labour	3·33
Possibility of retention of existing labour force (proximity to former location case)	2·83
Attractiveness of area (especially for key workers, managerial staff)	1·5
Remoteness from London	0·5
Strategic dispersal	0·5
Helpful local government attitude	
Proximity to local market	
Totals	46

Note: Replies on behalf of most factories refused to distinguish between two, and sometimes three, 'main' location factors. In these cases, a 0·5 or 0·33 value was allotted to each of the factors specified.

Source: As for Table 8.5.

Look at Fig. 8.8 which shows the pattern of re-distribution. There is a marked concentration of factories within a 160 km radius of London. Indeed this area contains almost 60% of all the factories. A similar trend to re-locate as near as possible to the place of origin was revealed in a more recent study of firm closures in South East London between 1970 and 1975. Of the 359 factories which closed, 92 (mostly the larger ones) were re-sited. Of these 48% of the moves were within Inner London and a further 32% within Outer London and the South East. A mere 3.3% chose to re-locate in Development Areas.

What is the perception of 'the North' of the London industrialist? Do you think he would be influenced by Figs 1.1 and 1.2? Referring back to Fig. 8.3 comment upon the distribution of factories in the remainder of Britain. In Fig. 8.8 do you notice any contrast in the size of the factories inside and outside the metropolitan area?

The overall pattern suggests that two groups of influences were at work resulting in the decision to locate either near the metropolis or far away in the Provinces. Using interview techniques, David Keeble was able to identify these forces and to assess their order of priority from the frequency of response. His significant findings are summarised in Tables 8.6 and 8.7. Look first at Table 8.6. Of outstanding importance is proximity to London. This perhaps reflects the market orientation of these kinds of industries: 48% of the firms questioned despatched 40% or more of their products to London and the South East while 11% despatched 80% or more to this area.

Worthy of comment is the third ranking factor. This links directly with the space preference studies of Gould and White introduced in Chapter 1. Does this factor express people's perception of pleasant countryside which yet remains accessible to all the attractions of the capital city?

Scrutinise Table 8.6 carefully and ask yourself how many of these forces are economic and how many are social ones. Analyse the responses listed in Table 8.7 and note the similarities and differences between these forces and those listed in Table 8.6. How do the

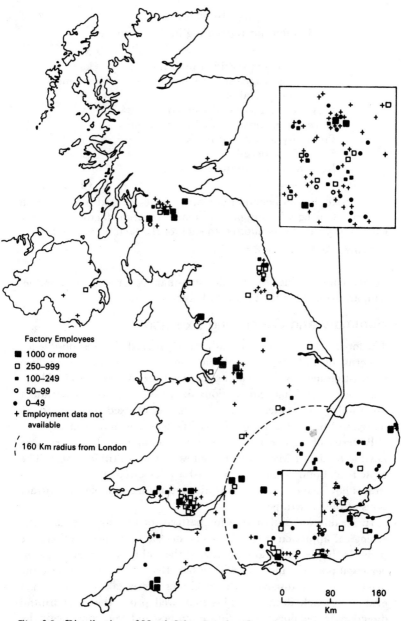

Fig. 8.8 Distribution of North-West London factories re-located since the war (*Keeble, D. E., 'Industrial decentralisation and the metropolis: the North-West London case'*)

Table 8.7

Reasons for re-locating in the Provinces

Factors specified by firms (arranged in rank order)	Main factor frequency
Availability of labour	6
Existence of associated company	5
Government pressure and/or inducements	4·5
Proximity to regional market	1·5
Strategic dispersal	1
Reasonable proximity to London	1
Totals	19

Note: Replies on behalf of several factories refused to distinguish between two equally important 'main' location factors. In these cases, a 0·5 value was allotted to each of the factors specified.

Source: As for Table 8.5.

factors contributing to the decision-making process in London compare with those for Bristol? (Tables 8.3 and 8.4.)

Summary and Concluding Exercise

The forces which have been traditionally regarded as responsible for patterns of industry have been considered together with two contrasting models. It would appear that the Weber model still has relevance in seeking explanations for heavy industries dependent upon bulky raw materials, but the rigidity of fixed points needs to be relaxed into the concept of a satisfactory feasibility zone.

Patterns of lighter industries are accommodated in the more flexible model of Myrdal which allows for a multiplier effect. The growth of London and the South-East reviewed in Case IV illustrates how even when de-centralisation is unavoidable, the attractions of the growth pole persist.

In seeking an explanation for patterns of industry, perhaps the ecological approach is helpful: some decisions are good, others are poor. If the decisions are good then the industry will thrive; conversely if poor the industry will wither. Recent studies illustrate the need to try to discover why decisions were taken rather than evaluating such decisions. This may well prove the most fruitful direction to be pursued in future studies and you may begin by working the situation exercise in the succeeding pages.

Further Reading

Alexander, J. W. (1963) *Economic Geography*, especially Part Nine. Prentice Hall.

Bale, J. R. (1977) 'Industrial estate development and location in post-war Britain'. *Geography*, vol. 62, part 2, pages 87–92.

Bechtol, Bruce E. (1970) 'A matter of perception: locational considerations of industrialists in Guatemala'. *The Californian Geographer*, 11, pages 15–20.

Bradford, M. G. and Kent, W. A. (1977) *Human Geography: Theories and their Applications*. Chapter 3. O.U.P.

Britton, J. N. H. (1967) *Regional Analysis and Economic Geography: A Case Study of Manufacturing in the Bristol Region*. Bell.

Hamilton, F. E. I. (1968) 'Models of industrial location'. Chapter 10 in *Socio-Economic Models in Geography*, edited by R. J. Chorley and P. Haggett. Methuen.

Harris, Chauncy D. (1954) 'The market as a factor in the localisation of industry in the United States'. *A.A.A.G.*, 44, pages 315–348.

Humphreys, G. (1976) 'Industrial change: lesson for South Wales'. *Geography*, vol. 61, part 4, pages 246–254.

Keeble, D. E. (1968) 'Industrial de-centralisation and the metropolis: the north-west London case'. *I.B.G.*, 44, pages 1–54.

Smith, W. (1955) 'The location of industry'. *I.B.G.*, 21, pages 1–18.

Taylor, M. J. and McDermott, P. J. (1977) 'Perception of location and industrial decision-making. The example of New Zealand manufacturing'. *New Zealand Geographer*, 33, 1977. Pages 26–33.

Warren, K. (1976) 'British steel: the problems of rebuilding an old industrial structure'. *Geography*, vol. 61, part 1, pages 1–7.

9 . Industry III — A Simplified Monte-Carlo Simulation Model

In the last chapter you were introduced to the many and varied factors which contribute to locational patterns of industry. Make sure that you are familiar with these forces, especially the ones shown to be significant in the case studies.

It is almost certain that in the past you will have played a geographical game. In the exercise which follows you will effectively be taking the decisions of an industrial entrepreneur or group of entrepreneurs. It is upon the basis of your decisions plus the part played by stochastic or chance factors, simulated here by random numbers, that the new pattern will be established. At the conclusion you will need to re-examine the basis of your decision-making in a self-critical way and be prepared to defend your decisions in discussion and debate with fellow students.

Depending upon the time and facilities you have available, the exercise may be completed in one of three ways but the preliminary steps are common to all three.

1. *The problem*
Imagine that 25 new 'light' industrial factories are to be built in the West Midlands during the next five years and you wish to predict the most likely areas in which these factories will be built.

In view of your knowledge of location theory what factors must you take into account and what data are required to enable a balanced, rational assessment to be made? List these factors and try to put them in rank order as in Tables 8.4–8.7.

2. *Available data*
A series of maps provides information about:

(a) In Fig. 9.1 the diversity of present day industry is indicated on a five point scale where 1 is low and 5 is high. Note the bulk of the area is too low to score on the scale. Some major towns outside the conurbation are indicated to help you.

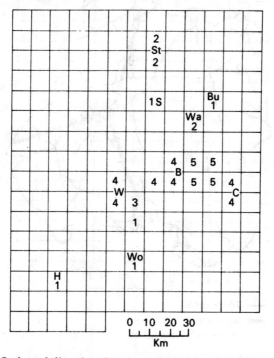

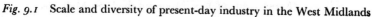

Fig. 9.1 Scale and diversity of present-day industry in the West Midlands

(b) The network of major roads and motorway accessibility points is shown in Fig. 9.2.

(c) Fig. 9.3 shows the designated areas:

1. The greenbelt where planning permission for industrial and residential development is extremely difficult if not impossible to obtain.
2. New towns and overspill schemes where such developments are actively encouraged.

3. *Simplifying assumptions*

(a) Electricity is equally available throughout the whole area.
(b) Labour relations are equally good throughout the whole area.

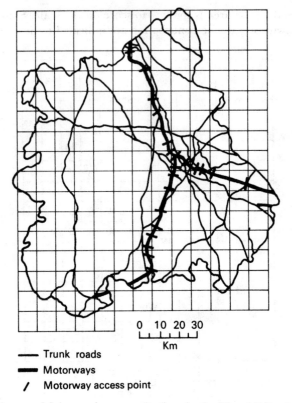

— Trunk roads
▬ Motorways
/ Motorway access point

Fig. 9.2 Major road communications in the West Midlands

(c) West of the line A–B on Fig. 9.3 land values tend to be lower and wage rates cheaper (though the latter may become subject to national rates) but *skilled labour*, accustomed to manufacturing is scarce.

The decision-making environment has now been established and it consists of:

1. Your imperfect knowledge of the area derived from the limited data maps and simplifying assumptions.
2. Your knowledge of location theory.
3. Factors revealed as significant in recent case studies.

In the simulation which follows, your assessment and judgment will influence the distribution of the most favourable locations **as**

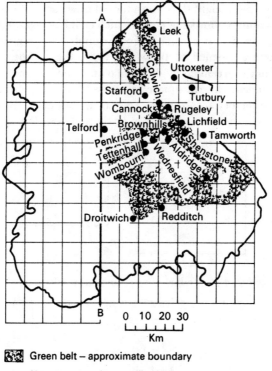

Green belt – approximate boundary

● New towns and overspill schemes

Fig. 9.3 Designated areas in the West Midlands

perceived by you. Since within this feasibility zone there is a strong chance factor determining actual locations (as, for example, in the case of car manufacture in Cowley), this chance element is simulated through the calling of random numbers as explained below.

Procedure

1. Decide a definite order of priority for the factors which you consider to be the most important determining the location of 'light' manufacturing industry. For example, you may decide proximity to existing industry is the most important factor followed by a motorway access point. It is advisable not to exceed six in number.

2. Assume the total number of points for any one square cannot

exceed 25. Weight the importance of these factors by allocating a maximum number of points which could be awarded for each factor in any one square. For example, suppose designated areas are deemed to be worth 10/25 then a square totally within the greenbelt might score 0 and a new town possibly 10.

3. Consider each grid square in turn and award points for each of the factors according to your own judgment. Enter these points in the same order in each square, as in Fig. 9.4, so that

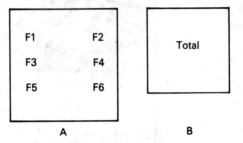

Fig. 9.4   Method of recording factor allocation

							3	4	1				
						16	13	9	3				
					16	19	13	9	7				
1	4	3	11	9	8	14	16	12	5				
3	4	4	13	13	13	14	21	16	13	15			
	4	11	16	16	17	16	19	11	16	2			
	1	10	11	13	18	9	15	17	16	19			
		4	6	12	8	8	19	16	14	17	17		
		3	7	10	12	9	13	23	19	16	17	14	
	1	4	5	9	10	17	13	10	13	12	17	13	
		2	6	5	6	14	17	13	15	18	17	15	
	2	3	7	5	7	16	14	10	10	9	10	13	
1	2	5	9	5	11	15	10	11	6	6	3	6	
	2	7	5	3	8	10	5	4		3			
	4	1	4	3									
			3										

Fig. 9.5   Factor allocation totals

you can identify your assessment at a later stage. The total score for the square should be entered on a separate grid. Such a series of possible totals are shown in Fig. 9.5.

4. It is now possible to proceed in three ways, each illustrating how areas of higher probability may be identified and how actual locations within these areas may be chosen. The third method is only possible if you have available a computer or computer terminal.

Method I. The simplified solution

Step 1: Shade those squares containing the highest values. You must judge which is the critical value. One way this can be achieved is by drawing a frequency histogram and determining the breaking point. In the accompanying example 16 was chosen.

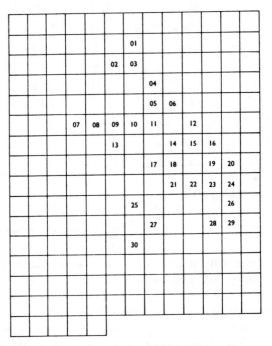

Fig. 9.6 Distribution of high value cells

Step 2: Number each of these squares 1–30 as on Fig. 9.6.

Step 3: Assuming not more than five factories may be built in any one square call random numbers (range 01–30) until 25 factories are located as shown in Fig. 9.7. In this way a chance element has been introduced to select the actual locations from those you considered feasible.

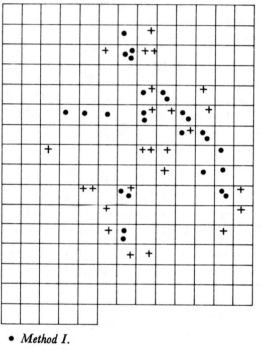

• *Method I.*
+ *Method III.*

Fig. 9.7 Location of 25 factories—simulated by random numbers

This is a shortened and simplified simulation in that the total area was divided into two zones: one where total allocations were below 16 and had no chance of a factory being built and one where totals were above 16. In the latter zone each square had an equal chance of being chosen no matter how high or low its weighting within the range 16–25. An alternative strategy is contained in Method II.

Method II. *The more complex simulation*

						1–3	4–7	8				
					9–24	25–37	38–46	47–49				
				50–65	66–84	85–97	98–106	107–113				
114	115–118	119–121	122–132	133–141	142–149	150–163	164–179	180–191	192–196			
197–199	200–203	204–207	208–220	221–233	234–246	247–260	261–281	282–297	298–310	311–325		
	326–329	330–340	341–356	357–372	373–389	390–405	406–424	425–435	436–451	452–453		
	454	455–464	465–475	476–488	489–506	507–515	516–530	531–547	548–563	564–582		
		583–586	587–592	593–604	605–612	613–620	621–639	640–655	656–669	670–686	687–703	
		704–706	707–713	714–723	724–735	736–744	745–757	758–780	781–799	800–815	816–832	833–846
	847	848–851	852–856	857–865	866–875	876–892	893–905	906–915	916–928	929–940	941–957	958–970
		971–972	973–978	979–983	984–989	990–1003	1004–1020	1021–1033	1034–1048	1049–1066	1067–1083	1084–1098
1099–1100	1101–1103	1104–1110	1111–1115	1116–1122	1123–1138	1139–1152	1153–1162	1163–1172	1173–1181	1182–1191	1192–1204	
1205	1206–1207	1208–1212	1213–1221	1222–1226	1227–1237	1238–1252	1253–1262	1263–1273	1274–1279	1280–1285	1286–1288	1289–1294
1295–1296	1297–1303	1304–1308	1309–1311	1312–1319	1320–1329	1330–1334	1335–1338			1339–1341		
1342–1345	1346	1347–1350	1351–1353									
	1354–1356											

Fig. 9.8   Random number allotment

In this case each square in the entire area will have an opportunity of being chosen in proportion to its total weighting.

Step 1:   Convert the weightings in Fig. 9.5 into a running total as shown in Fig. 9.8. Since probability must always sum to one it is necessary to convert the values in Fig. 9.8 into a probability matrix as shown in Fig. 9.9. This was achieved in a rather tedious way by normal graphical methods but could be done rapidly if you have a desk calculator available.

Step 2:   Call random numbers as before to locate the 25 factories. Again limit the maximum number of factories to 5 for any one square. A pattern generated in this way is shown in Fig. 9.10.

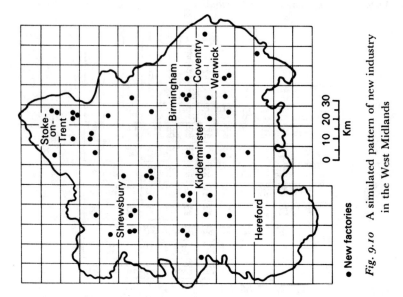

• New factories

0 10 20 30
Km

Fig. 9.10 A simulated pattern of new industry
in the West Midlands

Fig. 9.9 Probability Matrix

Method III. A Markov chain sequence

A much closer approximation to reality can be achieved by simulating the *multiplier effect* using what is known as the Markov chain technique. When a factory or group of factories is built this has an immediate impact upon the area which should be reflected in the weightings of each individual square. This on-going influence can be incorporated into the simulation by using a relatively simple computer program. In the example described below, weightings were adjusted after each group of five factories had been sited by calling random numbers as before. The adjustment used for one trial in this experiment is shown in Fig. 9.11. The square in which the factory

	1·2	
1·2	SITE 1·5	1·2
	1·2	

Fig. 9.11   Grid for adjustment of cell weightings

1	2	3	4	5	6	7	8	9	10	11	12	13
						3	4	1				
					16	13	9	3				
				16	19	13	8	8				
1	4	3	11	9	8	14	16	12	4			
4	4	3	13	13	13	14	21	16	13	15		
	4	11	16	16	17	16	19	11	16	2		
	1	10	11	13	17	10	15	17	16	19		
		4	6	12	8	8	19	16	14	17	17	
		3	7	8	14	9	13	23	19	16	17	14
	1	4	5	9	10	17	13	10	13	12	17	13
		1	6	5	6	14	17	13	15	18	17	15
	2	3	7	5	7	16	14	10	10	9	10	13
1	2	5	9	5	11	15	10	11	6	6	3	6
	2	8	5	3	8	10	5	4		3		
	4	1	4	3								
		2										

Matrix A

is sited has its weighting increased by a factor of 1·5 and those contiguous with it by 1·2.

The sequence begins with the same distribution of weightings portrayed in Fig. 9.5. Matrix A shows a computer version of this distribution: such small discrepancies in cell values which you may observe arise from necessary *rounding off* procedures.

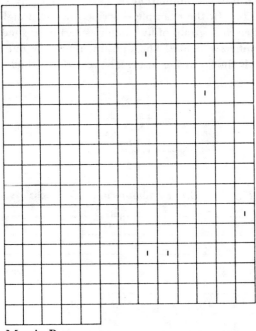

Matrix B.

A first cycle of five sites was established calling random numbers and these are shown in Matrix B. The impact of these new sites is immediately fed into the system and the weightings are changed as explained previously and shown in Matrix C. This procedure is repeated five times to simulate the multiplier effect (*ie.* the 25 factories are divided into five cycles each with five factories). The weighting of each cell prior to the final establishment of sites is shown in Matrix D. Study these values carefully and identify the ways in which they differ from the ones which remained static in the normal Monte Carlo Simulation shown in Fig. 9.5.

The final distribution of factory sites using this method is contained in Matrix E and has been superimposed upon the former one in Fig. 9.7 to facilitate comparison. You may well feel there is little difference between the two distributions but it should be remembered that over a longer time scale involved with perhaps the relocation of 100 factories any difference arising from the multiplier effect would become increasingly important until a point resembling *take-off* in the Rostow model of economic development would be reached.

							3	4	1			
						16	15	9	3			
					16	22	19	9	8			
1	4	3	11	9	8	14	19	12	4			
4	4	3	13	13	13	14	21	16	15	22		
	4	11	16	16	17	16	19	11	16	2		
1	10	11	13	17	10	15	17	16	19			
	4	6	12	8	8	19	16	14	17	17		
		3	7	8	14	9	13	23	19	16	17	14
1	4	5	9	10	17	13	10	13	12	17	15	
	1	6	5	6	14	17	13	15	18	20	22	
2	3	7	5	7	16	16	12	10	9	10	15	
1	2	5	9	5	11	18	18	19	7	6	3	6
	2	8	5	3	8	10	6	4		3		
	4	1	4	3								
		2										

Matrix C.

Method III is not only more realistic but more flexible. One could vary the different weighting of factors to simulate differing attitudes to industry. The rapid generation of alternative patterns in response to changed values of inputs – such as a growing motorway network – enables a much more dynamic approach. Above all, this may be achieved without tedious arithmetic on the part of the operator who is free to develop ideas and modify his strategies in the light of rapidly produced projections. After the initial preparation of the program which has to be done only once, each computer run occupies about 40 seconds of machine time. The program may be stored in a teachers' centre with computer facilities ready for processing data either taken to the centre or sent through the post. Alternatively, a computer centre may exist in your school or college.

							3	4	1			
					19	22	10	3				
				24	26	22	9	8				
1	4	3	11	9	9	14	22	12	4			
4	4	3	13	13	13	16	37	19	15	26		
	4	11	16	16	17	19	33	13	22	3		
	1	12	11	13	17	10	25	24	24	26		
		6	7	12	8	10	50	33	19	17	17	
		3	7	8	14	10	18	27	19	16	17	16
	1	4	5	9	14	25	15	10	13	12	20	22
		1	6	6	10	19	17	13	15	18	24	26
	2	3	7	6	12	19	16	12	10	10	15	18
1	2	5	9	5	13	18	18	19	7	6	3	6
	2	8	5	3	8	10	6	4		3		
	4	1	4	3								
		2										

Matrix D.

CONCLUDING TASKS

1. To what extent do you now appreciate more fully the decision making process in industrial location?
2. Did the role of the chance element help illuminate the empirical case studies which you have read?
3. Look at the distribution patterns generated by other members of your group. Try to account through discussion for marked similarities and differences between the patterns.
4. Discuss fully with other members of your group the choice and weighting of factors they employed. Did this weighting override the chance element?
5. If you had an opportunity to try more than one of the three methods described here, compare the advantages and disadvantages of each.

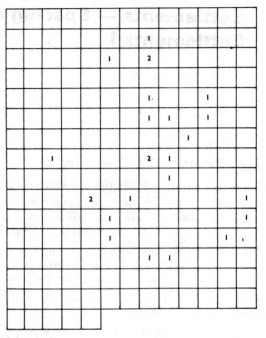

Matrix E

Further Reading

Keeble, David (1969) 'School teaching and urban geography: some new approaches'. *Geography*, 54, pages 18–33.

Wise, M. J. (1972) 'The Birmingham–Black Country conurbation in its regional setting'. *Geography*, 57, pages 89–104.

10 · Settlements — Spacing of Settlements I

Theoretical Models in the Search for Order

It is not surprising that the distribution of settlements in an area should appear complex and in many cases confusing to the interpreter. Settlements – whether hamlet or million city – represent a total summary of man's activities and of his way of life. Thus they reflect the attitudes and values of society which prevail at any given point in time. In fact it is this time element together with changes in the structure of society which significantly contribute to the complexity of settlement patterns in general and the morphology of individual settlements in particular.

In the past the important role of the physical environment in determining sites of settlements has been emphasised almost to the exclusion of other considerations. Description and explanation of patterns were attempted together rather than pattern identification preceding the explanation for that pattern. Springs were chosen as sites for villages, and hence spring line village patterns as in the Lincolnshire Wolds could be identified. The significance of gaps in the siting of towns is renowned as is the presence of a knoll for defensive purposes. The bridging point of a river is again a familiar classical example for explaining the presence of many towns and villages. Whilst abundant evidence of these may be found there are many sites in nondescript situations which could not be explained by physical factors alone. No attempt is being made to deny the significance of physical factors which have helped create a settlement pattern yet upon close examination of either map or ground we are often forced to ask 'why here and not there' when the physical terrain is identical.

One factor overlooked in considering physical forces only is that to fulfil basic human needs such as food and water, man requires land. Hence from their initiation settlements really competed for space and this competition persists and is as strong today as in the period of Anglo-Saxon peopling of the land. Parish boundaries are a reminder of the need for each settlement to have sufficient land to make it self-supporting. Hence on the fen margin one finds elongated parishes to incorporate complementary terrains. An individual settlement cannot therefore be considered in isolation but as part of a system of settlements. It is this concept of spatial competition and consequent organisation which underlies Christaller's Central Place Theory to be introduced later.

Look at Fig. 10.1 which shows the basic linkages within the system when an initial settlement is established. As in farming the physical constraints are subject to the perception level of the settlers and become less important as man's technology grows. The pattern of Iron Age settlements confined to the lighter soils and non-forested hill tops contrasts with that of the Anglo-Saxon villages. The market town pattern of Western Europe associated with an essentially rural community contrasts with the clustered agglomerations resulting from the industrial revolution. For example, with the help of an atlas or appropriate O.S. maps, compare the pattern of towns in East Anglia with that of West Yorkshire, or that of Southern Italy with the Ruhr.

Just as our control of environmental forces has changed, so human needs have extended to sophisticated levels with a highly complex society structure. It is these social forces which influence patterns within a settlement such as 'high-class housing' and 'ghettos', and the affluence of society which can support the out-of-town hypermarket.

Settlement patterns are both complex and dynamic and constantly adjust to changing conditions over time. A contemporary development is the deliberately planned town in a planned location – the so-called 'New Towns' such as Harlow and Telford in this country and Evry and Trappes in France. Furthermore, dynamism is generated by the *interaction* between settlements – a theme which is elaborated in Chapter 12.

Our first task is to try to detect an order in patterns of settlement and to understand the major processes which influence it. To achieve this, it is imperative to use more effective ways of *describing* the pattern and then develop more scientific ways of seeking an explanation. This is the objective of the remainder of the present chapter,

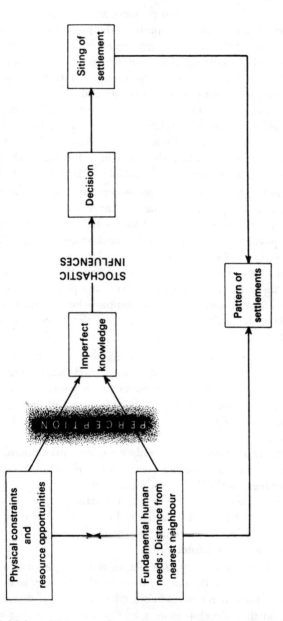

Fig. 10.1   Initial establishment of an individual settlement and its relationship to the overall pattern

though the order is partially reversed to introduce Christaller's central place model at an early stage in order to expedite the investigation.

CENTRAL PLACE THEORY

A convenient starting point in the analysis of settlement patterns is the work of Christaller whose thesis provides a framework for study. The essence of his theory is that a certain amount of productive land supports a settlement which performs essential services for that land. These services which today range from simple items such as providing groceries or hardware to highly sophisticated theatre performances, are called *central functions* and the settlements providing them *central places*; hence the name *central place theory*.

The premises upon which Christaller based his theory are not dissimilar to those of von Thünen, already considered – Chapter 5, page 81. He assumed an isotrophic surface facilitating equal ease of movement in every direction together with a uniform distribution of population and purchasing power, terrain and resources. Given these assumptions, the most economical use of space is that of a triangular lattice work as shown in Fig. 10.2. Each of these central

Fig. 10.2   Triangular lattice

places should ideally serve a circular area. The limitations of such a shape are revealed in Fig. 10.3 where the shaded areas are either unserved A or over provided B. Hence the hexagon emerges as the optimal shape (10.3C) for trading areas and thus overcomes the limitations of the circle.

From the earliest days of civilisation differences in the size of settlements had been evident leading especially to the classifying of

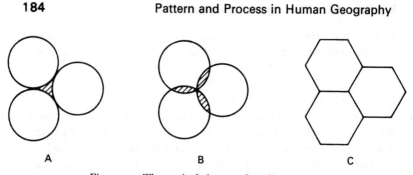

A   B   C

Fig. 10.3   Theoretical shapes of trading areas

settlements as urban or rural. Christaller himself identified seven orders of settlement as shown in Table 10.1. Within any given area there will be fewer higher order cities and towns in relation to the lower order villages and hamlets. However, for any given order, theoretically the settlements will be equidistant from each other, thus the higher order settlements will be further apart than the lower order ones. It follows from this arrangement that the area served by a central place will depend upon its order: the higher its order, the greater the area served. These relationships in the Christaller model are summarised in Table 10.1 and their spatial pattern shown in Fig. 10.4. This order of settlement is called a *hierarchy* of settlements and their hexagonal trading areas form what is known as a *nested hierarchy* since they fit together without overlap for any given order. The grouping in Fig. 10.4 is the arrangement when $k = 3$, k being the number of places dependent upon or served by the central place. For example, in Fig. 10.4, the highest order settlement numbered 3 serves itself and one-third of each of the six second order settlements. Look back at Table 10.1 and you will see that the theoretical number of settlements progressively divides the previous order by 3, namely 486–162–54...1. This is sometimes known as the *rule of threes*.

In the case so far described where $k = 3$, all the areas are served in keeping with the principle of least effort. Thus theoretically people go to the nearest centre providing the services they require, and this arrangement is really based upon a marketing principle. Although it is this retailing function of central places which is investigated and elaborated in this book, Christaller also recognised two other controlling principles shown in Figs 10.5A and 10.5B. In Fig. 10.5A, $k = 4$ and you will notice that as many places as possible

Table 10.1

Size and spacing of settlements

Order	Settlement type	Population (000)	Number of settlements	Distance apart (km)	Tributary area size (km²)	Population of area (000)
1 (lowest)	Hamlet	0·8	486	7	45	2·7
2	Village	1·5	162	12	135	8·1
3	Town	3·5	54	21	400	24·0
4	City	9·0	18	36	1200	75·0
5	County city	27·0	6	62	3600	225·0
6	Regional centre	90·0	2	108	10,800	675·0
7 (highest)	Capital	300·0	1	186	32,400	2025·0

Source: Based on Johnson, James H. (1967) *Urban Geography*, page 95. Pergamon.

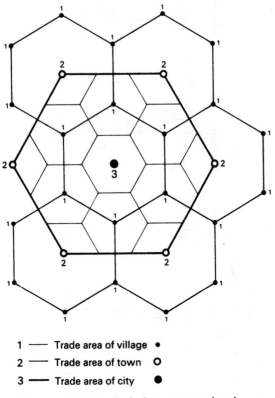

1 —— Trade area of village •
2 —— Trade area of town ○
3 —— Trade area of city ●

Fig. 10.4 The central place system when k = 3

are on the main transport routes which connect the higher order settlements so that the main influence is preference for access to a main transportation route. Hence Christaller himself relaxed one of

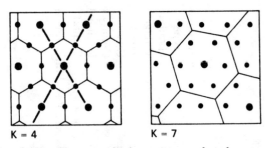

K = 4   K = 7

Fig. 10.5(A) and *(B)* The central place system when k = 4 and k = 7
(*Based on Haggett, P., Locational Analysis in Human Geography*)

his fundamental assumptions related to ease of movement. An example of this in the real world is the presence of a trans-continental railway such as the Trans-Siberian.

The administrative case where $k = 7$ is shown in Fig. 10.5B. Here the key controlling principle is central government. You will notice that all six lower order places owe allegiance to only *one* higher order instead of sharing their loyalties as in the previous cases. This principle is clearly illustrated in the organisation of local government in England where the hierarchy is:

parishes owe allegiance to one borough or district,
boroughs owe allegiance to one county,
counties owe allegiance to one central government at Westminster.

Returning to the case when $k = 3$, implicit in this hierarchical arrangement of settlements is an order in the goods and services provided by central places. The higher orders will perform all those of the lower ones, plus additional functions. From your own experience think of the kinds of goods and services available in a village compared with a market town and those of the market town with the city. This theme will be fully developed in Chapter 12, but an idea of the significance of a particular service may be obtained from Table 10.2 in which the number of people required to support a given activity is indicated.

Table 10.2

Some guidance about thresholds

A. British guidelines

Shop	Threshold
Boots the Chemist	10,000
Mac Fisheries	25,000
Barratts Shoes	20–30,000
Sainsburys Grocers	60,000
Marks & Spencers	50–100,000
John Lewis	50,000 for supermarket
John Lewis	100,000 for departmental store

Source: Chorley, R. S. and Haggett, P. (1965) *Frontiers in Geographical Teaching*, page 227.

B. Threshold population for selected functions in S. Ontario

Function	Threshold
General Food Stores	65
General Clothing	85
Banks	727
Lawyers	742
Dentists	1734
Opticians	2890

Source: Yeates, M. H. (1968) *An Introduction to Quantitative Analysis in Economic Geography*, page 105.

C. Threshold populations in Snohomish County

Function	Threshold	Function	Threshold
Filling Station	196	Chemist	458
Restaurant	276	Beautician	480
Tavern	282	Clothing	590
Doctor	380	Lawyer	528
Barber	386	Dry Cleaner	754
Dentist	426	Shoe Repairs	896
Fuel Merchant	453	Animal Feed Stores	526
Hardware	431	Farm Implement	
Furniture	546	Dealer	650
		Veterinary Surgeon	579

Source: Ambrose, P. (1969) Extract from *Analytical Human Geography*, pages 154–55, Longman, in which a much fuller list may be found.

Underlying central place theory are three key concepts. The first is called *the range of a good.* This is the maximum distance which people are prepared to travel in order to obtain a particular good or service. It is this upper limit which generates the hexagonal net, for at any given level of the hierarchy, locations could not be more widely separated. The distance will clearly be related to the frequency with which the service is required, for example, the daily purchase of bread compared with the very infrequent acquisition of furniture. It will depend too upon the value of the article and the length of the journey – or as we shall see later the perceived length of the journey.

The second concept is *the threshold* which indicates the *minimum* number of people required to support a particular function. In general the more specialised the function, the greater the number of people required. The threshold value really expresses the lower limit of the range of a good and indicates the minimum size of area to make its supply profitable. Guidelines for thresholds for a variety of functions are provided in Table 10.2. It must be emphasised these are only guidelines and the applicability of North American thresholds in Europe must be severely questioned.

The third concept is *spatial competition*, so that an area will be served with a minimum number of central places which together provide every good. As mentioned earlier, settlements require space to support them and if one is concerned with a retailing function of central places then they are competing for the customers distributed in space. Hence theoretically similar activities should tend to be located as far away as possible from each other. Notice the spacing of Marks and Spencers Stores in Fig. 10.6 which recognises that there is little advantage in clustering together yet must be so arranged as to serve the given distribution of population to best advantage. How does this idea differ from the scale economies resulting from agglomeration in farming patterns?

Central Place Theory has been described by William Bunge as 'the most perfect idea in geography'. What then are its weaknesses and strengths?

Substantial testing of Christaller's ideas is undertaken in the subsequent two chapters but it is clear that modifications are necessary from our present knowledge of the real world. Such modifications are largely caused by rigid assumptions such as the isotropic surface, and from changes in way of life, type of economy, transport media and town function since the time of the model's conception.

Uneven distribution of resources, as depicted by the presence of a coalfield or pleasant coastline, will lead to agglomeration of towns as shown in Table 10.3. Just as in the von Thünen model, a navigable

Table 10.3

Town spacing in an industrial region of England and Wales

Population size	Mean spacing (km)
20–30,000	9·8
40–50,000	12·6
75–100,000	16·0

Source: Haggett, P. (1965) *Locational Analysis in Human Geography*, page 109.

waterway distorted the ringed land-use pattern, so transport lines affect city growth especially along railways and trunk roads. The concept of threshold rests upon the number of people rather than the amount of space they occupy. Hence an uneven distribution will alter the theoretical pattern. Finally, whereas Christaller considered settlements as having only a central place function, in modern society this is merely one of several functions. Even when confined to

Fig. 10.6 The distribution of Marks and Spencer stores in England and Wales

the retailing case, not every good or commodity has the same threshold or range and thus service areas must vary and could scarcely be expected to conform to the rigid hexagonal network.

What are the strengths of the model?

Christaller provides us with a structure within which to think and from which hypotheses related to the search for order in the land-

THE MODIFICATION BY LÖSCH

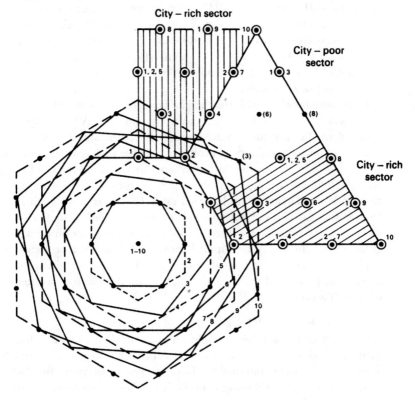

● Original settlements

◉ Centres of market areas of sizes indicated by figure

Alternative regional centres are in parentheses

Fig. 10.7 The ten smallest possible market areas. After A. Lösch (1954)
(*Carter, H., The Study of Urban Geography*)

scape may be derived and then tested. He suggests the optimum use of space in areas recently settled and of uniform terrain, for example, the Prairies and the Polder Lands. Important underlying concepts are introduced, especially the idea of spatial competition which is fundamental to any problem in human geography. Above all the pattern of settlement is conceived not as individual units but as a *whole interacting system* in which an order is distinguished.

The work of Lösch is difficult to understand and unravel. As in the Christaller $k = 3$ network, Lösch focused upon economic forces operating within the system. However, he made allowance for the fact that differing goods have different ranges and thresholds and created a profusion of various sized hexagons as shown in Fig. 10.7. The size of the hexagonal service area reflected the range and/or threshold of the particular service. You will notice too there are more values of k included.

One common element is that all the hexagons are centred on one point which is the highest order metropolitan city. All the super-imposed meshes are then rotated about this point and in this way zones containing many cities in contrast to those with few cities may emerge, as indicated in the 'city rich' and 'city poor' sectors in Fig. 10.7. Settlement rich and settlement poor sectors have been identi-fied by Peter Toyne around the cities of Exeter and Norwich in *Organisation, Location and Behaviour*, p. 219. Because there is no fixed k value in this arrangement, then it follows that the strict numerical groupings of the Christaller model shown in Table 10.1 no longer apply. However, it is suggested that order, if not a strict hierarchy, persists, and the third theoretical idea, the *rank size rule* is concerned with such an order.

THE RANK SIZE RULE

Christaller and Lösch both sought an order in the spatial distribu-tion of settlements as well as a numerical order. The rank–size rule introduced in 1913, but not really developed until 1941, by Zipf confines itself to establishing a numerical relationship between the settlements of a given area. This rule postulates that the size of settlements is inversely proportional to their rank. Thus if the popu-lation of a town is multiplied by its rank, the product will equal the population of the largest or highest ranked city. This city is known as the *primate* city. For example, Chicago, the second city of the United States, should have half the population of New York. The general relationship is expressed in the formula

$$Pr = \frac{P_1}{R}$$

where Pr = the population of city r; P_1 = the population of the largest city and R is the rank size of city r for the group of settlements being considered.

When the population is plotted against rank on log/log graph paper as in Fig. 10.8 it is seen that the hypothetical rank size rule is

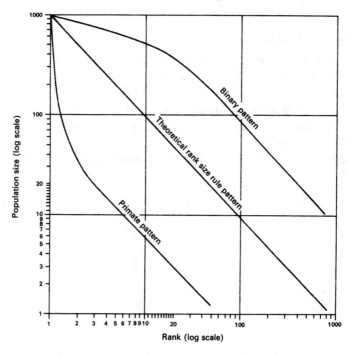

Fig. 10.8   Theoretical rank-size rule patterns

a straight line at an angle of $45°$. This is the theoretical norm against which real world settlement patterns may be measured.

Just as Lösch modified Christaller's ideas so Haggett has further extended the Zipf model to take into account historical and cultural differences. Look again at Fig. 10.8 and you will see convex and concave shapes. Where settlement is comparatively recent a number of cities of approximately the same size predominate. This is called a *binary* pattern and is displayed in the convex curve. The concave slope results from the converse case where the fall off from the first city is very abrupt. This is named a *primate* pattern.

Attention has been confined merely to the order and spacing of settlements in this chapter. The theoretical models introduced provide a sound base from which to derive hypotheses concerned with the search for order in these patterns. Empirical testing of these hypotheses by geographers is reviewed in the next chapter which also contains suggestions which you may undertake yourself.

Further Reading

Berry, B. J. L. (1967) *Geography of Market Centres and Retail Distribution*, Chapters 1–4. Prentice Hall.

Bradford, M. G. and Kent, W. A. (1977) *Human Geography: Theories and their Applications*, Chapters 1 and 4. O.U.P.

Carter, Harold (1972) *The Study of Urban Geography*, Chapter 2. Edward Arnold.

Haggett, Peter (1972) *Geography a Modern Synthesis*, Chapter 2. Harper & Row.

11 . Settlements — Spacing of Settlements II

Empirical Testing of Theoretical Ideas

TESTING THE CHRISTALLER–LÖSCHIAN MODEL

Case I. South West Wisconsin

Perhaps the earliest substantial testing of the spacing and size of settlements was carried out by John Brush in South West Wisconsin during the early 1950s. Look in the atlas and locate this area including, if possible, the counties of Vernon, Crawford, Richland, Sanx, Grant, Iowa and Lafayette.

Since this part of the American Mid-West fulfilled the postulates of the model – a relatively uniform terrain and an absence of manufacturing and urbanising influences – it is reasonable to expect the spacing, size and function of settlements to conform to Christaller's idea.

The basic observations of Brush are summarised in Table 11.1. Using population as a basis, he identified three orders of settlement:

Table 11.1

Spacing of settlement data in South West Wisconsin

	Hamlets	Villages	Towns
Number of settlements	142	73	19
Theoretical spacing (km)	8·5	16	31·7
Actual spacing (km)	9·4	15·8	34·0
Number of functions	2	18	42

Source: Based on data in Brush, John E. (1953) 'The hierarchy of central places in South West Wisconsin'. *Geographical Review*, vol. 43, no. 3, pages 350–402.

hamlet, village and town. The theoretical distances separating central places of the same order were postulated by applying the rule of threes so that a hamlet would serve one third the area served by a village and one ninth the area served by a town. From the measured distances in the real world it can be seen that the lower order settlements tend to cluster slightly, whilst the higher order ones disperse but the evidence of spatial order remains convincing. Equally there is a conformity to the expected number of settlements in each category and a clear hierarchy of function related to order of central place: the hamlet with two functions contrasting with the town performing 42 different functions.

Although these results of Brush were later called into question as we shall see on page 200 they offer strong evidence upon which to accept Christaller's hypothesis concerned with size, spacing and function of central places but not his idea of interaction between central places which is to be examined in Chapter 12.

Case II. Studies in South West Iowa and Saskatchewan
A similar numerical and spatial arrangement of settlements was identified by Berry in Saskatchewan. Table 11.2 summarises his

Table 11.2

Characteristics of centres in Saskatchewan 1961

| Classification | Number in 1961 | Average spacing in km | |
		1941	1961
Hamlet	404	14·5	15·3
Village	150	16·5	21·5
Town	100	24·6	31·7
Small seat	85	41·4	36·0
County seat	29	64·6	63·3
Regional city	9	191·8	108·0
Regional capital	2	230·4	230·4

Source: Berry, Brian J. L. (1967) *Geography of Market Centres and Retail Distribution,* page 117.

observations. You can see how the spacing of settlements increases in direct relationship to their number. However, an adjustment to the system is indicated when the 1941 pattern is compared with that for 1961. The distance separating the lower order places tends to increase whilst that for the higher order ones decreases. This decrease is especially marked in the case of the *regional city.*

This trend has resulted from two principal causes. As mobility has

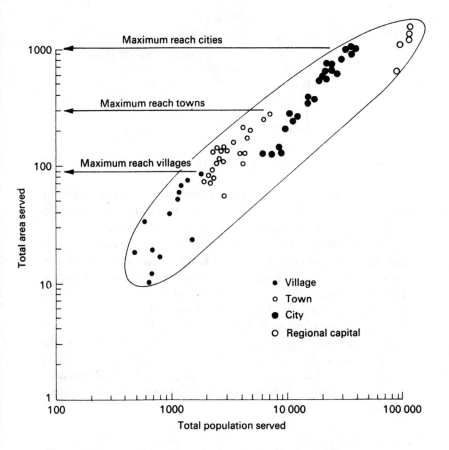

Fig. 11.1 Scatter diagram to show variations in levels of the settlement hierarchy (*Berry, B. J. L., Geography of Market Centres and Retail Distribution*)

increased, especially through the use of motor cars, so the need for lower order centres diminished. People decide to travel to higher order places to choose from a wider range of goods and to obtain an increased number of goods. In addition mechanisation of agriculture has resulted in a decline of rural population and the effect of this in Iowa between 1930 and 1960 is shown in Table 11.3. The trend is as indicated before in Saskatchewan: the higher order settlements are growing at the expense of the lower order ones and it is reasonable to expect a similar spatial adjustment.

Table 11.3

Change of central place populations in Iowa 1930–1960

Level of centre	Average annual growth rate %
Hamlet	−2·69
Village	−0·58
Town	−0·15
County seat	+0·44
Regional city	+0·94

Source: As for Table 11.2, page 116.

Attention is now turned to the trading areas of these settlement orders. Look at Fig. 11.1 which shows the postulated relationship between orders of central place. The range indicated for each of the four orders attempts to cater for variations and complexities in the real world. You will recall from your earlier work on correlation and regression in Chapters 4 and 5 how the *best fit* line has been drawn. The settlements would cluster closely about this line as indicated by the enclosing 'sausage'. Empirical evidence for trading regions in two familiar areas of North America is shown in Fig. 11.2. In both cases the general hypothesised trend is confirmed although the population of a centre at a given point declines with overall density; namely villages vary in size from 80–250 people in the wheatlands in contrast to the more densely peopled corn belt where the range is 380–700.

Case III. Your own test
It is quite possible for you to test the number and spacing of settlements within a small study area by using an O.S. 1:50,000 map and population data from the census returns. Choose an area which is able to fulfil Christaller's premises as far as possible. Such an area should be a rural one, as uncomplicated by relief variations as possible, and located away from the large conurbations to minimise the possibility of commuting villages being contained within it. Think carefully about the occurrence of such areas in Britain: they do exist. Classify the settlements into orders using population as a basis and record the number of settlements in each group. For each order determine the mean distance between settlements. This is achieved by taking each settlement within a given order in turn and

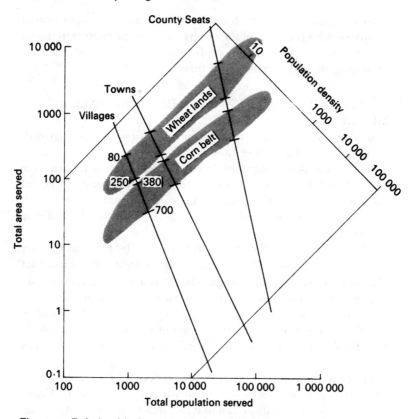

Fig. 11.2 Relationship between hierarchy of settlement, in two differing environments, to size of trade area and population served. (*Based on Berry, B. J. L., Geography of Market Centres and Retail Distribution*)

measuring to its nearest neighbour, adding all the values and calculating the mean. Results for an area around Taunton in Somerset are shown in Table 11.4. Does the previous numerical

Table 11.4

Spacing of settlements in the area around Taunton, Somerset

Level	Number	Mean spacing (km)
Hamlet/village	298	1.8
Towns below 10,000	9	11.0
Towns 10–30,000	2	41.5
Towns over 30,000	1	—

order and spacing persist? Clearly such an exercise is unsophisticated compared with the work of the geographical researchers introduced earlier but provides useful confirmatory evidence whilst only employing limited resources and time.

LÖSCH'S MODIFICATION OF THE CHRISTALLER MODEL

You will recall that one obvious factor promoting settlement growth is the presence of a road or railway.

When John Brush's work on Wisconsin is read, you will discover that although the numerical and spatial hierarchies exist, the actual pattern is a linear one rather than an hexagonal one in which $k = 3$. This arrangement of settlements reflects the railway connections.

This importance of the railway is developed by Berry in the case of Iowa. Fig. 11.3 shows three stages in the evolution and the impact of communications at each stage. The impact of the improved lines of communication clearly resulted in two *city rich* areas extending along the railway separated by a wide *city poor* zone. The situation was diversified, however, by the advent of paved roads as shown in Fig. 11.3C, although the basic dominance of the two rail routes persists.

In what other situations may we expect to find city-rich as opposed to city-poor sectors? Look at your atlas maps of the USSR and Australia and see if you can find parallels to the North American case. Could the coastal regions of Japan be regarded as city rich? Adverse physical terrain, especially when juxtaposed against a favourable mineral resource may create contrasting settlement patterns. For example, compare the city-rich coalfields flanking the city-poor High Pennines.

There would seem, therefore, to be some evidence to incorporate the Löschian modification into the basic Christaller model, as indicated through the work of Toyne in the previous chapter.

Do hexagonal lattices exist?

So far the problem of hexagonal lattices, common to the thinking of both Christaller and Lösch, has not been approached. However remote the possibility of such a pattern of hexagonal units may be this fundamental idea should be tested against the real world. How may this be done?

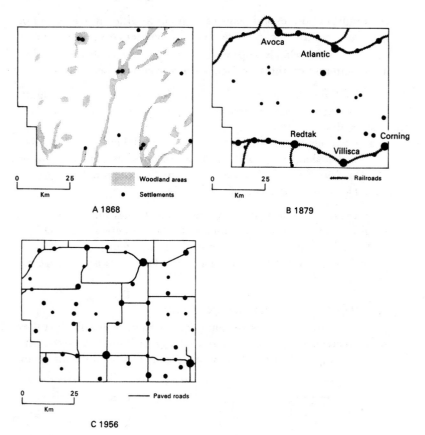

Fig. 11.3 Evolution of settlement patterns in Iowa (*Berry, B. J. L., Geography of Market Centres and Retail Distribution*)

Each hexagon of any given order will be in contact with six other hexagons of equal stature. Hence, if we examine areas served by a central place, they should be in contact with six similar areas. On the basis of published maps it is possible to test this assumption in the administrative case of $k = 7$.

Haggett examined the municipios in Brazil and discovered that on average they were in contact with 6·21 other municipios. Using the administrative maps published by the O.S. the idea may be tested by ascertaining the number of parishes with which each parish within a county is in contact. Results from the Vale of Pewsey in Wiltshire reveal the number to be 5·8. It is interesting to note that the results of both experiments carried out at different scales and in markedly contrasting physical and human environments should yield a number closely approximating to the theoretical norm of 6. When attempting this task for your own county proceed as follows:

1. Exclude all the parishes which are adjacent to the county boundary since information for parishes outside that boundary is absent.
2. Consider each parish in turn and count the number of parishes which share its boundary, *ie.* are immediately adjacent to or *contiguous* with it. For each parish record the number.
3. Determine the mean of this number.

With members of your group ascertain values for a number of counties and discover their closeness to the theoretical mean of 6.

A much more rigorous testing of the hexagonal spacing of settlements may be undertaken by a method known as *nearest neighbour analysis.*

NEAREST NEIGHBOUR ANALYSIS

Dot distribution patterns are commonly used in geography, yet they defy precise description. Look at the two distributions of settlement in Fig. 11.4 and attempt to write down a description of them.

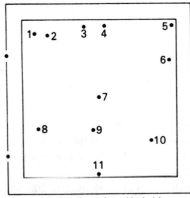

100 sq km Quadrat of the Yorkshire Wolds (Porous Chalk)

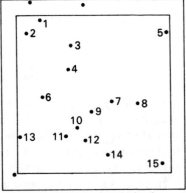

100 sq km Quadrat of the Vale of Pickering (Impervious Kimmeridge Clay)

0   5

Kms

Fig. 11.4 Contrasts in settlement patterns

Compare your description with that of your neighbour. Is it the same or different?

Nearest neighbour analysis will enable you to give a more precise description of the pattern, to derive an index which may then be correlated with other variables and hence facilitate the investigation of problems.

The basis of the method. Three categories of distribution are normally recognised as: clustered (nucleated), regular (uniformly dispersed) and random. Hypothetical examples of these are shown in Fig. 11.5.

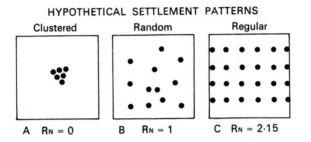

HYPOTHETICAL SETTLEMENT PATTERNS

Clustered   Random   Regular

A Rɴ = 0   B Rɴ = 1   C Rɴ = 2·15

Fig. 11.5 Hypothetical settlement patterns. Rn values indicate degree of randomness (*See Fig. 11.6*)

Look again at Fig. 11.4 and decide into which of these three categories you will place each of these two distributions.

In a random pattern, the location of any one point is in no way influenced by the location of the other points in the distribution. It is this random pattern which is used as the base from which all other distributions are measured, *ie.* the extent of deviation from randomness is measured by the *nearest neighbour statistic known as Rn*. This is achieved by determining the mean distance between dots and their nearest neighbour and comparing it with the value where the distribution is random.

The value of *Rn* may range from 0 = absolute clustering to 2·15 = perfectly regular (that of a Christaller network of central places). A random distribution has a value of 1·0. One other useful value is 0·23, that for linear clustering. This scale of *Rn* values is indicated in Fig. 11.6. Clearly then, this method presents another opportunity of testing the Christaller model. Look at Fig. 10.2 on page 183 which shows the distribution of a given settlement order as a series of dots. Such a distribution has an *Rn* value of 2·15. By applying this method of analysis to settlement patterns represented as dot distributions it is possible to determine not so much whether they conform exactly to the Christaller model but more importantly *how far* they conform to or deviate from the idealised theoretical pattern.

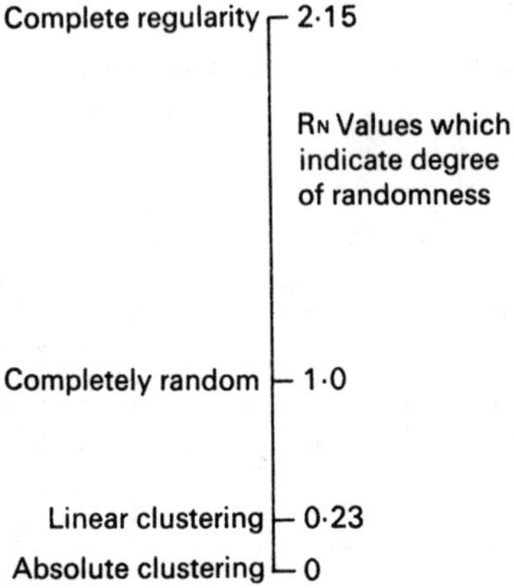

Complete regularity — 2·15

R_N Values which indicate degree of randomness

Completely random — 1·0

Linear clustering — 0·23
Absolute clustering — 0

Fig. 11.6 The Rn scale

Although this is one of the more rigorous methods of analysis, a number of procedural pitfalls may significantly affect the result. At the outset operational decisions should be taken and adhered to throughout. A satisfactory procedure is outlined below together with a worked example based upon Fig. 11.4.

Procedure

1. Define the boundary of the study area. Criteria used for this delimitation will depend upon the nature of the enquiry but are critical to the interpretation of the result. Useful boundaries may be geological ones *or* upland contained within a prescribed contour. Alternatively a quadrat may be used as a significant sample of an area as in Fig. 11.4. In an urban environment the Central Business District (C.B.D.) may be the unit involved.
2. Define the criteria for selection and exact placing of the dot. For example, what constitutes a settlement? Where is the centre of that settlement deemed to be? Arbitrary but unambiguous operational decisions must be taken: size of typeface on the 1:50,000 O.S. map is very helpful.
3. Dots on the periphery of the study area present a problem

because their nearest neighbour may be outside that area. This may be solved in one of two ways:

(a) by joining up these dots to form a buffer zone as in Fig. 11.7. One may measure to such dots, but *not* measure from them.

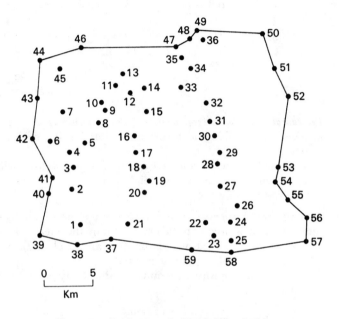

Fig. 11.7   Settlements in North Lincolnshire

(b) by resolving the issue when the original study area is defined by establishing an outer zone of dots as illustrated in Fig. 11.4. These outer dots will only be used when they occur nearer to a dot contained within the study area than any other dot within that area. For example, in the Vale of Pickering dot number 13's nearest neighbour is outside the study area as it is for dot number 8 in the Yorkshire Wolds. This latter area is used below to elucidate the procedure.

4. Number all the dots in the study area and from each in turn measure and record the distance to its nearest neighbour. An example is given in Table 11.5. *Note:* all measurements are to the point's *nearest* neighbour and it is possible to measure back to the previous point when relevant, for example, dots 1 and 2.

Table 11.5

Spacing of settlements in the Yorkshire Wolds (Fig. 11.4)

From point	To point	Distance km	From point	To point	Distance km
1	2	0·8	7	9	2·1
2	1	0·8	8	outside area	2·7
3	4	1·4	9	7	2·1
4	3	1·4	10	9	3·9
5	6	2·2	11	9	2·9
6	5	2·2			
				Total	22·5
				Obs mean	2·04

Procedural note when a large number of dots is involved:
a. Number the points as before and eliminate the peripheral ones.
b. Call random numbers to give a sample of 30 dots from which to measure to their nearest neighbour.
c. Proceed as before.

5. Add all the distances recorded in Column 3 and divide by the number of measurements taken to obtain the mean. This is known as the observed or measured mean (D obs). D obs in this Yorkshire Wolds quadrat is 2·04.

6. Determine the density of points in the study area by the formula:

$$\text{Density} = \frac{\text{Number of points in study area}}{\text{Area of study area}}$$

The units of area should be the same as those for measuring distances, *ie.* kms. In the Yorkshire Wolds this is:

$$\frac{11 \text{ (total number of points)}}{100 \text{ (area in sq. km)}} = 0·11$$

7. Calculate the expected mean in a random distribution ($\bar{r}E$) by the formula:

$$\bar{r}E = \frac{1}{2\sqrt{\text{density}}} = \frac{1}{2\sqrt{0·11}} = 1·51$$

8. Finally determine the random scale value (Rn) by the formula:

$$\frac{\text{Degree of}}{\text{randomness}} = \frac{\text{Observed or measured mean distance}}{\text{Expected mean distance in a random distribution}}$$

or

$$Rn = \frac{\overline{D} \text{ obs}}{\overline{r}E} = \frac{2 \cdot 04}{1 \cdot 51} = 1 \cdot 35$$

Refer now to Fig. 11.6 and interpret this Rn value which indicates a slight tendency towards regularity.

Whilst a desk calculator will accelerate the calculation of the Rn value, a computer program would further relieve you of much of the tedium and enable you to concentrate your energies upon interpreting the result. Such a program has been devised and is in use.

Interpretation of the Rn value

1. If the Rn value indicates a random distribution it *may* be that the pattern results from forces working at random but no firm conclusion should be drawn from this result. Whilst the method may be used to prove that a distribution is not random, it certainly cannot be used to prove that it is.

2. Of greater value is the indication of tendency towards clustering or dispersion for which the underlying causes may be sought. Nearest neighbour analysis is therefore helpful in isolating and defining a problem.

3. Interpretation will also depend upon the nature of the problem being investigated. For example, used to measure the strength of *functional adjacency* within an urban area, the hypothesis would be that the distribution of similar functions would tend to cluster. Clearly the strength of this tendency will be revealed thus enabling the hypothesis to be accepted or rejected. This is elaborated in Chapter 13, page 240.

In the present case of settlement patterns, if the hexagonal arrangements of settlements in a given order is present the Rn value would be 2·15 — that for complete regularity. In the Yorkshire Wolds, on the basis of this limited exercise the tendency towards such an idealised pattern is only very slight but at least such a tendency is towards regularity rather than clustering.

As with the chi-square values and rank correlation coefficients cited earlier, the Rn value should also be tested for statistical significance. Basically, as with sampling, the smaller the number of points in the study area the higher the Rn value must be to have statistical significance. One way this may be established is by calculating a z score as follows:

Step 1. Calculate the standard error of $\bar{r}E$ by the formula:

$$\bar{r}E = \frac{0 \cdot 26136}{(n \times \text{density})} \quad \text{where } n \text{ is the number of points.}$$

Step 2. Calculate the z score by the formula:

$$z = \frac{\bar{D} \text{ obs} - \bar{r}E}{\bar{r}E}$$

This value may then be looked at in the statistical tables and its validity ascertained. This procedure is somewhat lengthy and fortunately an alternative method of determining the statistical significance of the Rn value is to consult the very useful graph drawn by Pinder and Witherick whose paper is recommended reading. This graph is reproduced as Fig. 11.8.

As you will see the Rn value of 1·35 for the Yorkshire Wolds quadrat is just outside the 95% confidence level, but since such a small number of points is involved this is not surprising. When you have followed the nearest neighbour procedure to determine the Rn value for the Vale of Pickering you will find the result there to be statistically significant.

Nearest neighbour analysis has been applied to a number of differing areas in England and Wales. The investigation was confined to villages and hamlets and the results are summarised in Table 11.6. In addition to the Rn value, a relief index (RI) for each area has been calculated in the way described later in Chapter 15 on page 288. The higher the value of RI the more broken is the topography. Look at Table 11.6 and see if there is any supporting evidence for the Christaller model. Useful questions to ask yourself include:

Is the general tendency of the settlement towards dispersion (**2.15**) or clustering (**0**)?

Is there any suggestion that a more dispersed pattern occurs in areas of less broken topography as may be expected from Christaller's premise of an isotropic surface? Would regression analysis be a worthwhile technique to help answer this question?

How far do the results in Table 11.6 confirm the findings of L. J. King who used the nearest neighbour analysis to search for hexagonal

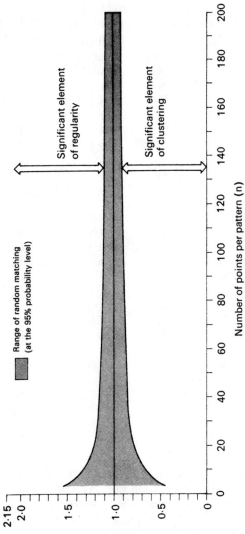

Fig. 11.8 The range of random matching: significant values for the Rn statistic (*Pinder, D. A. and Witherick, M. E., 'The principles, practice and pitfalls of nearest neighbour analysis'*)

Table 11.6

Spacing of settlement data for selected areas in England and Wales

Area	Density	Mean distance (km)	Relief index	*Rn* value
Abergavenny	20	2·5	12·78	1·286
West Sussex	36	1·7	12·66	1·38
Frome	36	1·8	2·63	1·45
Hay on Wye	16	1·8	6·6	0·73
Stafford	74	0·9	3·5	1·02
Brecon	16	2·4	17·33	1·20
Weston	29	1·6	4·73	1·40
Glamorgan	37	1·0	14·0	0·90
Monmouth	50	0·9	7·3	0·89
Peak District	26	1·7	5·91	1·11
Manchester	34	1·7	2·8	1·2
Fishguard	20	2·75	3·66	1·57
Birmingham	54	1·5	1·32	0·71
North Somerset	57	1·0	4·86	1·16
Lands End	25	1·0	34·63	0·76
Bridgnorth	54	1·5	8·06	1·35
Swindon	23	1·6	10·56	0·96
Birmingham SE	116	0·8	1·87	1·23
Bristol	60	1·0	1·3	1·15
Retford	24	1·8	1·05	1·37
Hereford	49	1·5	6·0	1·20
Shropshire	21	2·75	11·0	0·58
Birmingham S	26	1·8	5·33	1·35
Dorchester	35	1·6	11·9	1·27
Exeter	21	1·7	7·33	1·05

lattices in the USA? King investigated 20 sample areas and his *Rn* values ranged from 0·7 in Utah to 1·38 for Missouri and his general conclusion was that most settlement patterns were random. Remember, however, that the peopling of the USA took place at a completely different period of time, and in a larger and more varied physical environment than that of Britain.

SOME LIMITATIONS OF NEAREST NEIGHBOUR ANALYSIS

Although the usual limitations of a dot distribution map apply, they are minimised since our concern is with relative rather than absolute locations. The generalisation of the dot is not therefore particularly significant.

The boundary of the study area is *critical* because the size of the area will affect the Rn value. In general the larger the area the lower the Rn value. Hence if comparisons are to be made areas should be of the same order (as in the 100 sq. km quadrats). Even here sub-patterns within the area may be obscured.

Where an area is elongated, such as a river or glacial valley, distortion may occur, for example, pairs of towns on either side of a river or pairs of spring line villages on either side of a valley. A modification of the standard procedure of nearest neighbour analysis has been developed by Pinder and Witherick which may be found in the volume of *Geography* included as further reading. This article should be consulted if you embark upon an investigation in an elongated area.

TESTING THE RANK–SIZE RULE
Applying the rank–size rule is using another method to search for order in the landscape. Because of the consequences of colonial rule in large parts of the world, together with innate cultural differences and the variations in time span at which settlement has taken place, it would be unreasonable to anticipate rigid conformity to the rule.

SOME EMPIRICAL TESTS

Case I. The work of Berry
Indeed Berry has analysed 38 countries and found only 13 had rank–size distributions. Such countries were either the largest or had a long history of urbanisation. A further 15 countries demonstrated a primate distribution and in all cases urbanisation was a comparatively recent phenomenon. Does this suggest then that given time countries will conform to the rule? Look at Fig. 11.9 which shows the change in the USA since 1790. Notice how the original convex curve of a binary distribution has levelled off to approximate to the norm. What is also interesting and significant is that once the norm is achieved, population growth in the higher order cities is reflected proportionally by the lower order ones thus indicating the interdependence of settlements and hence their functioning as a system.

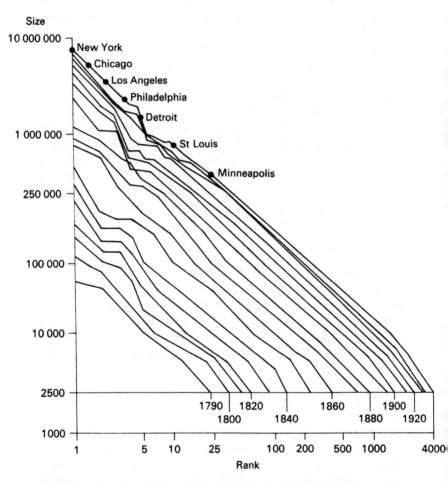

Fig. 11.9 The changing rank-size distribution of United States cities, 1790–1950 (*Berry, B. J. L., Geography of Market Centres and Retail Distribution*)

Case II. Brush in South West Wisconsin

The work of John Brush was cited earlier (page 195) and his testing of the rank–size rule in the study area is shown in Fig. 11.10. An *exponential* smooth curve relationship is revealed in Fig. 11.10A. When the data are transposed on to logarithm paper in Fig. 11.10B then the closeness of fit to the hypothetical norm may be measured.

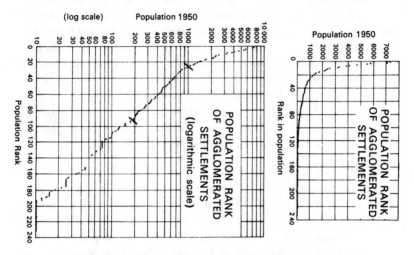

Fig. 11.10   The rank-size rule in South-Western Wisconsin (*Brush, J. E.*, '*The hierarchy of central places in S.W. Wisconsin*')

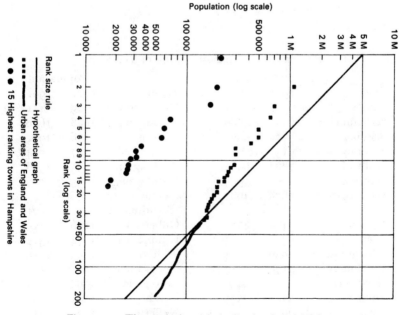

Fig. 11.11   The rank-size rule in England and Wales

Look carefully at Fig. 11.10B and you will observe two sets of
constant trend lines; that between 7000 to 1000 and between 800 to
200. The break between the two indicates that the fewer settlements
with more than 1000 people are disproportionately larger than the
many lower order settlements. This leads to the hypothesis that the
larger the area of study the more likely it is that it will comply with
the rank–size rule. Evidence for this is shown graphically in Fig.
11.11 where Hampshire figures are superimposed on those of Great
Britain. A further example using British data is contained in
Settlement Patterns by Everson and Fitzgerald.

Case III. Tests for you to carry out
   1. Do settlements in your home county conform to the rank–size
      rule or do they repeat the pattern of South West Wisconsin or
      Hampshire? Try to account for the pattern revealed. To
      undertake this you will need to extract the population data
      from the 1971 Census of Population for your area and re-
      arrange these data in rank order. These data may then be
      plotted and *interpreted* in the light of your local knowledge. An
      example of such data for the former East Riding of Yorkshire
      is contained in Table 11.7.

Table 11.7
Population in the East Riding of Yorkshire

Town	Population 1971	Population 1961	Town	Population 1971	Population 1961
Hull	285,970	303,961	Heslington	2029	451
Haltemprice	52,273	42,386	Woodmansey	1968	1648
Bridlington	26,776	26,023	Preston	1938	1902
Beverley	17,132	16,031	Patrington	1787	1724
Driffield	7895	6892	Walkington	1755	1336
Hornsea	7031	5955	Flamborough	1255	1706
Withernsea	5978	4981	Holme on Spalding Mr.	1712	1671
Norton	5424	4770	Gilberdyke	1666	1129
Filey	5336	4703	Hunmanby	1574	1512
Elloughton	4656	3174	Welton	1545	1240
Pocklington	4176	3452	North Cave	1526	1524
North Ferriby	3364	2450	Leconfield	1508	1412
Fulford	3265	2339	Leven	1504	638
Barlby	3022	3206	Nafferton	1331	1318

Dunnington	2983	2442	Stamford Br.	1206	674
Molescroft	2738	1453	Hutton		
			Cranswick	1163	1063
Thorngumbald	2709	773	Kirkburn	1148	1669
Hedon	2635	2460	Wawne	1142	376
Howden	2609	2282	Skidby	1072	839
Mkt. Weighton	2584	2185	Hemingboro'	1058	693
South Cave	2499	1521	Brandesburton	1048	1044
Bilton	2452	1934	N. Duffield	1029	783
Swanland	2303	1330			
Keyingham	2263	818			

Note: Only settlements with a population greater than 1000 have been included.

Source: Census of Population, 1971.

2. Using data from Phillips *Geographical Digest:*

   (a) Test the hypothesis that conformity to the rule is dependent upon time span by comparing a 'New World' country with a European country with long urban traditions.

   (b) Test whether or not the rank–size rule obtains within a planned economy. Useful data to use here would be that for the USSR derived from the *Geographical Digest* as before.

   (c) Apply the rank-size rule to the cities of Australia and Argentina. Why are they so different? Now read the suggested work of Johnston to help your explanation.

Summary

The last two chapters have examined theoretical ideas and the empirical evidence for the size and spacing of settlements. A brief summary may help clarify the issues for you.

1. A definite order in the size and spacing of central places was postulated by Christaller and modified by Lösch.

2. Evidence for such a hierarchy has been provided by both Brush and Berry who further demonstrated that the system could adjust to increasing mobility of people coupled with a declining rural population and an increasing urban population. Such adjustments, however, in no way negate the basic geometrical laws.

3. There would seem to be superficial evidence of an hexagonal arrangement of patterns though this is disputed when a more rigorous nearest neighbour analysis is employed.
4. The relationship between a population size and its rank in the hierarchy again reveals order, although it has been argued that settlements should be arranged in steps rather than in a straight line if they are to support the Christaller model.
5. The rank–size rule reveals an order in the landscape which is essentially a numerical relationship but Christaller sought not just a numerical order but a regular spatial distribution in addition.

A fundamental concept in central place theory is the interdependence and interaction between the central places. Attention is focused upon this aspect in the next chapter.

Further Reading

Brush, John E. (1953) 'The hierarchy of central places in Southwestern Wisconsin'. *Geographical Review*, vol. 43, no. 3, pages 380–402.

Everson, J. A. and Fitzgerald, B. P. (1969) *Settlement Patterns*, Chapter 5. Longman.

Haggett, Peter (1974) *Geography: A Modern Synthesis*, Chapter 12. Harper and Row.

Johnston, R. J. (1977) 'Regarding urban origins, urbanization and urban patterns'. *Geography*, vol. 62, part I, pages 1–8.

Pinder, D. A. and Witherick, M. E. (1972) 'The principles, practice and pitfalls of nearest neighbour analysis'. *Geography*, vol. 57, page 4, pages 277–88.

Pinder, D. A. and Witherick, M. E. (1975) 'A modification of nearest neighbour analysis for use in linear situations'. *Geography*, vol. 60, page 1, pages 16–23.

12 . Interaction Between Central Places

So far in the last two chapters, only the static relationships between central places have been considered. What is of more interest to the geographer are the linkages and interactions between differing orders of settlements.

From your reading in Chapter 10 you will already be familiar with the underlying concepts of the Christaller model: range of a good, threshold and spatial competition. Implicit too in this theory is that people behave entirely rationally and obtain their goods and services from the nearest central place which offers them. These ideas are explored in the present chapter in which theoretical models are tested against reality so that some evaluation of the processes at work may be accomplished.

Early Methods of Measuring Interaction

1. TOWN-BASED STUDIES

The area served by a town has interested geographers for several decades and early attempts to measure the interaction between a town and lower settlement orders were made through determining the *sphere of influence* of the town. Whilst the criteria used varied considerably the method adopted was a common one and a typical result is shown in Fig. 12.1. In this example Carter chose goods as depicted by the delivery area of a retail firm together with a variety of services, both social and commercial. It may well be that you are familiar with studies similar to the one illustrated or indeed may have undertaken one in the course of your fieldwork.

These earlier studies certainly illustrate the concept of the range of a good in relation to a single town studied in isolation. Compare, for example, the zone for the cinema with that of the insurance company in Fig. 12.1. However, the idea of spatial competition

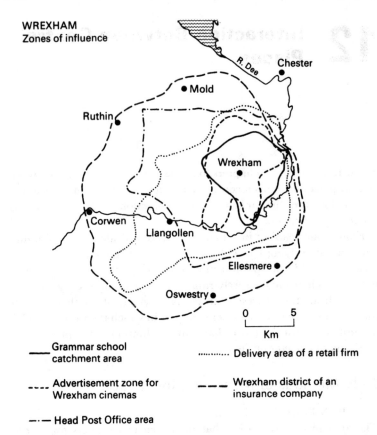

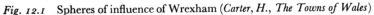

Fig. 12.1   Spheres of influence of Wrexham (*Carter, H., The Towns of Wales*)

between places and the functioning of the system as a whole is neglected. Why, for example, are all the zones in Fig. 12.1 elongated to the west of Wrexham yet severely compressed on the eastern side? Use your atlas and suggest reasons for this difference in pattern. Return to the problem again after completing this chapter.

2. COUNTRYSIDE-BASED STUDIES

A. *Towns and villages in Somerset*

A very significant contribution to understanding the relationship between higher and lower orders of settlement was made by the pioneer work of Bracey in the 1950s. It is essential you read his paper not least because it forms a good example of the scientific method being applied to an important problem.

Instead of using the town as his base, Bracey investigated the movements of people in the villages and discovered which towns were used for what services. Look at Table 12.1 which summarises

Table 12.1
Classification of goods and services employed in Somerset by Bracey

Description

Group I. *Clothing shops:* gents' outfitting, ladies' outfitting, boots and shoes.

II. *Household goods shops:* hardware, electrical, radio, furniture.

III. *Medical services:* doctor, dentist, optician, dispensing chemist.

IV. *Other professional services:* bank, solicitor, chartered accountant, auctioneer.

Source: Bracey, H. E., 'Towns as rural service centres: an index of centrality'.

the categories and subdivisions of the services listed by Bracey. Do you consider these to be the most essential ones today? Why were no food stores included in his survey?

The people questioned in each village were the schoolmaster, clergyman, chairman of the parish council and 'other responsible persons'. They were asked in which town they *usually* obtained each service. What are the weaknesses of such a survey and how could you improve the data collection? Refer back to Chapter 2 for specific details.

Each of the 15 services was allocated one point. If a village used only one town for a service that town scored one point; if two towns, then each town scores half a point and so on. It is important to note that in his research design Bracey acknowledged and allowed for the fact that villages use more than one town as in the shared principle of the Christaller model, and that towns were thus competing against each other. The town scores were used to build up an *index of centrality* – an idea to be discussed later (page 228).

Scores, with a maximum of 15, were awarded for individual villages; these scores indicated the shopping habits of those villages. As before, if a service was obtained at the nearest town to the village, then the village scored one point. If more than one town was visited

for the service the point was halved. Village scores out of a possible
15 maximum are shown in Fig. 12.2 for the area served by Bridg-

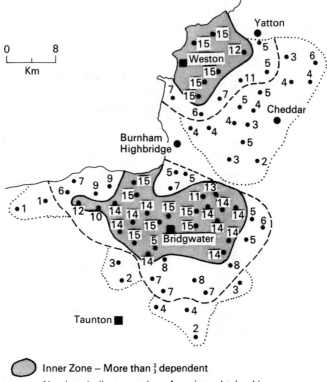

Fig. 12.2 Trading areas of Bridgwater and Weston delimited by Bracey
(*Bracey, H. E.*, '*Towns as rural service centres: an index of centrality*')

water and Weston. Thus Bracey obtained a quantitative measure of
a town's sphere of influence and as you will notice from studying
Fig. 12.2, there appears to be a marked decrease of this influence
with increasing distance from the town.

A number of limitations were acknowledged by Bracey himself;
some services were ignored, he concentrated only on the usual habits
and made no allowance for stochastic influences, all villages were
treated as equal despite differing populations and all services were

awarded the same scoring, irrespective of their differing significance. Although such limitations are less rigorous than the premises of many model builders, they do not materially detract from the essential *order in the landscape* identified by Bracey. Through his index of centrality a hierarchy of service centres emerged. The three zones of decreasing dependence shown in Fig. 12.2 were a recurrent feature throughout Somerset and hence bear the hallmark of a conceptual model: especially important is the intensive zone of no competition juxtaposed with a zone shared between centres as in the Christaller model. One interesting result was that Bracey discovered that whilst shopping areas overlap, those providing professional services do not. In the true spirit of scientific investigation a new problem arises during the examination of the original one and could provide a model for your own hypothesis testing in fieldwork.

This work of Bracey has been commented upon in some detail because his contribution is regarded as significant. Pause and ask yourself how he has contributed to both the methodology of investigation and the conceptual understanding of relationships between settlements. After reading this chapter return to ask yourself what problems he neglected completely in the light of present trends.

B. Cities, towns and individuals in East Yorkshire
Some fifteen years after Bracey completed his studies in Somerset a most thorough survey of shopping habits in relation to central place theory was undertaken by John Tarrant in Eastern Yorkshire. Again this is an important work recommended as further reading and only brief extracts are included here.

Using sampling techniques Tarrant investigated the shopping habits of varying groups of people for a comprehensive range of goods and services. He distinguished between differing social groupings, for example, the movement pattern of farmers and farm-workers; between people using differing modes of transport, car or bus; between delivered and non-delivered goods and between people in villages and dispersed households. The summary here is merely confined to the range of a good and the emergence of a hierarchy of shopping centres.

The area consists of one primate city – Hull – with a population of more than 300,000, and smaller market towns of Beverley, Driffield and Hornsea. The movements of people are summarised in

trip lines such as those on Fig. 12.3 which show the locations where
people buy their bread and groceries. It is clear from these maps that
these two commodities tended to be bought in the nearest central
place (purchases within the village are excluded).

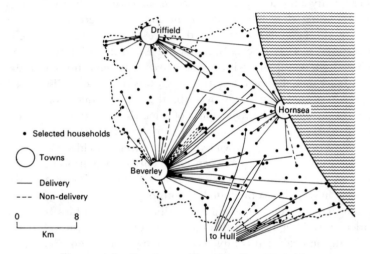

Fig. 12.3(A)   Purchases of bread in East Yorkshire

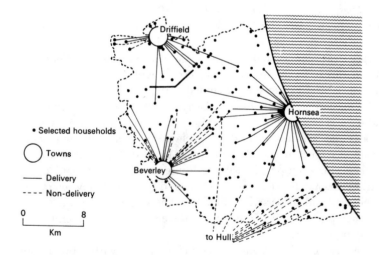

Fig. 12.3(B)   Purchases of groceries in East Yorkshire (*Tarrant, J. R.,*
'Retail distribution in Eastern Yorkshire in relation to central place theory')

What happens, however, when progressively higher order goods such as hardware, clothes and furniture are considered? Look at Fig. 12.4 and examine closely how the movements of people change

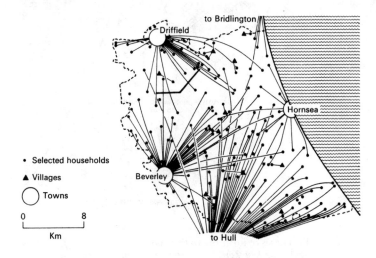

Fig. 12.4(A)   Purchases of hardware in East Yorkshire

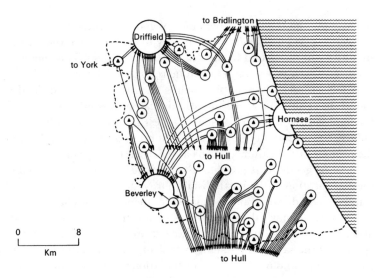

Fig. 12.4(B)   Purchases of shoes in East Yorkshire (*Tarrant, J. R.*, '*Retail distribution in Eastern Yorkshire in relation to central place theory*')

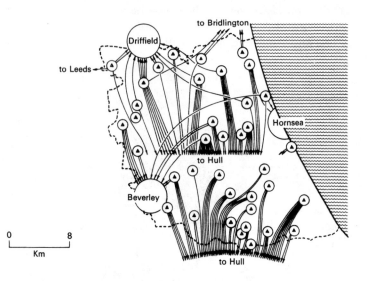

Fig. 12.4(C) Purchases of furniture in East Yorkshire (*Tarrant, J. R.*, 'Retail distribution in Eastern Yorkshire in relation to central place theory')

in their purchases of the three kinds of goods. Is there evidence for the range of a good and of a hierarchy of centres? Are these commodities still purchased in the nearest central place? This theme of the nearest centre's attraction will be returned to later.

A fair summary of shopping habits for goods other than food is found in Table 12.2. Examine this carefully and identify the predominant trends. In particular note the distinctive role of the village, towns and city in general (column 2) and the attraction of the primate city (column 3). Look at the distances travelled to obtain the named goods. Is it possible to categorise these goods and relate the classification to the mean distance travelled? Is there a relationship between distance and estimated frequency of purchase?

The three empirical studies discussed illustrate how the methodology of the geographer has changed in approaching what is essentially the same fundamental problem: that of finding order in the landscape and of offering an explanation for it. Attention is now turned to models of interaction which attempt to formulate general laws or probability norms.

Table 12.2

Shopping for goods other than food: village sample in East Yorkshire

Good	Col. 1 Mean distance (km)	Col. 2 % shopping in towns and city	Col. 3 % shopping in Hull
Post office	6·29	6·0	1·3
Primary school	3·62	0	0
Secondary school	7·01	100	—
Grammar school	8·85	100	—
Bank	10·84	100	31·6
School uniform	11·49	100	52·4
Brushes	12·53	84·5	34·5
Saucepans	12·81	90·4	37·1
Television	13·03	99·0	48·0
Shirts	13·55	100	53·0
Shoes (male)	14·58	100	57·0
Shoes (female)	15·77	100	58·7
Baby clothes	16·96	100	58·6
Easy chair	17·26	100	72·6
Raincoats	18·39	100	73·8
Bedroom suite	18·42	100	78·6

Source: Tarrant, J. R., 'Retail distribution in Eastern Yorkshire in relation to central place theory'.

Theoretical Models of Interaction

Theories which attempt to predict the amount of interaction between two places are derived in the first instance from the basic gravity model which owes its origin to Newtonian physics:

> 'Every particle of matter attracts every other particle of matter with a force proportional to the mass of each and to the inverse square of the distance between them'.

Translated into geographical terms the expected movement between two towns A and B may be obtained by multiplying the population of town A by that of town B and then dividing the product by the square of the distance separating them. This is expressed in the formula

$$\text{Movement A–B} = \frac{\text{Population A} \times \text{Population B}}{(\text{Distance})^2}$$

When applied to real world problems, modifications to the above formula become necessary. For example, in predicting the retailing attraction of a town, is its population the best measure to employ? People are interested in variety, numbers and scale of shops. Whilst it may be assumed the provision of shops will relate to population size, this may not be the case. Attempts have thus been made to arrive at the *functional strength* of a town. Such an index would try to overcome differences in scale such as the multiple chain supermarket compared with the small family grocer and also the diversity which arises from trying to equate the importance of a confectioner with that of a furrier.

Since efficiency of models must depend in part upon the precision of their inputs it is worth considering some of the approaches made in arriving at a satisfactory measure of functional strength or potential attraction, which may then be substituted for population in the gravity model.

MEASURES OF FUNCTIONAL STRENGTH

1. Direct measurements
One example of this is Bracey's index of centrality introduced earlier. However, simply to add together all the differing functions results in a weak index. Why? An alternative is to single out certain key functions and categorise places on the basis of how many outlets of each particular function they possess. Smailes' definition of a town – a settlement which contains a Woolworth stores, four banks and a cinema – is an example of such selectivity. Although subjective and generalised this procedure helps overcome the overwhelming number of functions and outlets found within a major town. However, the criteria upon which the selection is based should be clear and ready for revision. For example, Smailes chose the cinema in 1944; would he do so today or would the bingo hall and the bowling alley be more appropriate?

A third method may be to grade functions and allocate points, for example, a supermarket 5, a grocer 1 and a bank 3. A total score to summarise the range and number of amenities in a town could then be calculated. Once again this is very subjective.

2. Indirect measurements
Christaller himself used telephone calls in the 1920s to indicate the

Table 12.3

Distribution of selected retail establishments in West Yorkshire and North Humberside

Town	Population	Total Retail Establishments	Grocers	Clothing and Footwear	Furniture	Jewellery
Bradford	293,756	2,823	643	536	124	90
Hull	285,472	2,543	538	426	100	106
Leeds	494,971	4,657	851	906	177	191
Sheffield	519,703	4,817	1,067	764	183	199
Aireborough	29,477	230	53	35	8	7
Barnsley	75,330	723	199	148	26	31
Batley	42,004	291	82	30	15	8
Bentley	22,888	144	52	15	4	5
Bingley	26,540	228	46	40	12	11
Bridlington	26,729	468	66	88	22	52
Brighouse	34,111	293	81	38	10	13
Castleford	38,220	448	84	107	22	20
Colne Valley	21,188	167	56	20	4	N.A.
Dearne	25,029	231	78	29	7	5
Dewsbury	51,310	573	129	115	20	23
Doncaster	82,505	1,101	196	247	49	48
Haltemprice	52,239	266	54	31	3	9
Halifax	91,171	1,018	233	207	47	46
Harrogate	62,290	741	116	162	61	38
Huddersfield	130,964	1,382	312	267	51	57
Ilkley	21,828	221	42	48	18	7
Keighley	55,263	664	173	118	39	22
Morley	44,340	322	100	45	14	5
Pontefract	31,335	245	56	48	15	12
Pudsey	38,125	330	84	63	6	10
Rothwell	28,353	153	57	19	3	N.A.
Rotherham	84,646	710	154	115	30	32
Shipley	28,444	286	54	60	13	13
Spenborough	40,693	313	105	42	14	4
Wakefield	59,650	660	122	147	41	33
York	104,513	1,220	239	217	61	65

Source: Census of Distribution, 1971.

volume of business. Green argued that bus companies discovered 'by a process of trial and error' where people demand to make journeys and this was reflected in the density of their networks. Functional strength would then be indicated by degree of accessibility within the network (see Chapters 14 and 15 for a fuller explanation of this idea).

Whilst they are useful indirect measures, the kind indicated fail to take into account the strength generated within the town itself, being preoccupied exclusively with movements from town to town or between town and country.

3. An index of centrality
In an endeavour to minimise many of the problems and weaknesses of earlier measures discussed, Wayne Davies has introduced a formula which it is relatively simple to operate in conjunction with the *Census of Distribution*:

$$C = \frac{t}{T} \times 100$$

where C = coefficient of location of the function
t = number of outlets of function t in one town
T = total number of outlets of function t in the whole system.

A worked example will illustrate this method. Table 12.3 contains details of selected retail establishments in the former East and West Ridings of Yorkshire extracted from the *Census of Distribution*. Suppose your study area consisted of the towns Doncaster, Sheffield, Barnsley and Rotherham. Begin by abstracting the relevant data which has been partially done in Table 12.4.

Table 12.4

Selected data for a study area in South Yorkshire

	Furniture	Clothing
Doncaster	49	247
Sheffield	183	764
Barnsley	26	148
Rotherham	30	115
Total	288	1274

To determine the functional strength of Sheffield apply the formula above and you discover furniture = 63·5 and clothing = 59·9

What are the values for grocers and jewellers? Add all four values
together to obtain Sheffield's functional strength. Now repeat the
procedure to obtain indices for the other towns. Is the rank order of
functional strength synonymous with the rank order for population?
(See Table 12.3.)

Although more sophisticated methods of determining functional
strength as more valid inputs for the gravity model have been
introduced, it may well be that you need to rely upon population.
It was hinted earlier that it is reasonable to expect a correlation
between population size and urban amenity however measured.
Look at Table 12.5 which indicates the population and number of

Table 12.5

Relationship between population size and urban amenities in part of
Central England

Column number

1	2	3	4	5
			Number of retail	
		Rank	establish-	Rank
Town	Population	order	ments	order
Coalville	26,159	8	400	7
Corby	36,322	7	273	10
Derby	132,325	3	1991	3
Grantham	25,030	9	362	8
Heanor	23,867	10	315	9
Leicester	273,298	2	3842	2
Lincoln	77,065	4	898	4
Nottingham	311,645	1	4064	1
Peterborough	62,031	6	777	5
Scunthorpe	67,257	5	676	6

retail establishments for a study area in the Midlands. A Spearman
Rank Correlation (page 57) yields a value of $+0.92$ which is
statistically significant at the 99% confidence level. Perhaps then you
should not feel too disquieted about employing raw population data
provided that you remain alert to their limitations.

REILLY'S LAW OF RETAIL GRAVITATION
In 1931 W. J. Reilly formulated what has become known as Reilly's
Law of Retail Gravitation which states:

'Two centres attract trade from intermediate places in direct proportion to the size of the centres and in inverse proportion to the square of the distances from these two centres to the intermediate place'.

Suppose therefore that town A is located between towns B and C then the formula expressing this law is

$$\frac{\text{Volume of trade to } B}{\text{Volume of trade to } C} = \frac{\text{Population } B}{\text{Population } C} \times \frac{(\text{Distance } A\text{–}C)^2}{(\text{Distance } A\text{–}B)^2}$$

An example will illustrate the prediction of this model. Stafford (population 47,814) is 25·6 km distant from Stoke on Trent (276,300) and 27·2 km distant from Wolverhampton (150,385). Using the above formula a value of 2·1 is obtained and thus indicates that the attraction of Stoke on Trent is just over twice that of Wolverhampton for people living in Stafford. Using the Census of Distribution and substituting specific retail functions for population it is possible for you to use this model to establish a hypothesis which you may then test by fieldwork.

Usually a version of Reilly's Law is employed to predict the boundary line separating the trade areas between two places. This line is known as the 'breaking point' and may be calculated from the formula:

$$Bxy = \frac{\text{Distance } xy}{1 + \sqrt{\dfrac{\text{Population } x}{\text{Population } y}}}$$

where Bxy represents the distance of the breaking point from the smaller of the two settlements.

Again, an example will illustrate this. Hereford (43,950) and Leominster (6830) – on Fig. 12.5 – are 20·8 km apart and using the formula, the breaking point for trade between the two establishments is 5·9 km from Leominster.

Three empirical examples of this law in action will now be examined.

Case I. Somerset

Turn back to Fig. 12.2. If the breaking point between Weston-super-Mare and Bridgwater is calculated it falls at Burnham-Highbridge. This hypothetical location is upheld by the empirical evidence of Bracey already discussed.

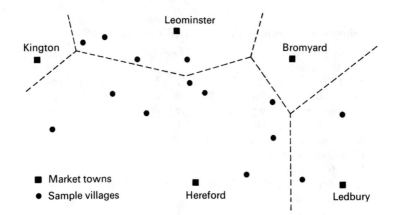

Fig. 12.5   Spheres of influence of Herefordshire market towns predicted by Reilly's law of retail gravitation

Case II. *East Yorkshire*

Again return to Figs 12.3B and 12.4A upon which the breaking point between Beverley and Driffield and that between Driffield and Hornsea have been superimposed. Does the evidence again support this predicted theoretical boundary? Insert similar boundaries on the remaining maps of the area. At what point does the theoretical boundary cease to be upheld by the field evidence? Suggest reasons for this breakdown and state how the model may be modified to be tested again. Think of the inputs to the model.

Case III. *Herefordshire*

Using 'breaking point' theory the urban sphere of influence of Hereford was simulated as shown in Fig. 12.5. For individual villages on each side of the line, a random sample of the population was obtained by using the electoral rolls. A questionnaire was designed which took into account the needs of the villages today. Thus the pattern of people's shopping movements was obtained and results for the Leominster/Hereford boundary are summarised in Table 12.6.

Table 12.6

Shopping patterns within Hereford's sphere of influence

Good

% purchasing good in	A	B	C	D	E	F	G	H	I	Mean
Hereford	57	66	71	82	46	14	83	65	55	59
Leominster	24	23	22	18	32	14	6	27	33	22

A = basic foods other than milk.
B = hardware and electrical.
C = shoes and clothes.
D = furniture.
E = dentist, auctioneer and vet.
F = post office.
G = entertainment.
H = hairdresser.
I = chemist.

This table shows the percentage of people within Hereford's simulated sphere who actually bought their goods in Hereford or in Leominster. Examine this table carefully. Overall 59% do clearly use Hereford whilst 22% use Leominster and the remainder (19%) elsewhere. Of greater significance, however, is the breakdown. 81% go to town for basic foodstuffs rather than obtain them in the village. Does this reflect the increasing mobility of people, supermarket attraction and the results of multipurpose journeys? The latter is to be discussed later. The professional services in category E show a similar tendency to that discovered in Somerset by Bracey, namely that boundaries for the professional services are not directly related to the competitive retail field. Although the difference between 46 and 32 may seem large, it should be remembered that this is significantly reduced when the standard error of 7 and 6·5 respectively is taken into account. Does the value in category F support the view of Tarrant that the only true village level good today is the post office? What evidence is found in Table 12.6 for the range of a good? Is the predictability of the Reilly model justified? Although this study of Herefordshire is less sophisticated than those of Bracey and Tarrant it provides an example of what may be accomplished at the pre-university stage. How would you improve the methodology for a similar study to be undertaken by yourself?

Whilst Reilly's model may seem to work fairly well in rural areas, because distance however measured – whether as time or cost – is at a premium, it is a very rigidly deterministic model as is the original Christaller one. It is reasonable to suppose that the model would have less meaning in a densely populated area where many options are open to shoppers and frictional distances are minimised.

HUFF'S PROBABILITY MODEL

D. L. Huff's model attempts to predict the *probability* of people's purchasing habits by taking into account the relative attraction of all the centres within the study area. Stated in its simplest terms the formula for the general case is: probability that consumer from centre 1 will purchase goods in centre 1 is:

$$P_1 = \cfrac{\dfrac{\text{Number of shops in Centre 1}}{\text{Total time taken or distance travelled to reach them}}}{\dfrac{\text{Summation of the shops in the study area}}{\text{Summation of times taken or distances travelled to reach them}}}$$

This may be adapted as indicated below.

Instead of using population as an index, one commodity – clothing – may be selected from the Census of Distribution. Suppose we are attempting to predict the probability of people living in Stafford purchasing clothing in (a) Stafford, (b) Wolverhampton and (c) Stoke on Trent. The number of clothing shops in the towns as shown in the Census of Distribution is Stafford 119, Wolverhampton 133, and Stoke 77. In the latter two towns only the shops listed as in the central shopping area have been taken into account since it is unlikely that visitors would be attracted to peripheral shops. Notice too that no account is taken of the size of the shop or indeed of its fashion and this is a limitation upon the model as worked here. Distance rather than time is being used as a factor in the calculations. The predicted probability that a consumer at Stafford will visit Stafford to purchase clothing is:

$$P_{\text{Stafford}} = \cfrac{\dfrac{\text{Number of clothing shops in Stafford}}{\text{Distance travelled to reach them}}}{\dfrac{\text{Summation of clothing shops in the three towns}}{\text{Summation of distances travelled to reach them}}}$$

We are now able to substitute using the appropriate data

$$P_{\text{Stafford}} = \cfrac{\cfrac{119}{3}}{\cfrac{119}{3} + \cfrac{133}{27\cdot2} + \cfrac{77}{25\cdot6}} = 0.83$$

The distances separating the towns are given on p. 230 and the internal distance of 3 km is derived from studies introduced in Chapter 13 as indicative of distances travelled within an urban area of this size. Similar calculations are then made to determine the probability of consumers living in Stafford purchasing clothing in Stoke and Wolverhampton by substituting the respective numbers of clothing shops on the top line of the formula and of course entering the distance separating Stafford from the particular town. Values of 0·07 and 0·10 were obtained respectively for Stoke and Wolverhampton.

The sum of probability values always equals 1 and in real terms this value tells us there is an 83% probability that people living in Stafford will buy their clothes in that town, a 10% probability of purchasing clothes in Wolverhampton, and only a 7% probability of visiting Stoke for this specific purpose. Contrast these levels with those for Tayside and Crawley in Chapter 14.

The Huff model may be used to generate a hypothesis for field-work as in the case presented below. Look at Fig. 12.6A. The predicted shopping habits of people living in Ledbury in relation to

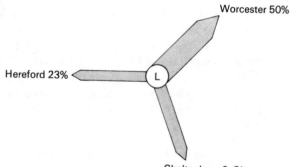

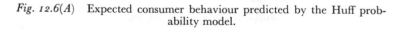

Fig. 12.6(A)   Expected consumer behaviour predicted by the Huff probability model.

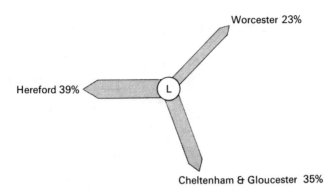

Fig. 12.6(B)   Observed consumer behaviour

the surrounding towns of higher order – Worcester, Hereford and the twin towns of Cheltenham and Gloucester – are shown here. Compare these values which would have resulted from the rigid Christaller hypothesis, namely 33% to each of the three.

These expected patterns were tested using a stratified random sample of 100 and one question only was asked: when you last shopped outside Ledbury, in which town did you shop? The results are shown in Fig. 12.6B revealing a marked discrepancy between the expected and observed values (note 3% shopped in towns other than the three listed). A chi-square test reveals that the result has a 99% chance of being correct and the hypothesis must be rejected. How can the hypothesis be re-tested? Some suggestions include: instead of using population, feed in a more sophisticated measure of functional strength; should time or cost distance be substituted for linear distance? What of historical ties? Was the correct question asked and on an appropriate day of the week? Perhaps one needs to draft a questionnaire to discover the *perception levels* presented by the three towns.

Look at Fig. 12.7 which shows the distribution of several towns in South Yorkshire. To ensure that you are able to set up a simple hypothesis testing exercise generated by the Huff model work out what is the predicted probability of people living in Wath purchasing jewellery in the other towns on the map. Details of the numbers of jewellers for each town is contained in Table 12.3.

Once again the tedium of calculation may be avoided by using a computer program. One currently in use at school level, which

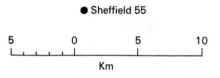

Fig. 12.7   Distribution of selected South Yorkshire towns

enables probability contours to be drawn is that contained in *Gravity Model* developed in the Hertfordshire Advisory Unit for Computer Based Education.

Summary and Concluding Exercise

Although useful, the gravity models pose a number of problems and their limitations should be realised. What values are fed into the models and how subjective are they? Assumptions are made about travel costs being directly proportional to distance; yet length of journey is progressively less significant since certain fixed costs are involved in making a journey no matter how short it happens to be. Should therefore a constant be added to the distance in any gravity formula?

At the end of the next chapter we shall consider many other variables such as: the assumed rational behaviour of people, social grouping and age of purchasers, their personality traits and perception levels. After reading pages 264–271 you should re-assess the helpfulness of the models introduced here.

Interaction between central places would seem to depend upon functional strength – however measured; distance – measured in time or km or cost and the range of a good. Despite limitations the examples used in this chapter are a helpful initiation into this complex process and you are asked to work the following exercise.

Look at Fig. 12.8 together with the data in Table 12.7. Suggest which of the seven urban areas you would use for shopping if you lived in (*a*) Ferryden (*b*) Monifieth (*c*) Friockheim. Your answer will partially depend upon the good required but in any event the choice of destination will have become more difficult as you answered *a*, *b* and *c* in turn. Can the models introduced in this chapter help predict answers to questions such as these?

First determine the sphere of influence of the towns by using Reilly's Law. The distances in Table 12.8 will help you. Trace the town locations from Fig. 12.8 and plot these boundaries. To what extent do they confirm or challenge your original suggestions? Calculate the functional strength of each town and substitute these

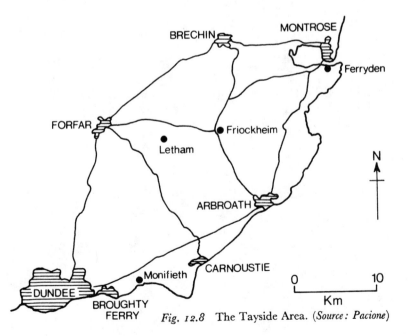

Fig. 12.8 The Tayside Area. (*Source: Pacione*)

values in the formula for population. Does this significantly alter the boundaries?

Suppose you are living in Friockheim. Use the Huff Model to predict the probability of buying (a) clothes (b) food (c) general goods in each of Arbroath, Forfar, Brechin and Montrose. Check back to see how the probability level relates to your first assessment.

After reading the next chapter you should return to this exercise and reconsider the predictions.

Table 12.7

Facility Provision in Tayside

Town	Popl.	All Retail Outlets	Food shops	Super-market	Depart-ment stores	Cloth-ing shops
Arbroath	22,921	540	76	3	3	23
Brechin	6,685	531	42	2	0	14
Broughty Ferry	12,522	753	42	1	2	11
Carnoustie	6,568	588	34	1	1	6
Dundee	181,842	2,755	60	3	9	36
Forfar	10,897	574	63	3	3	26
Montrose	10,096	600	59	1	2	26
Totals	251,531	6,341	376	14	20	142

Source: Michael Pacione (1975) 'Preference and Perception' *T.E.S.G.* vol. 66, no. 2, p 84–92 and unpublished Ph.D. Thesis (1973), University of Dundee.

Table 12.8

Distances (km) between towns in Tayside

	A	B	B.F	C	D	F	M
Arbroath	0	22	27	11	27	24	21
Brechin		0	43	35	43	13	14
Broughty Ferry			0	11	5	22	48
Carnoustie				0	11	24	21
Dundee					0	22	48
Forfar						0	45
Montrose							0

Further Reading

Ambrose, P. J. (1969) *Analytical Human Geography*, pp. 226–42. Longman.

Bracey, H. E. (1953) 'Towns as rural service centres: an index of centrality with special reference to Somerset'. *I.B.G. Transactions*, no. 19, pages 95–105.

Dickinson, Robert E. (1967) *The City Region in Western Europe*. Routledge and Kegan Paul.

Everson, J. A. and Fitzgerald, B. P. (1972) *Inside the City*, Chapter 8. Longman.

Pacione, Michael (1975) 'Preference and perception – an analysis of consumer behaviour'. *T.E.S.G.*, lxvi, 2, pp. 84–92.

Tarrant, J. R. (1967) 'Retail distribution in Eastern Yorkshire in relation to central place theory'. University of Hull. *Occasional Papers in Geography*, no. 8.

Taylor, Peter J. (1975) 'Distance decay models in spatial interaction'. *Catmog* no. 2. Geoabstracts. University of East Anglia.

13 . Patterns and Relationships Within the City

INTRODUCTION

An outstanding characteristic of the twentieth century landscape is the growth of towns. In England whilst only 16·9% of the people lived in towns in 1801, today more than 80% of the population is classified as urban. This trend is repeated throughout the developed world as illustrated by two examples: today the USA and Japan both have more than 69% of their populations in towns whilst in the early years of the century they had 45% and 19% respectively.

It is not therefore surprising that much interest in urban geography has been generated and that many books have been written on this subject. Two books have been selected as essential reading at the end of this chapter since they are complementary to each other and are particularly lucid in their explanations.

Because of the importance of urban geography you will almost certainly have undertaken some field investigation within a town and may well be aware of the difficulties of the urban scene. A major problem is that of mere scale in terms of area or distance, and except in the case of the small market town, sampling techniques must be employed in the fieldwork undertaken. Cities also are complex: they have a number of distinct functions: business and commercial, residential, industrial and administrative. They have evolved over a long period of time and change is continuously taking place. For example, the decline of inner city industrial zones contrasts with the development of peripheral trading estates: houses which were once upper class mansions are now frequently broken into flats and house working-class communities. Urban renewal and decay may well exist side by side.

The morphology of a town may again be influenced by the presence of a river or group of hills. The former is illustrated in the case of Sunderland to be introduced later in this chapter, whilst the latter hypothesis could well be tested in Bristol or Bath.

Historical, cultural and physical forces thus contribute to the most sophisticated expression of man in space – the city. Is it therefore possible to find an order within the urban landscape and a repetitive pattern which accommodates the complexities and difficulties outlined? The spatial arrangement of common elements has been summarised in a number of models which are now considered.

Models of Urban Structure

1. THE CONCENTRIC ZONE MODEL OF BURGESS

Look at Fig. 13.1A. To what extent does this recall the simple form of von Thünen's model?

This is the simplest of the models to be discussed and within its limitations, which Burgess himself recognised, provides a useful starting point for investigating a smaller town. The concentric zones are arranged in a logical order from the city centre designated as the *central business district* or C.B.D. What functions would you expect to find in the C.B.D.?

Zone two is a transitional one which contains many of the smaller original industries of the town together with the older houses. Currently this is often an area of re-development adjacent to dereliction and the description 'twilight' zone is perhaps very apt. Can you identify such a zone in a city familiar to you?

Zones three, four and five are all by definition residential ones and become more affluent as distance from the C.B.D. increases until the commuter belt is eventually reached.

Burgess derived his model intuitively from observations of a large number of American cities, but especially it is related to Chicago in the 1920s. For these reasons the model is limited by both culture and time. In many pre-industrial European cities the élite lived in elegant houses very close to the city centre. The pattern of the 1920s has been distorted too by peripheral high-density housing estates which are characteristic of the 1960s.

Despite weaknesses the model provides a simple and useful framework for the initial stages of thinking. Carter has suggested that within the C.B.D. the principle of zoning may be applied vertically to land use on different floors as illustrated in Fig. 13.11. Such a suggestion may form the basis of a fieldwork exercise carried out by yourself.

2. THE HOYT SECTOR MODEL

Much later than Burgess, Hoyt developed his model in 1939. He confined his attention to the residential structure only, basing this structure on rental values in some 142 cities. The general pattern deduced by Hoyt is shown in Fig. 13.1B.

A

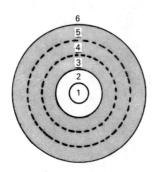

BURGESS: Concentric Ring Theory

B

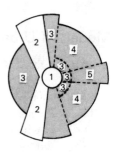

HOYT: Sector Theory

C

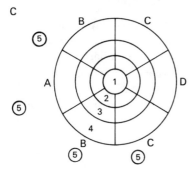

MANN: The structure of a
hypothetical British city

D

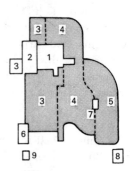

ULLMAN HARRIS:
Multiple Nuclei Theory

1 Central business district
2 Commercial/Wholesale,
   light manufacturing/
   "Twilight" transition
3 Low class   ⎫
4 Middle class   ⎬ Residential areas
5 High class   ⎭

6 Manufacture
7 Outlying business district
8 Suburban residential area
9 Industrial suburb

Fig. 13.1(A–D)   Models of urban structure

The control of this pattern is *directional* rather than distance from the centre, although the latter cannot be entirely discounted. Hoyt identifies sectors of differentiation – not unlike the city-rich, city-poor sectors of Lösch – and these sectors too are related to communication axes. In the basic model shown in Fig. 13.1B clearly a radial transport network is assumed. A second control is the centripetal/centrifugal force more commonly called 'push and pull'. A simple example of the latter in operation is industry being attracted to a line of communication, then high class housing is repelled by the industry. Look carefully at Fig. 13.1B and notice how this principle operates.

3. MANN'S MODEL OF A BRITISH CITY

In 1965 Peter Mann devised a model of the structure of a hypothetical British city as shown in Fig. 13.1C. This model is based upon the three cities of Sheffield, Nottingham and Huddersfield. You will notice that he combines the idea of zones and sectors. Since he assumed the prevailing wind to blow from the west, industry is found in sector D on the east, whilst high class housing is as far away as possible on the west. In zone 3 of sectors C and D small terraced houses are located. What type of housing are you likely to find in B3? This model is a helpful source of hypotheses for urban fieldwork in medium-sized cities. This model also emphasises that zone and sector models are not necessarily inconsistent with each other but may indicate differing attributes such as prestigious residential areas. You will read later how zones and sectors together may be used to analyse urban patterns in Sunderland.

4. THE MULTIPLE NUCLEI MODEL OF ULLMANN AND HARRIS

This model assumes that cities grow not from one central point but from the integration of a number of separate nuclei. These separate locations act as growth points and may include airports, a new-type industrial trading estate, the waterfront of a port or a railway station. Equally the heart of a small town or village may become enveloped within a growing city and itself become a growth point and appear as a suburban shopping centre. Can you think of any former villages which are now suburbs in your own city? Two examples where twin central shopping areas exist are Bristol and Hull. Bristol has a post-war shopping centre, Broadmead, near the site of the heavily bombed 'Old Market' area which was the working man's shopping centre until 1940. It also has a high class shopping centre in the more genteel area near the university. In Hull the two points of growth are the medieval port and the nineteenth century railway station.

Look at Fig. 13.1D which shows the arrangement of the component parts of the model. This is more complex than the others and hence approaches closer to reality. It is also a more flexible model and able to take into account peculiarities of site and the fashions of history – in particular the changing whim of what constitutes a favoured residential location.

During growth a degree of specialisation develops leading to an agglomeration of particular functions. Examples include the emergence of Harley Street in London as the medical centre or the jewellery quarter in Birmingham. Are you able to identify similar functional zones in your own city? Is there a street in which estate agents or solicitors' offices tend to cluster?

Equally as in the other models some activities will repel others. As the city grows so *diseconomies* of scale may commence leading to a duplication of functions. This arises from the need for functions to be readily accessible, and once a city centre becomes too congested, decentralisation and duplication begin to take place.

MODELS TESTED AGAINST REALITY
As in previous chapters, research evidence of the testing of the various models is now introduced.

Case I. Chicago
The special association of the Burgess model and Chicago has already been mentioned. Look at Fig. 13.2A. To what extent is the model supported by the real world evidence? In which zone would you expect to find the heavy industry associated with Chicago today? Notice the complicating factor of differing cultural groups and their distribution. Is this tendency being repeated in larger British cities today?

Case II. Calgary
Fig. 13.2B shows a schematic arrangement of land use in Calgary. Note the predominantly industrial belt to the south east and the adjacent low value houses. What advantages are there for the high

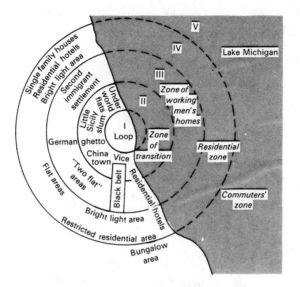

Fig. 13.2(A) Urban zones in Chicago in the 1920's (*Park R. E., Burgess E. W., McKenzie, R. D., The City*)

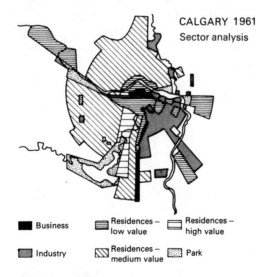

Fig. 13.2(B) Calgary 1961: land use and its interpretation by sectors (*Smith, P., 'Calgary: a study of urban patterns' Economic Geography 38, 1962*)

value residences? Is the overall pattern one which lends support to Hoyt's sector model?

Case III. Sunderland
A comprehensive investigation of Sunderland has been undertaken by Robson and a summary of housing types in relationship to areas of industry and the C.B.D. is shown in Fig. 13.2C. The zone of

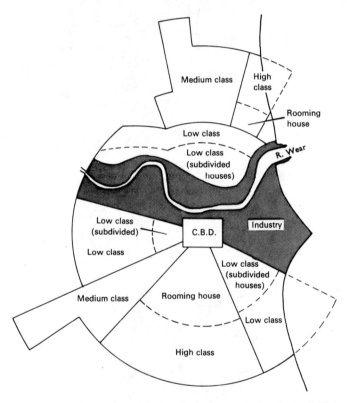

Fig. 13.2(C) Idealised model of ecological areas in Sunderland (*Robson, B., Urban Analysis*)

industry is located along the river with the C.B.D. on the south side. There is a marked difference in the spatial arrangement of the housing on the two sides of the river. To the north, housing types are predominantly in rings whilst to the south a sectoral pattern prevails. To what extent does this combination reflect the Mann model?

The 'pull and push' forces mentioned earlier seem to operate here.

The C.B.D. is the focus around which the housing is organised and it exerts a centripetal or pulling force. The pushing or centrifugal force is that of industry repelling housing. Note that low class housing is adjacent to industry on all sides and the difference in pattern to the north and south may be explained by the C.B.D. which acts as a buffer zone and enabled the sectoral arrangement to be established. Eventually a sectoral pattern has established itself in the north where the high class housing is attracted to the coast. It is interesting to see that there is no sector of such housing types on the southern coast.

Case IV. Sydney
Many large cities reflect the traits of all the models, the dominant ones being dependent upon physical, cultural and historical characteristics. Look at Fig. 13.2D which is a schematic arrangement of

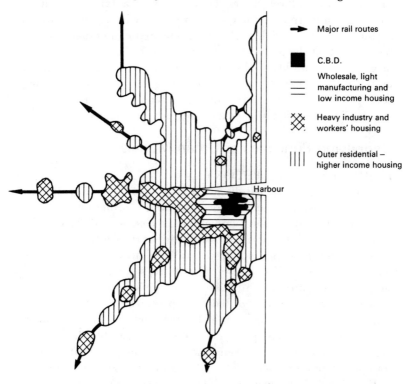

Major rail routes

C.B.D.

Wholesale, light manufacturing and low income housing

Heavy industry and workers' housing

Outer residential – higher income housing

Harbour

Fig. 13.2(D) The composite structure of Sydney (*Rutherford, J., Logan, M. I., and Missen, G. J., New Viewpoints in Economic Geography*)

Sydney's morphology. On the south side of the harbour the concentric zones are elongated along the major routeways in a manner reminiscent of the von Thünen model. Superimposed upon this pattern are several 'district centres' – shown here as industry and housing–designed to be self-contained and self-generating. Although this is not so clear an example of the multi-nuclei model as Los Angeles, it illustrates the idea that models do not exist in isolation from each other but may be used in conjunction in examining the complexity of urban morphology in the larger cities of today.

Burgess ignored the effects of transport and assumed an isotropic surface whilst Hoyt recognised the impact of increased accessibility. The more complex models of Mann and Harris/Ullman approximate more closely to the real world.

From the ideas introduced you will conclude that all models have their strengths and weaknesses. They do provide a framework within which urban morphology maps which you may have constructed as a result of your own fieldwork can be analysed more easily. Always remember that the map is the starting point rather than the end of investigating a problem. However, as in the case of models studied in the earlier chapters an understanding of their underpinning concepts facilitates an understanding of landscape and provides a source of relevant hypotheses to be further investigated.

Underlying Principles of Urban Models

1. BID RENT: THE THEORY

Common to all the models discussed is value of the land. Just as in the rural landscape crops compete for land so differing functions compete within the town. Competition is keenest at the centre for two reasons. First it is normally assumed that the centre is the most accessible location. Second, since available area increases as the square of the radial distance from the centre, so land is in its shortest supply at the centre. Fig. 13.3 shows the simplest form in which the principle of economic rent or bid rent operates and a clear relationship between this diagram and the Burgess model is easily identified.

If the premise is accepted that the more accessible the site the higher its potential rent, then land values will be greater along transportation axes, especially roads, and even higher at the intersection of routes. Hence instead of forming a conventional line graph a more accurate representation is shown in the rent cone diagram

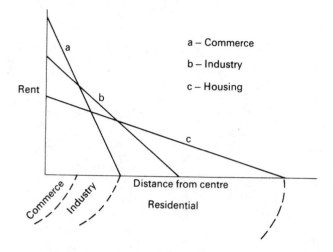

Fig. 13.3 The relationship between land values and land use inside the city

shown in Fig. 13.4. Land values reach a peak in the centre away from which they decline rapidly. Values form ridges along principal routeways and troughs in between the routeways, only to rise into mini-peaks at routeway intersections.

Empirical evidence to support this idea of bid rent in Exeter is illustrated in Fig. 13.4. What are the spatial implications?

Case I. Rateable values and distance from the centre
Since rateable values are partially based upon rent potential, the rateable value of a property, which may be obtained from inspecting the rate book in the local government offices, is a strong indicator of its bid rent.

Several studies of the pattern of rateable values have been undertaken: two accessible ones are found in Robson's study of Sunderland and in Everson and Fitzgerald, *Inside the City*. Look at Fig. 13.5 which shows the rateable values per unit area for Hanley in Staffordshire. Visual inspection would support the general hypothesis. Using tracing paper plot isopleths of the critical values shown and see how their shape conforms to and differs from the model.

Case II. Rateable values and distance from the centre
A full analysis of values has been undertaken and plotted as a rent

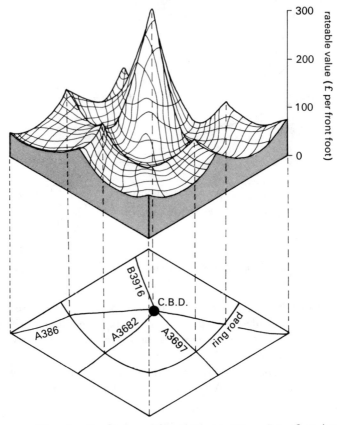

Fig. 13.4   The urban land value surface in Exeter (*Toyne, Peter, Organisation, Location and Behaviour*)

cone for the city of Exeter by Peter Toyne. This is illustrated in Fig. 13.4 The support of this example for the theoretical arrangement is remarkable and the overt relationship of the crests and peaks to the road network is very clear.

Unless you are able to work within a group, if you attempt to test this hypothesis within your own town the exercise may prove difficult and lengthy. A useful expedient may be to determine the mean rateable value for a street by applying sampling techniques. Plot these values on a 6-inch or 25-inch map at the mid-point of the street and measure its distance from the centre of the C.B.D. You

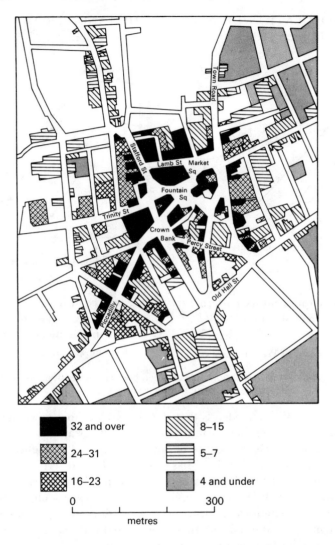

Fig. 13.5 Rateable values per unit area in Hanley, Staffs. (*Herbert D.,*
Urban Geography)

may then draw isopleths on the map and in addition have two
variables which may profitably be used in regression analysis to
determine the strength of their relationship.

2. POPULATION DENSITY AND DISTANCE FROM THE CENTRE

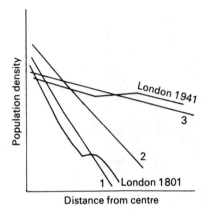

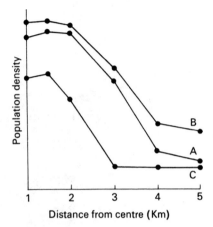

KEY

1 = earliest 19th century pattern.
2 and 3 = successive periods.

A   Changes in Western Cities

KEY

A = Mean condition.
B = Rate along major routeways.
C = Rate in the interstitial areas.

B   Relationships in Exeter

Fig. 13.6(A and B)   Relationships between population density and distance from the centre.

Implicit in all the models is that the higher class housing is mainly located on the periphery whilst terraced dwellings are contained in zones 2 and 3. Hence density of population should be higher near the centre. The C.B.D. itself has sometimes been described as the 'dead-heart' of the city because so few people actually live there. Ignoring the C.B.D. the principle of distance decay should operate and there is empirical evidence to support this. In Fig. 13.6A the changing general trend over time is illustrated with that for London superimposed. The steepness of the gradient from the early nineteenth century contrasts with that for the mid-twentieth century and results from the immobility of people then compared with now. The increased mobility of people will be commented upon in Chapter 15. Fig. 13.6B is a case study of Exeter and reveals how the lapse rate is less steep along major routeways and more steep away from them. What problems are suggested in these two diagrams for further investigation? Once again this could be tested for any large city by determining the density of population for each of the wards from the Census of Population and measuring its distance from the centre.

SOME DEVIATIONS FROM URBAN MODELS

As in the classical models considered earlier in this book, these urban ones also depend upon economic determinism accompanied by rational decision-making. However, more and more society is developing a social conscience and just as industrial patterns are modified by social necessity so urban patterns too are being altered. The periphery of the city is no longer the preserve of higher class housing since many corporation housing estates are located there – often consisting of high rise flats – as inner city dwellers are re-housed. The population density and distance relationship may therefore eventually become inverted. You will find evidence of this in Robson's book and possibly field evidence in your own town. Can you think of possible reasons for this change?

Shops may wish to substitute a larger land area with adequate parking facilities for an allegedly accessible location within the C.B.D. Hypermarket and out-town discount stores are just appearing on the British scene despite opposition. The first hypermarket to open was at Caerphilly in 1972 but others are emerging at Telford,

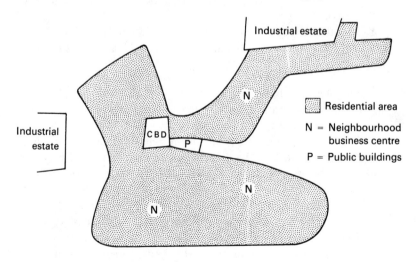

Fig. 13.7 Functional zones in Harlow New Town

Washington, County Durham, and Chandler's Ford, Southampton. This trend is being pursued by the major supermarket chains.

The third deviation is deliberate planning in a new town area, for example, Harlow shown in Fig. 13.7. The C.B.D. remains the focus but industry is found on the periphery of the town on a series of estates. The residential areas sandwiched between these two consist of several planned neighbourhood units each with its own smaller business district and containing a mixture of housing classes. Such an overall arrangement stands in marked contrast to the Burgess model introduced at the beginning of the chapter.

The Form and Functions of the C.B.D.

Since the C.B.D. is common to all models and forms the focal point of all towns and cities a brief discussion of its attributes is needed, especially since interaction between other areas and the C.B.D. is discussed in the last section of this chapter.

The C.B.D. is the heart of the city and its functional hallmarks are:

1. Public and government buildings are found here together with professional and business offices, especially the financial ones.
2. Very specialist, prestigious shops offer high level goods (see Table 13.1) together with branches of the major chain groups.
3. Social amenities are concentrated here: theatres, cinemas, hotels.
4. Manufacturing is absent except for printing of newspapers.
5. There are no substantial areas of residential accommodation.

Three characteristics of form include:

1. The height of buildings: office blocks such as Centre Point in London and multi-floored departmental stores are complemented by multi-storey car parks.
2. The height of building results from high land values and high rates. Look back at the distribution in Hanley in Fig. 13.5.
3. Accessibility – especially when public transport is being used. This is reflected in both motor car and pedestrian densities and flows. Once the C.B.D. ceases to be accessible, partially as a result of the phenomenal increase in traffic density, then decentralisation will begin. What kinds of evidence would indicate this is taking place? Is there any evidence in your own town?

DE-LIMITING THE C.B.D.

These expressions of form and function have been combined effectively to delimit the C.B.D. Rateable values converted into a rates index, *ie.* rateable value per foot of frontage is a common device and would be a useful initial indicator. Within this area further tests may be carried out: absence of residence and heights of buildings may be readily ascertained. Pedestrian flows, however, require teamwork and are more difficult to arrive at. An alternative to counting shoppers is to collect information from them at bus stations and car parks. Remembering the need for tact and courtesy as mentioned earlier, merely ask which shops have been visited. From responses a quantitative pattern of actual usage may be constructed to help identify the limits of the CBD. In a recent exercise in Newcastle 1,470 questionnaires revealed 13 particularly attractive shops – designated magnet stores – which accounted for 74% of all shop visits. What do you think are the magnet stores in your city? How would you test your estimate?

An example of pedestrian flows in Leicester in 1968 based upon 92 count stations is shown in Fig. 13.8 and indicates not only the maximum flows within the central area but shows how the density decreased with increasing distance from the C.B.D. What evidence can you find on the map to explain this density in the centre? Why do you think it declines so rapidly? Look carefully to identify the detailed pattern of this distance decay and suggest explanations for its shape.

The way in which these measures may be combined to identify a hard-core area of the C.B.D. where all attributes – highest rateable values, buildings and pedestrian flows – are present is indicated in *Teaching Geography No. 11* which summarises the work of a sixth-form field exercise in Norwich. This could become the model for you to adapt for your own field-work.

INSIDE THE C.B.D.

The forces already recognised operate within the C.B.D. itself. A study of Bolton, Lancs., contained in *Briggs' Fieldwork in Urban Geography* reveals how certain functions occupy key positions. Banks seem to occupy corner sites of major intersections in Bolton whilst solicitors are in narrower side streets.

From this study of Bolton it is also clear that certain functions tend

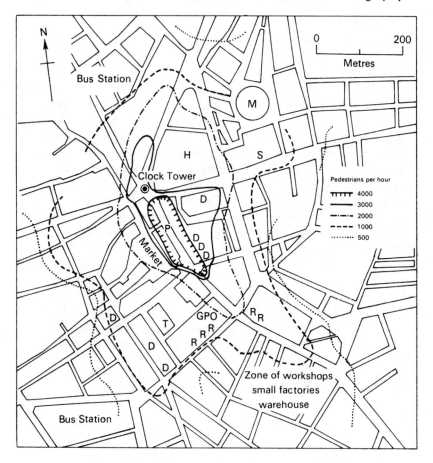

KEY D Departmental store.
     H Haymarket Centre (shopping precinct, theatre, restaurants).
     M Multi storey car park.
     P Pedestrian precinct.
     R Restaurants.
     S Sainsburys.
     T Town Hall.

Fig. 13.8 Leicester Central Area: average pedestrian flows (*Lewis, G. J., 'Pedestrian flows in the central area of Leicester' East Midlands Geographer, Vol. 6, Pt. II, page 82 with additional help from Patrick Bailey, University Department of Education*)

to occur adjacent to each other. This phenomenon which is very apparent in larger cities, for example, diamond merchants in Hatton Garden, repeats itself in smaller cities, and in *Teaching Geography No. 11* full details are given for constructing a functional-adjacency matrix. An alternative to this laborious method is to plot a number of key functions perhaps the identified magnet stores or such as those shown for the centre of Cardiff in Fig. 13.9. A visual inspection of the arrangement reveals a distinct clustering of finance houses and an agglomeration of furniture stores. More quantitative measure is possible through the application of nearest neighbour analysis (page 202): indeed, it is possible by this means to discover whether or not some functions are more agglomerated than others. Reasons for this ob-

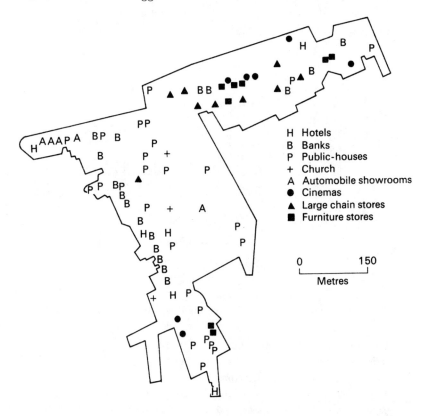

Fig. 13.9 The distribution of selected functions within central Cardiff
(*Carter, Harold, The Study of Urban Geography*)

served functional adjacency seem related to scale economies which arise from proximity of similar activities and to historical forces. How else could one begin to explain the distribution of public houses in the medieval core of Cardiff? Earlier it was suggested that the principle of zonation might be applied vertically resulting in an arrangement such as that shown in Fig. 13.10. To what extent is this pattern true of the C.B.D. of your own city?

Although emphasis has been placed upon the importance of the C.B.D. as the highest order central place within an area its primary position is now being challenged in countries free from planning controls. In the U.K. the growth of out-town shopping centres has

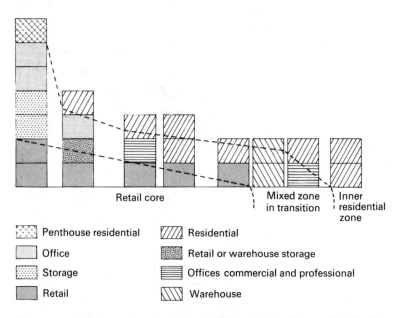

Fig. 13.10 Land use in relation to building height (*Carter, Harold, The Study of Urban Geography*)

not only been prevented but through re-development plans and pedestrian precincts the C.B.D. has been strengthened. How far is this true of your town? In North America 'greenfield' sites, such as the Yorkdale Centre, Toronto, located near express ways with 50,000 sq. m. of floor space and 4,000 parking spaces are common place. These are having a marked effect upon the trade of the C.B.D. of the larger urban areas in particular. In the Mid-West the C.B.D.'s share of trade has dropped by 10–16%. The larger towns have suffered most, for example Detroit's C.B.D. has declined by 30%. Departmental stores have suffered most with falls varying 26–50%. Some 60% of people gave parking and congestion as reasons for not shopping in central Seattle.

A similar growth trend of out-of-town centres can be identified in Europe. For example, France possessed only 4 hypermarkets in 1967 but had 212 by 1973. Will this change of fashion spread to the U.K.? What will happen here if it does? Already, the impact of new Sainsbury stores in out-town locations at Bretton and Kempston is being felt by supermarkets in the C.B.D.'s of Peterborough and Bedford respectively.

Inter-Action within the Urban Area

Effectively the city is not just one central place but a whole group of central places each located in different parts of the city and ranging from lowest order to highest order. Three easily recognisable orders within the hierarchy are:

convenience goods centres: baker, butcher, greengrocer, post office.
neighbourhood shopping centre: convenience goods plus hairdressing, dry cleaning and hardware.
central business district: full range of amenities.

With a hierarchy of central places within the urban area it is reasonable to expect similar interaction patterns as between town and country.

What evidence is there of threshold and the range of a good?
The threshold concept is subsumed in the hierarchy outlined above and more specifically illustrated in Table 13.1. Although the data are confined to exotic items, the available variety of champagne and cigars is far greater in the C.B.D. than elsewhere whilst the price ranges for watches and jewellery show the same trend. The range of a good, so well illustrated in Tarrant's study between town and country, is equally true for intra-urban interaction. Look at Fig. 13.11 which summarises shopping patterns in Zurich. Lower order goods are obtained in the neighbourhood centre whilst the bulk of the higher order is bought in the C.B.D.

What evidence is there that goods are bought at the nearest centre offering them? You will recall that this was an essential premise of central place theory and was called into question in the earlier investigations discussed in the last chapter. How true is this for intra-urban behaviour? Do consumers minimise the distance travelled?

Table 13.1

Range of goods in three business districts of Zurich at three different levels of the urban hierarchy

| | Number of kinds | | Price range (francs) | |
	Cham-pagne	Cigars	Wrist watches	Jewellery
Neighbourhood centre	1	112	40–200	30–210
Regional centre	3	205	60–950	50–1050
C.B.D.	20	501	100–20,000	100–30,000

Source: H. Carol, 'The hierarchy of central functions within the city'. 1962.

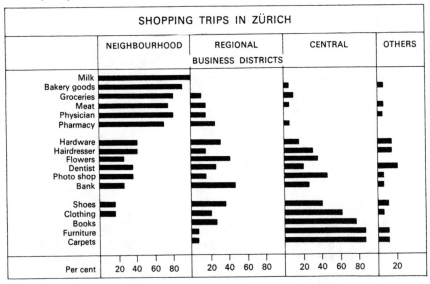

Fig. 13.11 Shopping trips made by the residents of a Zurich suburb. (*Carol, H., 'The hierarchy of central functions within the city' I.G.U. Symposium in Urban Geography 1962*)

Case I. Christchurch, New Zealand

Clark and Rushton examined the hypothesis that people shopped at the nearest centre which offered a good and their overall findings are summarised in Table 13.2.

Table 13.2

Shopping patterns in Christchurch, New Zealand

Commodity	% using nearest centre
Groceries	39·3
Meat	22·4
Vegetables	35·8
Dry cleaning	32·9
Beauty care	25·3
Banking	25·0

Source: Clark, W. A. V. and Rushton, G. 'Models of intra-urban consumer behaviour and their implication for central place theory'.

This most seriously calls into question the nearest centre hypothesis and an alternative explanation must be sought. One possibility is the increased public transport facility within an urban area and the number of alternative centres located within what may be considered a reasonable distance. Although Table 13.2 summarises the overall findings in fact the detailed analysis is shown in Fig. 13.12 where it can be seen that for all commodities other than banking, the probability of patronising the nearest centre declines as its distance from the consumer increases. We shall return to possible solutions of this problem later.

Case II. Leeds, West Yorkshire
Although Ross Davies was concerned primarily with the differing shopping habits of distinct socio-economic groups, his findings contribute to the examination of the nearest centre hypothesis. Study Table 13.3. Davies isolated two areas where all variables except income were neutralised. Look first at the numbers of movements made by the two groups and make general statements about the differences you observe. Now turn to the direction of movements. Is there a significant difference in the range of a good for differing income levels? It would seem that higher income groups have greater mobility than low income ones which are much more circumscribed. What evidence is there in Table 13.3 for this statement? Although similar overall trends to the pattern in Zurich are apparent there are significant differences between the groups. If we assume the local parade and the neighbourhood centre to be the

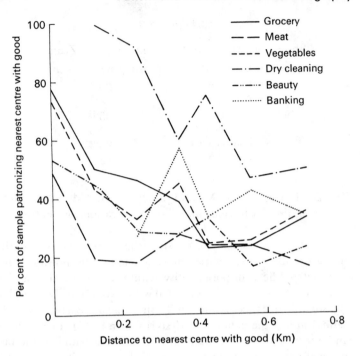

Fig. 13.12 Patronage of nearest centre as related to distance from the consumer (*Clarke, W. A. V., Rushton, G., 'Models of intra-urban consumer behaviour and their implications for central place theory'*)

nearest centre offering the goods specified in Table 13.3, how far is the nearest centre hypothesis substantiated? How do these results compare for the overall figures for Christchurch?

These two studies help re-introduce the basic problem considered earlier, namely, upon what basis do shoppers decide where to shop?

Clearly those people with a higher income have a greater choice – not only of goods but of locations. Look again at Fig. 13.12 Clark suggests that where the nearest centre is within walking distance a high proportion of consumers will patronise it, but beyond that point patronage declines with increasing distance. Even a distance of 50 metres seems critical in making the decision. Clark also discovered that whilst people seemed very conscious of the nearest centre for groceries, meat and vegetables this is less true for the other goods investigated.

Table 13.3

Effect of consumer income differences on shopping movement
behaviour in Leeds

	Group 1	Group 2
Background	Middleton (S. Leeds)	Street Lane (N. Leeds)
	Low income (median 733)	High income (median 1276)
	3 miles from C.B.D.	3 miles from C.B.D.
	Frequent public transport	
	65 stores with 24 functions	78 stores with 25 functions

18 functions common to both

	Destination	No.	No.
Number of movements	Hairdressing	62	87
	Shoe repairs	61	90
	Bank	47	96
	Cakes	91	78
	Cooked meat	99	88

		%	%
Direction of movements	I To local shopping parades		
	Groceries	81	57
	Meats	75	54
	II To neighbourhood centre		
	Chemist	92	78
	Hardware	50	23
	Hairdressing	52	40
	III To C.B.D.		
	Convenience goods	13	18
	Groceries	15	31
	Cakes	14	24
	Adult clothing	96	84
	IV To other retailing centres		
	Convenience	6	25
	Groceries	4	31

Source: Derived from Davies, Ross L. 'Effects of consumer income differences on shopping movement behaviour'.

One important hypothesis to arise from the study of behaviour in Christchurch is the idea of a zone of *indifference* within which shoppers have no particular preference for one centre or the nearest centre and this raises the important question of how shoppers perceive distance. Is this a parallel case to the farmer's attitude in choosing crops (Chapter 6)?

HUMAN DECISION-MAKING AND SHOPPING MOVEMENTS

With the exception of Case II considered above, so far all the discussion and examples have confined their attention to the functional strength of the central place and its linear distance from the consumer, and to single purpose journeys. What of the consumer himself – his age, sex, degree of affluence, personality, attitudes and values? What perception does he have of the central place? Is this conjured up by amenities themselves, accessibility, parking or overall quality of the environment? Do consumers ever make journeys for only one

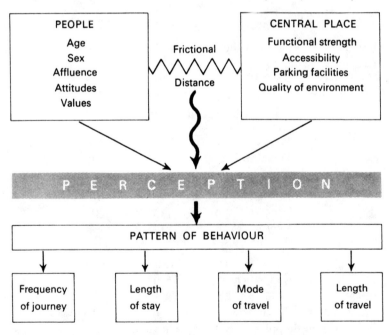

Fig. 13.13 The contribution of perception to shopping behaviour patterns
(*Spence, P. S.*)

good? Recently studies have focused upon perception and the contribution this makes to patterns of movement. The linkages between the elements in this system are shown in Fig. 13.13.

We should begin by examining how shoppers perceive distance as this is perhaps a key factor in decision-making when a shopper can choose between several locations offering the same kinds of facilities.

1. Distance perceived as time

A study of habits of people using Yorkdale, which is a regional shopping centre in Metropolitan Toronto, was undertaken by Spence. He sought to discover (i) whether people perceived distance as time distance or territorial distance, and (ii) whether an order in shopping patterns exists despite the many variables involved. To achieve this he divided the area around Yorkdale into six time zones placed at 5-minute intervals and employed a stratified random sample.

Spence discovered that people described distances in terms of time especially as territorial distance from Yorkdale increased and their perception was remarkably accurate regardless of the actual distance travelled, sex, social status or frequency of visit.

A remarkable orderliness in shopping habits was revealed. There was a significant percentage decrease of people shopping for everyday items with increasing distance supporting by implication the nearest centre hypothesis. Specific item shopping – for items such as clothes and furniture – increased with distance hence indicating the range of a good.

2. Subjective distance

Thompson established a very careful research design in four areas of San Francisco to test whether or not distance affected decisions of shopping destinations. Each of the four areas contained a large departmental store and a discount store in close proximity to each other and offered a similar range of goods. Yet when shoppers were questioned they regarded the discount houses as more distant than the departmental stores. In all cases they also over-estimated times and distances and the error increased with real distance. Thompson concludes that subjective feelings about a location can therefore influence your evaluation of its true geographical position. The distance perceived in your mind he termed subjective distance.

Urban models have been introduced and their strengths and

weaknesses discussed. Once again attention needs to be focused upon the underlying concepts rather than the rigid form of the model. These concepts provide interesting hypotheses to be tested through your own fieldwork. Whilst the interaction within the urban area supports some aspects of central place theory, the nearest centre hypothesis must be seriously questioned in the light of the evidence. People's perception is an important factor which must be built into future models attempting to predict patterns of human behaviour.

In a study in Erlangen in Southern Germany, Gunter Meyer tested a number of hypotheses:

Hypothesis 1. Perception of distance in the C.B.D. varies with the degree of consumer preference for a particular street. The results from 244 respondents are found in Table 13.4. You will see that lengths of preferred streets are underestimated whilst those disliked are overestimated, confirming the findings of Thompson in San Francisco.

Table 13.4

Perception of distance and street preference

| | Percentage perceiving the distance | | |
	Too short	Correctly	Too long
A Preferred street	50	30	20
B Less Preferred street	34	36	30
C Disliked street	22	32	46

Source: Meyer

Hypothesis 2. Perception of distance varies with direction: the length of a shopping street is perceived as shorter if it leads in the direction of the shopper's residence. Study the results of the survey in Table 13.5. Do you accept the hypothesis? Use the chi-square test to determine the statistical significance of the results. Remember to turn percentages into actual numbers.

Table 13.5

Distance perception and direction towards
the shopper's residence

Direction of street from C.B.D.		Number of respondent's residences in relation to C.B.D.	percentage perceiving the distance		
			Too short	Correctly	Too long
1. Leading South	N	30	30	13	57
	E	52	34	33	33
	S	116	47	31	22
	W	46	31	41	28
2. Leading North	N	30	60	23	17
	E	52	35	27	38
	S	116	28	40	32
	W	46	30	46	24

Source: (based on Meyer)

Hypothesis 3. Perception of distance varies with frequency of visit
Look at Table 13.6. It is clear that estimates of the lengths of
shopping streets are strongly related to frequency of use.

Table 13.6

Distance perception and frequency of visit

Street	Percentage perceiving the distance		
	Too short	Correctly	Too long
Most frequently visited	52	28	20
Less frequently visited	36	39	25
Rarely visited	18	34	51

At this point pause to sum up the conclusions which may be drawn
from Meyer's study but in using these as guidelines for your own
investigations, remember that the distances involved were in the
range 400–500 m. Furthermore he found even within this range
perceived distances were on average 31 % longer than actual distances.
This average conceals a wide range of estimate as shown in Table 13.7.

Table 13.7

Actual and perceived distances.

	Road 1	Road 2	Road 3
Actual length (m)	500	450	430
Extreme Respondent A	100	80	100
Extreme Respondent B	2000	1500	2000

Source: Meyer

A second important consideration is the assessment of the central place by the shopper. How does he perceive this? A very full investigation of the Tayside Region by Pacione revealed the rank order of preferences listed in Table 13.8.

Table 13.8

Rank order of preferences in the consumers' value system

RANK ORDER

Preference

1. Retail establishments having quality and fashionable merchandise.
2. Establishments offering competitive prices and bargain shopping.
3. Reliability of establishments.
4. Variety of establishments in the towns retailing the type of good required.
5. Ease of accessibility to town and convenient car parking facilities.
6. Ability to combine the shopping trip with other activities in the town.
7. Atmosphere and appearance of the shopping town.

Source: Michael Pacione (1975) *Preference and perception – an analysis of consumer behaviour. T.E.S.G.,* lxvi, 2.

Study this list of preferences. What pattern are you able to detect? It may help to ask yourself how the preferences 1–4 differ from those 5–7. How are they related to the idea of magnet stores introduced earlier? On the basis of these criteria the attractiveness of the towns as shopping centres were ranked as in Table 13.9.

Note the low rank order of Dundee, despite its size. Other studies too show that shoppers dislike large metropolitan cities. Notice that

Table 13.9
Consumer evaluations and numbers of
banks in Tayside

Col	1	2	3	4
	Rank Order	Attractiveness	Accuracy of Perceived Distance	No. of banks in town in Col. 3
	1	Montrose	Montrose	5
	2	Forfar	Broughty Ferry	6
	3	Broughty Ferry	Forfar	3
	4	Arbroath	Arbroath	12
	5	Brechin	Brechin	6
	6	Dundee	Dundee	15
	7	Carnoustie	Carnoustie	2

Source: Pacione

accuracy in perception of distance is again related to preference. Of particular interest is that only 25% of shoppers bought their clothes in the nearest town. Return to your exercise at the end of the last chapter and assess the predictive value of the models used.

By experimentation Pacione concluded the best measure of functional strength to be the number of supermarkets, department stores and banks and travel time be substituted for linear distance.

Summary and Concluding Exercise

Problems associated with Central Place Theory arise from the way society lives in the closing decades of the twentieth century. It is a highly mobile world of working wives, two car families and home freezers. Despite these complicating variables when you have followed through the suggested reading you may be surprised to find many of the theoretical concepts remain intact. Of course people with cars and more money travel further as do the young. Although multipurpose trips are made, food items account for some 80% of all shopping journeys, more than 50% of all journeys are less than 4 km, 71% of shopping is carried out on single purpose trips and 93% of people use a maximum shopping pattern in the week irrespective of income level, number of children or car ownership. Perhaps the need is to review our idea of a central place rather than central place theory.

Although the rigid nesting hexagons should be replaced by realistic overlapping trade areas to accommodate present day complexities, there is sufficient research evidence to suggest that a satisficer principle operates in consumer choice. For although differing consumers will have differing needs and aspirations, they nearly always choose the nearest centre which satisfies their particular set of desires.

Look at the data in Table 13.10A. The mean number of centres used is 3.05 and the mode 2. How do these findings of Potter in Stockport relate to those of Bracey and Tarrant? Do they confirm a hierarchy of centres? What explanation can you offer for the variation in numbers of centres used? A further analysis by Potter is shown in Table 13.10B. To what extent do these data substantiate the findings of Davies in Leeds?

Table 13.10A.

Frequency of centres used by residents in Stockport

No. of centres used	No. of people
1	9
2	67
3	55
4	38
5	16
6	4
7	3

Table 13.10B.

Variations in use according to social class of consumer

Social Class	Mean no. of Centres	Mean distances of Centres (km)	Mean angle of usage field
I	4·45	3·30	83
II	4·27	3·00	45
III	2·87	1·85	23
IV	2·27	1·57	19
V	2·00	0·65	15
Economically inactive	2·54	1·65	14
All respondents	3·05	2·04	28

The social class corresponds to the classification used by the Registrar General. The angle of usage field was determined by drawing two radii from the town centre which encompassed all the centres used by the consumer together with his place of residence.

Return now to Fig. 10.4 on p. 186. Join by a line any second order place to the third order. Join the first order place located south east of this chosen second order one also to 3 as in Fig. 13.14. Measure the angle at 3. How does this compare with the mean of 28° in Table 13.10B.? What may be concluded from this?

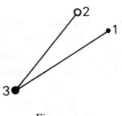

Fig. 13.14

Crawley like Harlow and other new towns was built as a planned environment where it is reasonable to expect central place theory to hold since there are two levels of shopping hierarchy optimally located in space. Day questioned 241 people living in 3 estates and his findings are summarised in Table 13.11.

Table 13.11
Shopping destinations of consumers in Crawley

percent shopping in

Good	C.B.D.	Local Parade	Another Town
	1·6 km	0·8 km	
Food	59	37	4
Furniture	82	—	28
Clothes	37	—	63

Source : Day.

In the light of what you have read, how would you explain this pattern? Think particularly of the work of Pacione and the idea of an indifference level.

Further Reading

*Briggs, K. (1970) *Fieldwork in Urban Geography*. Oliver and Boyd.

*Everson, J. A. and Fitzgerald, B. P. (1972) *Inside the City*. Longman.

Carter, Harold (1972) *The Study of Urban Geography*. Arnold.

Clark, W. A. V. and Rushton, Gerald (1970) 'Models of intra-urban consumer behaviour and their implications for central place theory'. *Economic Geography*, 46, pages 486–97.

Davies, Ross L. (1969) 'Effects of consumer income differences on shopping movement behaviour'. *T.E.S.G.* March/April 1969, pages 111–22.

Day, R. A. (1973) 'Consumer shopping behaviour in a planned urban environment'. *T.E.S.G.* vol. 63, no. 2, pages 77–85.

Meyer, Gunter (1977) 'Distance perception of consumers in shopping streets'. *T.E.S.G.* vol. 68, no. 6, pages 355–361.

Potter, R. K. (1977) 'The nature of consumer usage fields in an urban environment' *T.E.S.G.* vol. 68, no. 3, pages 168–175.

Rawling, Eleanor (1975) 'Supermarket for Llandovery – an exercise in field research'. *Teaching Geography*, vol. 1, no. 1, pages 7–10.

Robson, B. T. (1975) *Urban Social Areas*. O.U.P.

Spence, P. S. (1971) 'Orderliness in the journey to shop', *T.E.S.G.* Jan./Feb. 1971, pages 22–34.

Thompson, Donald L. (1963) 'New concept: subjective distance'. Reprinted in Ambrose: *Analytical Human Geography*, pages 197–203. Longman

* Essential reading.

14 · Transport Networks I — Measurement of Structures

Distance and Change in Spatial Relationships

A recurrent theme throughout the pages of this book has been the distance separating locations and how to traverse the distance. Bid rents for crops or urban land use were shown to depend upon distance from market and city centre respectively. Distance decay

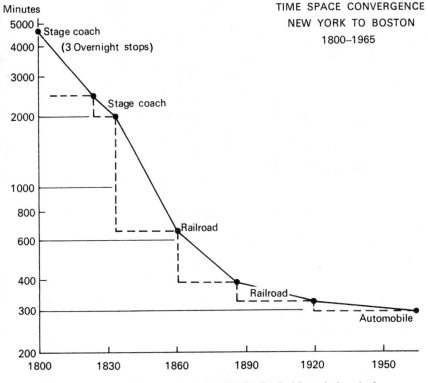

Minutes

TIME SPACE CONVERGENCE
NEW YORK TO BOSTON
1800–1965

Stage coach
(3 Overnight stops)

Stage coach

Railroad

Railroad

Automobile

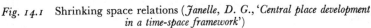

Fig. 14.1   Shrinking space relations (*Janelle, D. G., 'Central place development in a time-space framework'*)

273

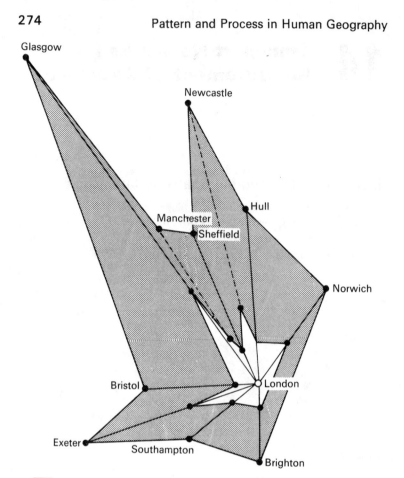

Glasgow

Newcastle

Hull

Manchester
Sheffield

Norwich

Bristol

London

Exeter
Southampton

Brighton

▨ Time saved with motorcoach compared with stagecoach

Fig. 14.2 Shrinking Britain

has been identified as an all-important force influencing many patterns from agricultural land use to urban shopping habits. In the interactive systems we have examined, a key aim is to minimise this frictional distance and thus increase accessibility between places. Examining the changing spatial relationships between places is essential to an understanding of geographical problems.

Look at Fig. 14.1 which indicates one instance of how two cities have changed their relative position in space. Whilst in 1800 the journey from New York to Boston took nearly 5000 minutes, the same journey in 1965 took a mere 300 minutes. This vast difference may be explained by improved technology: three modes of transport are indicated. This is not, however, the complete answer, for even in the stage coach era the journey time was halved. How can you account for this? Consider your answer again after reading this chapter.

During the last ten years the most significant impact upon surface travel in Great Britain has been made by the growing motorway network. Fig. 14.3 shows the predicted changes in travelling time around Birmingham in 1980. Many of the motorways facilitating this shrinkage have already been built. What implications do these changed spatial relationships have for shopping and commuting?

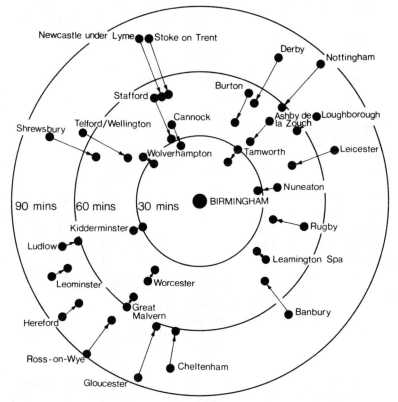

Fig. 14.3 Convergence of West Midland towns on Birmingham 1960–80.
(Source: based on Williams, A.F.)

This shrinkage of distance, measured in journey time, is a world wide phenomenon. The Moscow–Vladivostok Express takes 212 hours to cover the 9337 km journey, whereas by air this can be traversed in less than 24 hours. The 'shrinkage' of Britain over time is indicated in Fig. 14.2 where stage coach and motor coach journey times are plotted from the data in Table 14.1. This phenomenon has been described as *space convergence* and as geographers we must

Table 14.1

Transport data for Great Britain

London to	Distance (km)	Bearing (degrees)	Journey times (hrs)			
			Stage coach	Motor coach	Rail	Air
Bradford	302	335	—	5	2	1
Brighton	80	182	$7\frac{3}{4}$	2	1	—
Bristol	189	270	$12\frac{1}{4}$	$7\frac{1}{4}$	$1\frac{3}{4}$	—
Cardiff	253	270	$17\frac{1}{2}$	6	$2\frac{1}{4}$	—
Carlisle	480	334	$32\frac{3}{4}$	$8\frac{1}{2}$	$4\frac{1}{2}$	$1\frac{1}{2}$
Edinburgh	629	339	43	11	6	$1\frac{1}{4}$
Exeter	272	254	$18\frac{3}{4}$	$7\frac{1}{4}$	3	—
Glasgow	641	325	$42\frac{1}{2}$	12	$6\frac{3}{4}$	$1\frac{1}{2}$
Hull	315	356	$18\frac{1}{2}$	$4\frac{1}{2}$	4	1
Leeds	288	339	$21\frac{1}{2}$	$4\frac{1}{2}$	2	1
Manchester	293	328	$19\frac{1}{2}$	$5\frac{1}{2}$	3	$\frac{3}{4}$
Newcastle	429	346	$30\frac{1}{4}$	$8\frac{1}{2}$	4	1
Nottingham	200	335	$12\frac{3}{4}$	$4\frac{1}{2}$	$1\frac{1}{4}$	—
Norwich	184	036	12	5	$2\frac{1}{4}$	—
Sheffield	241	335	17	4	$2\frac{1}{2}$	—
Southampton	127	234	9	$3\frac{1}{4}$	$1\frac{1}{4}$	—

Sources: 1. Directory of Stage Coach Services 1836 by Alan Bates. Times are for Royal Mail only.
2. Associated Motorways Timetable.
3. British Rail Timetables.
4. B.E.A. and B.M.A. Timetables.

remain constantly alert to adjust our ideas and perceptions of spatial relations as they change with the opening of a new motorway or with the supersonic flight of Concorde.

NETWORK TERMINOLOGY

This chapter is not concerned with assessing the relative merits of different modes of travel, important though these are. Our purpose is confined to exploring different forms and structures of transport *networks* and to evaluate them as entire systems rather than as individual routes within the system. What then is a network?

The simplest definition is that of Kansky: 'a set of geographic locations inter-connected in a system by a number of routes'. In Fig. 14.4 there are several networks in which the locations are represented by dots and the connections by straight lines. Such networks are known as *topological* ones. Topology, as you may already know from your studies in mathematics, is often called 'rubber sheet geometry'. In other words distances and directions no longer matter:

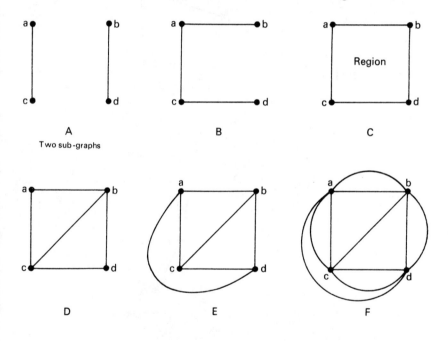

Fig. 14.4(A–F)   Progressive integration within networks

the qualities of a topological network is that it must retain its original number of locations and linkages. Topological representation is not new: the London Underground map is a topological one and British Rail now publish their maps in topological format. What then are the advantages of topological maps?

In the first place they communicate information much more clearly because they eliminate irrelevant factors. They are more flexible and may be drawn on several bases – time, cost or linear distance – depending upon their purpose. In addition they lend themselves to rapid analysis as we shall see in this and the following chapter and their format enables a computer to be used in predicting changes and consequences of such changes in a given network. They are especially useful for solving routing problems, both simple and complex.

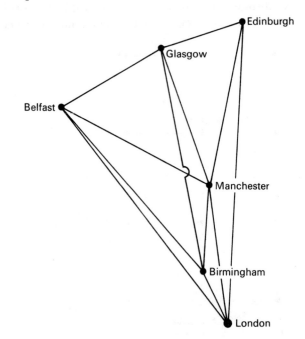

Fig. 14.4(G)   Example of a non-planar network

Traditionally the maps we use in geography are topographical ones. How may such a map be converted into a topological one? Look at Fig. 14.5 in which the topographical map of a road network in A has been converted into a topological one in B. Note that all the roads have been converted into straight *edges* and the towns into

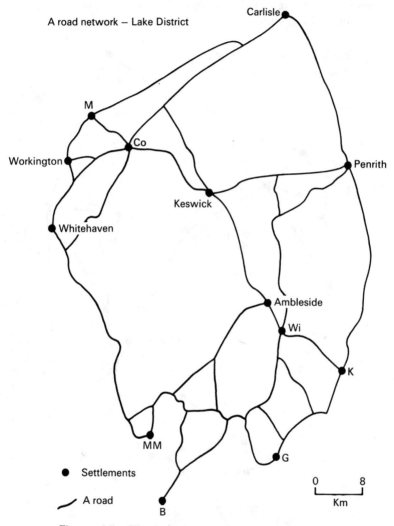

Fig. 14.5(A) The A road network in the Lake District

nodes. All road junctions also appear as nodes. A node is defined as a point of origin or destination, a significant town en route, or a junction of two or more edges. An edge is a link between any two nodes. It is important to grasp the topological equivalent of the topographical and to realise that edges may be arcs as well as straight lines. Look at Fig. 14.6B on page 286 which is the topological equivalent of Fig. 14.6A.

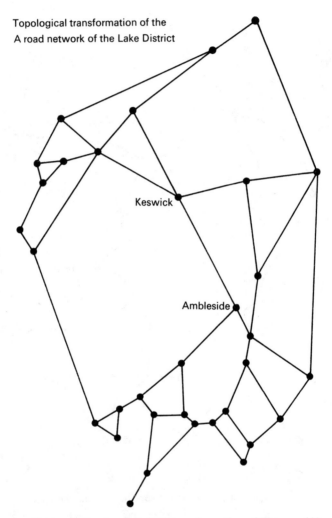

Topological transformation of the
A road network of the Lake District

Keswick

Ambleside

Fig. 14.5(B)   A topological transformation of Fig. 14.5(A)

Networks are really graphs and the terminology and rules of graph theory apply to them. Definitions with which it is essential for you to become familiar are now introduced with reference to Fig. 14.4 in which four nodes remain constant.

In A, two sets of two nodes are each connected but remain as distinct pairs. Each pair of connected nodes is called a *sub-graph*. B is a *connected graph* since all nodes are linked, and the edges linking them form a *path*. C is also a connected graph, but since it begins and ends at the same node it is called a *circuit* and encloses a *region*. How many regions are there in D and E? Look at Fig. 14.4E; notice that all the nodes have a direct link to every other node in the network. This is known as a *complete* graph and the network is said to be *fully integrated*. The addition of further edges as in Fig. 14.4F does not improve the linkages in the system and these additional edges are deemed *redundant*.

Think back over your studies in regional geography and try to identify real world examples of the six networks portrayed in Fig. 14.4. It may help you to examine contrasting regions of physical difficulty and stages of economic development.

It is important to distinguish between *planar* and *non-planar* graphs. In a planar graph the edges are on a two-dimensional surface, so that when they intersect they form nodes as in Fig. 14.4E. Rail and road networks are examples of planar graphs. When edges move in three dimensions, they may cross without intersecting and hence do not form a node. This is a non-planar graph and the example of air routes in the United Kingdom is shown in Fig. 14.4G. Thus the crossing of a trunk road and motorway is not a node unless it is also an access point. Discussion in these chapters is confined to planar graphs.

Basic relationships between nodes and edges
Three simple but essential relationships must be understood:

1. There is a minimum number of edges needed to connect all nodes and this may be calculated by the number of nodes minus one $(n - 1)$. In the case of Fig. 14.4 this would be three edges so that B is *minimally* connected.
2. The number of possible ways in which nodes may be connected is governed by the number of nodes *factorial* divided by 2:

$$\left(\frac{n!}{2}\right)$$

which in this case is

$$\frac{4 \times 3 \times 2 \times 1}{2} = 12$$

The factorial of the number of nodes is divided by two because each link is traversible in each direction.

3. There is a maximum number of edges to provide *complete* connectivity without any being redundant. This may be calculated by

$$\frac{n^2 - n}{2}$$

where n is the number of nodes in the network. Thus in Fig. 14.4 the number would be 6 and this completely integrated network is illustrated in Fig. E.

Description and Measurement of Networks

In river studies the subjective descriptions of drainage patterns such as dendritic, radial and trellised have been replaced by stream ordering within the basin and consequent determination of fundamental associations between such variables as stream order and stream length. Similar more precise forms of measurement are also applicable to networks in human geography. The advantage of deriving indices should by now be clear: namely that comparison of variables is facilitated and statistical relationships between them established. Three are selected here: density, shape and connectivity.

Density may simply be expressed as the number of edges per unit area. In Fig. 14.4, B has three edges and D five, thus the latter has a greater density. Similarly nodal values may be ascertained by the number of edges which meet at a node. Notice in Fig. 14.4 how the nodal value of A changes with increasing integration from D through E to F. In a complex network it may be possible to distinguish a hierarchy of nodes similar to that of Christaller, introduced in Chapter 10.

The shape of a network – whether it is dispersed or compact – may be measured by the diameter index. In its simplest form this is the number of edges traversed to cross from one extremity of a network to the other by the shortest route. Again in Fig. 14.4 the value in B would be 2 but in E, 1. The lower the index the more compact the network.

This diameter may be refined to include linkages between each node and all other nodes in the network. These shortest path linkages for Figs 14.4C and E are recorded in matrices A and B. The measure of dispersion 16 for C is reduced to 12 for E. These measures of dispersion are also known as the *gross accessibility index* of the network whilst the total for each individual node is called the *Shimbel index*. Also contained in the matrices are the simple diameter index scores for each node. These have been ringed for node a: these values are known as the *associated number* of the node. In all three cases, the lower the number, the greater the degree of accessibility predicted.

To	a	b	c	d	Total		To	a	b	c	d	Total
From a	–	1	1	②	4		From a	–	1	1	①	3
b	1	–	2	1	4		b	1	–	1	1	3
c	1	2	–	1	4		c	1	1	–	1	3
d	2	1	1	–	4		d	1	1	1	–	3
					16							12

Shortest path matrices

A for Fig. 14.4C. B for Fig. 14.4E.

A measure of how well nodes are connected in a particular network is of special relevance to the geographer. Three ways of determining connectivity are introduced here:

1. *The cyclomatic number* relates the number of edges, nodes and sub-graphs and is expressed in the formula $e - n + g$ where e is the number of edges, n the number of nodes and g the number of sub-graphs. Whilst the value of g is normally 1, this is not always true. For example, in Fig. 14.4A its value is 2. The cyclomatic number for Fig. 14.4A is $2 - 4 + 2 = 0$ and for Fig. 14.4D $5 - 4 + 1 = 2$. Calculate the values for E and F. This measure is not such a strong one as the other two.

2. *The beta index* again relates edges and nodes by dividing the number of edges by the number of nodes

$$\frac{e}{n}$$

This is a useful index because where the network contains no circuits, the B value is less than 1, where only one circuit the value is 1 whilst more complex networks have values of more than 1. Thus in Fig. 14.4 the beta value for B is 0·75, for C 1·0 and E 1·5. This particular index is normally considered to be a sensitive indicator of growth in a network such as the motorways of Britain.

3. *Efficiency of the network.* It was observed earlier that there are minimum limits and maximum limits for the number of edges in relation to the number of nodes. The percentage efficiency of a network may be calculated by comparing the observed number of edges with the maximum possible without duplication of linkages. For this use the formula:

$$\frac{e}{\frac{n^2-n}{2}} \times 100$$

Look yet again at Fig. 14.4. The network in B is 50% efficient.

$$\left(\frac{3}{\frac{16-4}{2}} \times 100\right)$$

The complete network in E is 100% and in F 183% thus reintroducing the concept of redundancy within a network. Any value in excess of 100% indicates a surplus of edges which may be removed without detriment to the efficiency of the network as a whole. It was this concept which has underpinned much of the drastic pruning by British Rail since the Beeching Report.

An alternative method for determining efficiency is by calculating the alpha index using the formula:

$$\frac{e-n+g}{2n-5}$$

This formula compares the cyclomatic number with the maximum possible value of the cyclomatic number in a complete graph. The range (0–100%) is perhaps more convenient than that for the redundancy index in that when the value is 0 then every link is vital as in Fig. 14.4B; as before, 100 indicates the complete network as in Fig. 14.4E.

The derivation of indices without relevant application is a somewhat tedious and sterile operation but it is essential to understand the procedure if they are to be used and interpreted with meaning. To reinforce such understanding and calculation draw six nodes on several different pieces of paper and connect each group of six in differing ways. Describe and measure each of the networks in turn and carefully record the indices. It is now possible for you to formulate and test hypotheses about the relationships between accessibility and connectivity, accessibility and density, nodal value and the node's accessibility within the network. For example, does the rank order of nodal values correlate significantly with their accessibility index (Shimbel index)?

TWO INTRODUCTORY NETWORK PROBLEMS

1. The Konigsberg bridge
The first problem is one dating back into the eighteenth century and from which has developed graph theory and topological transformation. The problem is a routing one in the Prussian city of Konigsberg devised by the mathematician Euler in 1736. Fig. 14.6A shows the topography of the city with seven bridges linking four land areas. Is it possible to visit each of the four areas of land and return to your point of origin crossing each bridge once and only once? You will

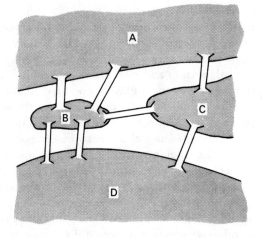

Fig. 14.6(A)   The Konigsberg bridge problem

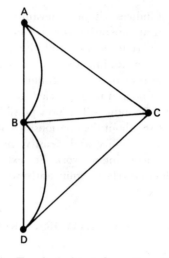

Fig. 14.6(B)   Topological transformation of Fig. 14.6(A)

already be familiar with the trial and error approach of solving mazes. Can a topological transformation as shown in Fig. 14.6B help solve the problem? Since each node has an odd number of edges meeting there (3 or 5) then the answer must be that the prescribed route and conditions cannot be fulfilled. Why?

2. A 'climax' network

Fig. 14.7A shows an over developed railway network in West Yorkshire as it appeared in the 1930s. Its density reflects the industrial history of the area and the dominant part played in its economy by coal, textiles and steel. It was developed in a period prior to planning and in the highly competitive atmosphere of the pioneer traditions of railway building throughout the world.

Fig. 14.7B shows the British Rail network in the same area in the 1970s. How does the efficiency of this network compare with that of the earlier one? This is an impossible question to answer unless the number of nodes to be served is specified, so assume that the network is merely to provide efficient linkages between the five named towns. Once more efficiency needs more precise definition: do we assume the towns should be minimally linked? If so, how many edges would be required and to what extent is there still a degree of redundancy in Fig. 14.7B? This minimum requirement may well be the case

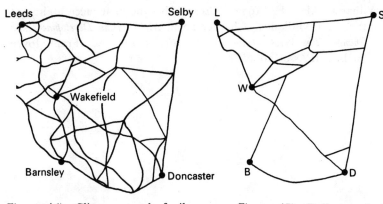

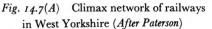

Fig. 14.7(A)   Climax network of railways
in West Yorkshire (*After Paterson*)

Fig. 14.7(B)   Rail network of
West Yorkshire in 1975

advanced by British Rail in order to reduce running costs. However, the rail user may well prefer the network to be completely linked. How many edges would be required to retain complete connectivity? Are there still too many edges in 14.7B and do they form the most appropriate pattern? Suppose British Rail decided to scrap all existing track and build a new network. Which pattern would be an optimum one to build? This *concept of minimisation* will be developed in the next chapter where the underlying concepts which help explain network patterns are examined.

Further Reading

Briggs, K. (1972) *Introducing Transport Networks*. University of London Press.

Cole, J. P. (1970) 'Notes on distance and location in human geography', Bulletin no. 25, *Department of Geography, University of Nottingham*.

Haggett, Peter (1972) *Geography A Modern Synthesis*, Chapter 14. Harper and Row.

Janelle, Donald G. (1968) 'Central place development in a time–space framework'. *The Professional Geographer*, XX, pages 5–10.

Tidswell, W. V. (1971) 'An introduction to the analysis of road networks, *Teaching Geography*, no. 15. Geographical Association.

Williams, Alan F. (1977) 'Crossroads: the new accessibility of the West Midlands'. Chapter 20 in *Metropolitan Development and Change. The West Midlands: A Policy Review.* (ed) Frank Joyce for British Association.

15 · Transport Networks II — Search for Order and Explanation

As with other geographical phenomena there is a great diversity in the shape and degree of integration of network patterns. Is it possible to find a satisfactory explanation for the variety of patterns and to identify the controlling forces?

The first substantial modern study of transport networks was undertaken in 1963 by Kansky who identified five factors or *independent variables* which influence network patterns. These he listed as relief, shape, size, population and degree of economic development. For each factor he devised a statistical index to facilitate comparisons between regions and countries and an extract of these is given in Table 15.1. How these indices were derived is explained below. These data also enable Kansky's assumptions about the general relationship between network integration and the five independent variables to be tested by regression analysis as explained in Chapter 5, page 89.

FACTORS CONTRIBUTING TO NETWORK STRUCTURES

Relief

It cannot be disputed that relief remains a barrier to movement despite technological advances. Rivers, river estuaries and highland zones are traditionally cited as impeding the development of road and rail building. How may this topographical influence be summarised into a statistical index for comparison with other areas and evaluating its influence compared with other variables.

The method used by Kansky involved the following steps:

1. Locate three random transects across the study area by calling random numbers

289

Table 15.1

Relationship of transport network to independent variables

	Tech Scale	Demog scale	Size	Shape	Relief	Energy Consumption	Imports per Capita	Index of Railways
1. Tunisia	351	32	4·7	2·7	5·5	0·18	1·66	
2. Ceylon	323	14	4·4	2·5	3·5	0·15	1·65	0·87
3. Ghana	355	15	4·9	2·5	2·8	0·18	1·69	0·92
4. Bolivia	370	18	5·6	2·1	20·0	0·18	1·42	0·90
5. Iraq	344	25	5·2	2·4	2·2	0·13	1·82	0·99
6. Nigeria	394	0	5·5	2·2	3·6	0·11	1·15	0·99
7. Sudan	410	6	5·9	2·1	4·5	0·13	1·21	0·99
8. Thailand	400	9	5·3	2·2	5·4	0·13	1·29	0·99
9. France	125	38	5·3	1·5	12·0	0·36	2·13	1·42
10. Mexico	222	19	5·9	2·4	21·0	0·26	1·60	1·16
11. Yugoslavia	241	16	5·0	2·6	23·2	0·21	1·53	1·18
12. Sweden	154	55	5·3	2·9	8·3	0·38	2·50	
13. Poland	182	25	5·1	2·2	3·1	0·35	1·61	
14. Czechoslovakia	159	38	4·7	2·7	14·0	0·40	1·99	1·36
15. Hungary	221	29	4·6	2·5	6·0	0·31	1·79	1·38
16. Bulgaria	279	47	4·6	2·4	13·0	0·20	1·62	1·12
17. Finland	202	46	5·1	2·8	0·35	0·36	2·30	
18. Angola	438	28	5·7	1·8	1·4	0·15	1·45	
19. Algeria	323	26	6·0	1·2	1·5	0·17	2·01	1·02
20. Cuba	256	37	4·6	3·0	12·8	0·32	2·11	
21. Rumania	258	23	5·0	2·1	25·0	0·23	1·64	1·16
22. Malaya	256	17	4·7	2·2	19·5	0·22	1·99	
23. Iran	372	12	5·8	2·4	8·5	0·15	1·17	0·89
24. Turkey	283	8	5·5	2·7	19·5	0·20	1·88	1·02
25. Chile	239	24	5·5	3·1	66·8	0·28	1·81	1·24

Source: Compiled from Kansky, K. J. (for explanation see text).

2. Construct cross-sections along each transect. For each cross-section the straight line distance is regarded as 100% and the surface distance expressed as a percentage of this. The latter will always be larger than 100 unless the terrain is perfectly flat.

3. Sum the differences of the two percentage figures and divide by three to obtain the relief index. For the study area of the former county of Herefordshire an index of 6·3 was derived from the measurements recorded in Table 15.2.

Table 15.2

A relief index for Herefordshire

	Straight line distance	Per cent	Surface distance	Per cent	Differ-ence
Axis 1	1·8	100	1·9	106	6
Axis 2	4·9	100	5·2	106	6
Axis 3	5·7	100	6·1	107	7

Mean difference = 6·3.

The lower the index, the more favourable is the relief. Check your impressions of relief in the countries listed in Table 15.1 against the statistical index.

Although a useful measure of relief as a barrier, this method has weaknesses. Does it indicate the barrier effect of rivers, and river estuaries such as the Severn and Humber? An index of less than 1 might be expected in the Fens yet the drainage pattern exerts a marked influence upon the shape of the transport network.

Shape

The concept of optimal shape was introduced in Chapter 14. It is reasonable to assume that an elongated country such as Norway or Chile would have a very different network than a compact one such as France. To test this hypothesis it is essential to measure shape statistically to facilitate the degree of correlation between shape and network integration.

Shape may be measured in one of three ways:

Method I.   Divide the length of the longest axis which may be drawn in the study area (Axis 1 in Fig. 15.1A) by the length of the perpendicular to the boundaries from the mid-point of the longest axis (Axis 2 in Fig. 15.1A).

Method II.   Divide the area of the smallest circle which will circumscribe the study area as shown in Fig. 15.1B, by the area of the study area itself.

Method III. Divide the area of the smallest circle which will circumscribe the study area by the area of the largest circle which may be contained within it as in Fig. 15.1C.

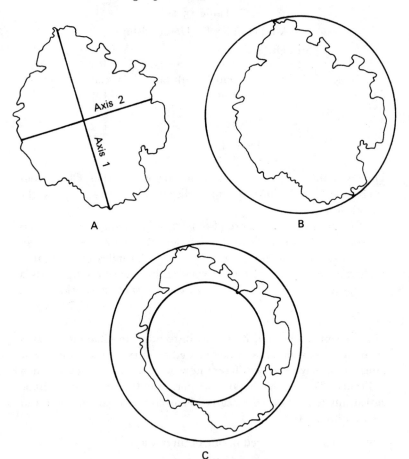

Fig. 15.1   Methods of measuring shape

Of the three methods described, the first is the simplest and is the one employed by Kansky. Despite weaknesses – a circle and a square both give the same optimal index of 1 – it provides a useful and satisfactory method of measuring compactness on a comparative scale. Results of all three methods applied to the same study area are summarised in Table 15.3. Method I seems as efficient as the others and its simplicity commends its use in preference to them. Whilst the methods have been applied within politically defined units they may be used in any areas defined according to differing criteria such as population density or a coalfield.

Table 15.3

Shape indices of selected countries and counties

	Method I	Rank	Method II	Rank	Method III	Rank
Japan	7·14	4	8·28	4	82·2	4
India	1·65	1	1·05	3	6·25	1
USSR	3·7	2	0·39	1	9·35	2
Italy	5·2	3	1·01	2	24·01	3
Lincolnshire	1·78	3	1·64	3	3·86	3
Herefordshire	1·37	1	1·47	2	2·96	1
Wiltshire	1·56	2	0·63	1	3·00	2

Size

Equated as area by Kansky, size may be more important in terms of the medium of transport used than the actual network. However, this factor will be reflected in the density of a particular network; for example, the distances travelled in Great Britain are so short that canals cannot compete with roads and railways and therefore have declined in comparison with those of continental Europe. Similarly the challenge of road transport to rail is caused by the shortness of haul which increases the tonne-km rate due to disproportionate handling costs for such short journeys. This is resulting in a growing motorway network juxtaposed with a shrinking railway one.

Population

Kansky was concerned with contrasting national areas and devised an index taking into account not only density of population, but also relative birth and death rates. A high population density with an appropriate degree of affluence will generate a demand for transportation links and hence affect the network. The growing motorway network in Britain is a good example of response to an affluent, high density population. In your own studies you may be reduced to considering population density only, although in the case of national areas this may be combined with Gross National Product (G.N.P.) obtainable from the *Ginsburg Atlas of Economic Development*.

Technological scale

The index derived by Kansky was based upon the work of Berry who used 43 measures of economic development and combined them mathematically. Two such measures – energy consumption and imports, both on a per capita basis – are included in Table 15.1. In interpreting the technological scale in this table (15.1) note that the *lower* the index the *greater* the technological advantage of the country. Care will therefore need to be exercised when feeding this index into a regression analysis. The relationship between the structure of the network and the stage of economic development was one suggested in the Taaffe, Morrill and Gould model introduced later in this chapter. Using either the technological scale or energy consumption as a measure of economic development, and the Beta index as a measure of network integration, test the hypothesis that the two variables are significantly related. Look back to Chapter 5, page 89, for detailed instructions for regression analysis.

The five variables employed by Kansky provide a useful framework for seeking an explanation of a network in any area even though detailed statistical indices may be elusive. Return to the A road network in the Lake District shown in Fig. 14.5. How effective are these five forces in explaining the pattern of the network as a whole and subsections of it, such as the Workington–Whitehaven coalfield?

Extraneous factors

Kansky himself acknowledged that the structure of a network may well be affected by forces located outside the study area. An obvious example is the traffic generated through the network by ports and their connections outside the area, in turn demanding a higher density network inside the area. Hence as in regional geography boundaries are very significant. The influence of the political boundary between Canada and the USA may be mapped by tracing the railway network along the border from your atlas. How many links are there between the two countries? How does this number compare with the density of the network in the border region? Other influences are social, historical and chance ones. It could be argued that the former two are subsumed in the Kansky hypothesis yet networks too result from human decision-making and must take into account the behavioural concept of minimisation and especially chance factors amongst others. You will already appreciate the latter if you have played *Railway Pioneers*. These themes of decision-making and chance will be assessed later.

A SEQUENTIAL MODEL OF NETWORK EVOLUTION

The evolution of a network linked to stage of economic development has been hypothesised by Taaffe, Morrill and Gould, with special reference to West Africa. From this study a more general model has been deduced. Look at Fig. 15.2A which identifies the stages through which a network is presumed to pass. Initially small scattered ports each have a tiny hinterland and there is no linkage between them. Stage two sees the emergence of one or two ports developing more rapidly than others and these major ports develop longer lines of inland communication resulting in a third stage of intermediate centres. These stages are well exemplified in West Africa itself where the cocoa area north of Accra and the Enugu coalfields provided the economic stimuli.

It is not until stage four is reached that nodes become interconnected reaching a high degree of integration in the penultimate stage five. The final stage is reached with the emergence of high priority 'main streets' resulting from a particular demand. Implicit throughout the model is the concept of growth point and growth pole consistent with the idea of city-rich and city-poor sectors advanced by Lösch and quoted in Chapter 10 on page 191.

This model has been applied in the context of other developing areas: the case of East Africa by Hoyle and of Malaysia by Marion Ward. The latter is shown in Fig. 15.2B. Although useful in seeking an explanation for the initial development of a network, the Taaffe model does not take into account human decision-making in more advanced, affluent and sophisticated society. Attention is now turned to an alternative approach although it should be realised that it may well build upon the earlier evolutionary network contained in the sequential model.

The Model
Ideal-typical sequence of transport development

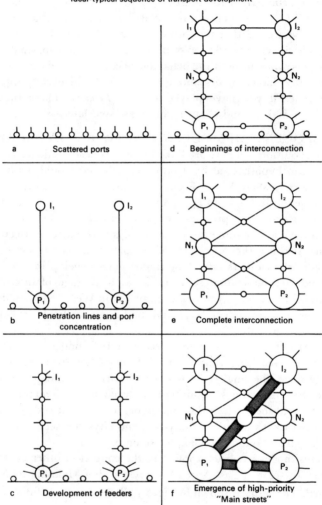

Fig. 15.2(A)   Idealised sequence of network development (*Taafe, E. J., Morrill, R. L., Gould, P. R., 'Transport expansion in underdeveloped countries'*)

The Reality

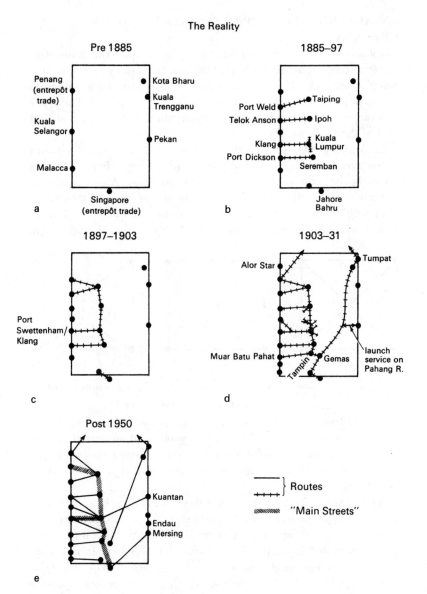

Fig. 15.2(B)   Idealised sequence applied to Malaya (*Ward, M. J.*, '*Progress in transport geography*', *Trends in Geography*)

AN ALTERNATIVE APPROACH TO NETWORK EXPLANATION

Emphasis in earlier chapters has been placed upon the concept of minimisation, and this all-important idea is equally relevant in a study of networks. However, another question must be asked: from whose point of view should the network be minimised? There are two major viewpoints to be considered: that of the road user and that of the road builder.

Look at Fig. 15.3A which shows a completely integrated network where every node is connected directly with every other node. This is clearly the most advantageous for the road user. A special case of minimisation for the road user is that known as the travelling sales-man problem, where the road user wishes to visit a number of nodes in a given order and return to his point of origin as in Fig. 15.3B.

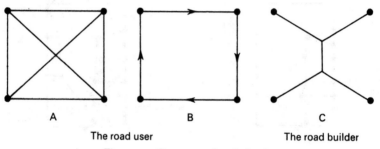

A   B   C

The road user   The road builder

Fig. 15.3   Concepts of optimisation

This problem is a very fundamental one since much of the role of transport is delivery and collection of goods and services. Unfortunately the solution is highly complex and is a staggering task even for a computer. Haggett suggests there are some 475 million ways of connecting 13 points!

The strategy adopted in solving this complex problem is first to connect the points in a random path as in Fig. 15.4A. Next remove three edges as in Fig. 15.4B and reconnect them to see if a shorter path results in Fig. 15.4C. The procedure is repeated until a minimal path emerges, and is akin to combining matrices until a stable one is established. This method has been computerised and a mathematician, Shen Lin, of Bell Telephone Laboratories, has developed a way of obtaining *satisfactory* solutions, but not the *unique* solution to the travelling salesman problem which contains a maximum of 145 nodes.

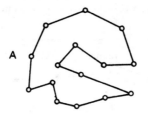

A

Start with a random path . . .

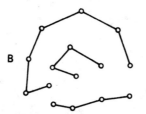

B

Break it into three sections . . .

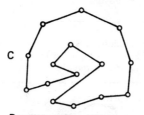

C

Reconnect them differently and
see if a shorter path results.
Repeat

Fig. 15.4   Solving the travelling salesman problem (*Abler, R., Adams, J. S., Gould, P., Spatial Organisation*)

In reality, the topological solution to the problem is helpful only when an isotropic surface is to be traversed or when air transport is used. Computer programs need to take into account available roads and in many instances variable road surfaces, as in the Ghana example of Shen Lin's work shown in Fig. 15.5. Optimal routes for the delivery of fish from coastal ports to inland locations have been computed. In Fig. 15.5A an isotropic surface was assumed whilst in Fig. 15.5B the problems of the real environment were taken into account. Study these two routes carefully and try to assess the impact of environmental factors upon the idealised solution. Return to this problem when you have become familiar with the detour index on page 304.

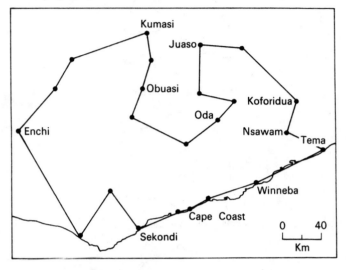

Fig. 15.5(A)   The travelling salesman's path among twenty-three towns in southern Ghana, assuming an isotropic surface (*Abler, R., Adams, J. S., Gould, P., Spatial Organisation*)

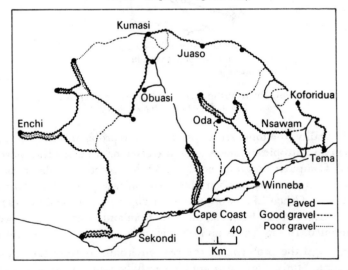

Fig. 15.5(B)   The travelling salesman's path in the real world of varying quality of road surface (*Abler, R., Adams, J. S., Gould, P., Spatial Organisation*)

Computer programs in the commercial world are now widely used in route planning and English Electric offers a program which takes into account six diverse variables including ten different vehicle capacities, the daily time for delivery and collection and visits to be made first or last during the trip.

The third case for minimisation is that of the road builder. Refer back to Fig. 15.3C on page 298 where the concept is illustrated. As in the travelling salesman problem, the solution is complex but a satisfactory answer may be obtained by using a hardware model described by Dr. Morgan in *Models in Geography*. This mechanical method was applied to minimising the network between market towns in Herefordshire and the result is shown in Fig. 15.6. Of

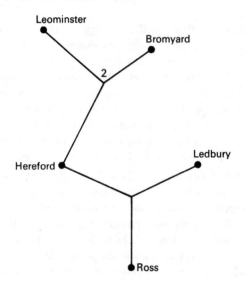

Fig. 15.6   A minimal road network

particular significance in this type of solution is the 120° angle of intersection. Notice this is the same angle as that at the junction of hexagons in the idealised Christaller network of settlement patterns. An alternative to the hardware model is to construct on tracing paper an intersection of three edges at an angle of 120° as at 2 on Fig. 15.6. Slide this on a map to discover the minimum distance connecting any three towns. For a study area of your choice trace off the towns as nodes and by the re-section method just described join all the nodes together without crossing any lines and measure the total distance of your minimal network. Knock out one link and substitute another to see if the total is decreased. Repeat the process, attempting to improve the network by trial and error, until you reach the most satisfactory solution. Such a procedure is, of course, irksome after the first two or three attempts and you may find the construction and operation of the simple yet effective hardware model more fun and more rewarding. Again at planning level a computer would be employed in the solving of this problem.

Case study of an optimal network: cost–benefit analysis
In reality an optimal network is often a compromise solution: it is this element of compromise which prevents it from becoming an optimum one.

In a recent book, Brian Fullerton suggests that road networks in Britain could be designed on two principles. The first of these is an administrative one linking London with regional centres and providing outside links via ports. This network, which he called 'primary', totals 1550 km in length and it is shown on Fig. 15.7. The second principle is an economic one designed to provide the maximum number of people with the maximum route km. To achieve this and provide east–west links between sea ports a secondary network of a further 1250 km is added as in Fig. 15.7.

Look at the graph in Fig. 15.7 which shows the relationship between percentage of people living within 9 km of the network per 1000 km of road. The primary and secondary network together thus cater for some 70% of the population at a minimal cost given the premises of essential links with London and the major ports. Look at the current map of the motorways and assess its pattern in relation to that in Fig. 15.7. What problems do people in remoter areas face and why are they not likely to have these problems alleviated? The graph in Fig. 15.7 will help you answer this. To what extent do you think this network also incorporates Kansky's five variables?

ACCESSIBILITY WITHIN A NETWORK

In the last chapter you were introduced to recording the shortest paths between nodes in matrix form and from this of deducing the dispersion of the network. The edges in the system could have been weighted to reflect the linear distance separating the nodes in a topographical network.

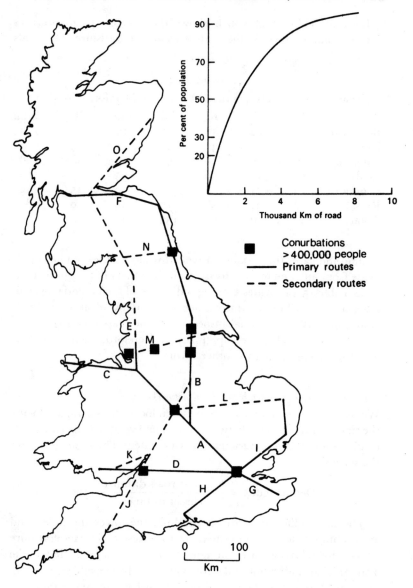

Fig. 15.7 A minimal/optimal road network for Britain (*Fullerton, B., The Development of British Transport Networks*)

Look at Table 15.4 which shows the shortest path distances between market towns in the study area of Herefordshire. The totals

Table 15.4

Road distances between market towns in Herefordshire (km)

	Br.	H.	K.	Ld.	Lm.	R.	Total
Bromyard	0	22	42	19	19	38	140
Hereford	22	0	32	24	21	24	104
Kington	42	32	0	56	22	56	208
Ledbury	19	24	56	0	35	19	153
Leominster	19	21	22	35	0	45	142
Ross	38	24	56	19	45	0	182
Total	140	104	208	153	142	182	

column indicates the distance travelled when a series of journeys is made from any one market town to all the others in the study area. Thus Table 15.4 provides a strong indication of the potential of each town as a distribution centre since a hierarchy of accessibility is established. Whilst a visual inspection of the map – see Fig. 15.8 – would have revealed the supremacy of Hereford, such a method could not have ranked the other towns.

Measuring efficiency in a topographical network
When the shortest road distance between locations is compared with the straight line distance between those same locations then an index of directness or *detour index* may be calculated. This is achieved by the formula:

$$\text{Detour index} = \frac{\text{Shortest road distance}}{\text{Direct distance}} \times 100.$$

The more efficient or direct the link, the lower the index and maximum efficiency is indicated by 100. Results for Herefordshire market town linkages are contained in Table 15.5. Immediately the least efficient individual links are evident and the problem isolated. An explanation may be sought or alternatively planning improvements may be focused upon them. The mean for each town indicates its overall efficiency whilst the mean for the network enables comparison with others to be made.

Table 15.5

Detour indices between market towns in Herefordshire

	Br.	H.	K.	Ld.	Lm.	R.	Total	Mean
Bromyard	0	107	118	109	120	127	581	116
Hereford	107	0	118	125	108	125	583	117
Kington	118	118	0	125	108	125	594	119
Ledbury	109	125	125	0	115	109	583	117
Leominster	120	108	108	115	0	127	578	116
Ross	127	125	125	109	127	0	613	123
Totals	581	583	594	583	578	613		118

The effect of relief as a barrier to movement was mentioned earlier in this chapter and by comparing relief indices with mean detour indices it is possible to test this hypothesis using the data provided in Table 15.6. This may be accomplished either by regression analysis or Spearman Rank Correlation (page 57) and preliminary calculations to expedite the procedure have been included in Table 15.6.

Table 15.6

Relief and detour indices for ten regions of England and Wales

Region	Relief index	Rank	Detour index	Rank	d	d^2
Cumberland and Westmorland	91·9	9	230	9	0	0
Yorkshire	9·0	4	117	1	3	9
Gloucestershire	11·3	5	156	7	−2	4
Devon	34·0	8	282	10	−2	4
Staffordshire	3·0	1	118	2	−1	1
Oxfordshire	4·9	2	145	6	−4	16
Nottinghamshire	6·8	3	137	4	−1	1
Denbighshire	98·0	10	211	8	2	4
Kent	15·0	6	125	3	3	9
Sussex	22·0	7	142	5	2	4

Mean relief index = 29·6.
Mean detour index = 166·3.

IDENTIFYING CHANGE IN A NETWORK

In Chapter 14 dramatic changes in the railway network in Britain in general, and West Yorkshire in particular, were revealed. Three examples of change resulting from new links are now introduced. The first case is the improvement in the road network from the

Table 15.7

Journeys via Severn Bridge: advantage expressed as a percentage saving

	BA	BR	CA	CH	G	H	MT	MO	N	R	S	T	W-s-M
Bath			50			25	32	42	57	39			
Bristol			59			25	36	52	66	44			
Cardiff	50	59									11	41	49
Cheltenham													
Gloucester													
Hereford	25	25										15	19
Merthyr Tydfil	32	36										25	29
Monmouth	42	52										30	38
Newport	57	66									13	43	52
Rhondda	39	44									11	31	37
Swindon			11			15	25	30	13	11			
Taunton			41			19	29	38	43	31			
Weston-super-Mare			49						52	37			

opening of the Severn Bridge, the second is concerned with improved accessibility in the London Underground network following the opening of the Victoria Line. Finally the question of where is the 'crossroads' of Britain is objectively assessed.

The Severn Bridge

The Severn Estuary formed a marked barrier to movement and to measure the improvement resulting from the building of the Severn Bridge, distances between selected towns in the region before its opening were compared with journey lengths after the opening. The percentage saved on each journey is indicated in Table 15.7. Plot on a sketch map of the area those journeys which show more than 50% advantage. Does the pattern add credence to the concept of Severnside as a *functional* region?

In addition to a re-alignment of linkages, flows through existing links are affected by major projects such as the Severn Bridge. Traffic which previously was routed via Gloucester could now use alternatives. Changes indicated by traffic census returns are approximately a 10% decrease in flow on the A38 and A40 whilst the A45 and A417 have increases of almost 30%. Locate these roads in a current road atlas and suggest reasons for the changes in flow.

The London Underground network

Change in the Severn Bridge area was analysed through topographical analysis. The London Underground network is normally represented in a topological format and Cooper measured the impact of the building of the Victoria Line upon the entire network. To do this he constructed shortest path matrices to record linkages between each node and every other node in the network. This long task was performed twice: prior to and after the building of the Victoria Line. From these matrices the associated number of each node was ascertained and the nodes placed in rank order. Clearly nodes with the lowest associated number are the most accessible in the network as a whole. By comparing changes in nodal values, the impact of the new line could be assessed for each individual node whilst comparison of gross accessibility indices indicated the overall impact. The gross accessibility of the entire network was reduced from 15,956 to 15,050 and the significant changes in individual scores are shown in Table 15.8.

Look at a current map of the London Underground, such as the one in your diary, and locate the nodes named in Table 15.8. From Table A you will notice that Victoria itself shows the greatest increase in accessibility. In fact it has changed from being the least accessible of the main line stations to the most accessible, sharing first place with Euston. What do you notice about the location of those nodes in Part A of the table? Why do you think those nodes in Part B have remained relatively inaccessible?

Table 15.8A
Nodes with Greatest Gain

Node	Percentage loss of links	Rank Before	After	Change in rank
Victoria	29·28	47	15·5	31·5
Sloane Square	22·81	50	29·5	20·5
Warren Street	20·35	26	9	17
Euston	17·01	27	15·5	11·5
Green Park	16·48	15	5	10
St. James's Park	13·89	34	27	7
Hyde Park	12·89	28	21	7
Knightsbridge	10·16	39	35	4
Oxford Circus	10·00	2	1	1

Table 15.8B
Least accessible nodes

	Accessibility rank Original network	Second network
1. Tower Hill	53·5	54
2. Aldgate	53·5	52
3. High Street, Kensington	52	53
4. Gloucester Road	51	49
5. Cannon Street	44	48
6. Notting Hill Gate	49·5	50
7. Bayswater	48·5	51
8. Queensway	46	47

Source: Cooper. 'A graph theoretic analysis of the effect of the Victoria line on the underground network of Central London.'

The Motorway Network

In Chapter 1 contrasting viewpoints of the location of the 'Cross-roads of Britain' were presented. They were based upon people's perception levels. If the term 'crossroads' is assumed to be synonymous with the most accessible node in the motorway network, then analysis similar to that of Cooper enables an objective evaluation of its position to be made. The results of Mill's analysis of the 1000 mile motorway network already built and that of the 2000 mile network projected for the mid 1980's is detailed by Williams. Three measures of accessibility were employed. Two of these – nodal accessibility and shortest path -- will be familiar to you from the last chapter. The third measure, valued path, is a refinement of the shortest path matrix, weighting each link according to the time taken to traverse it. Table 15.9 shows the rank order for the major conurbations. Look at this together with Fig. 15.8 which categorises the positions of all the nodes used into four groups of descending accessibility. The rank order of locations on the map takes into account all three measures used by Mills.

Table 15.9
Accessibility rankings of the major conurbations

Node	Nodal Accessibility		Shortest Path		Valued Path	
	A	B	A	B	A	B
Birmingham	2	1	5	1	2	1
Bristol	3	15	15	17	16	27
Leeds	13	13	5	15	9	16
Liverpool	—	30	—	30	—	21
London	6	3	13	12	18	28
Manchester	15	5	10	8	14	13
Newcastle	21	37	21	39	21	34

Note A = 1000 mile network
    B = 2000 mile network
    39 = total number of nodes in network

Identify the changes in accessibility which will result from the improved network. Which conurbations gain and which lose? Return to Figs 1.1 and 1.2; it is now possible for you to form a valid judgment and one which you can defend?

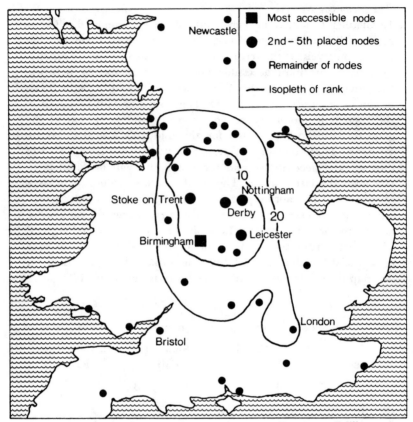

Fig. 15.8 Totalled accessibility rankings in 2000 mile scheme (Mills 1974)
(*Source: based on Williams, A. F.*)

PREDICTION IN NETWORKS

Predicting flows through a network
Throughout this book the predictive nature of models has been emphasised. Two examples of prediction are now examined. The first is concerned with predicting flows in a network and the second with predicting which new link in a network would effect the maximum improvement in the network as a whole.

Predicting flows in a network may be achieved by use of the simple gravity model

$$\frac{(P_1 \times P_2)}{d^2}$$

already discussed in Chapter 12 on page 225. Predicted flows between the market towns of Herefordshire are recorded in Table 15.10 and

Table 15.10

Matrix of desire for movement in 000's of units as derived from the simple gravity formula

	Br.	H.	K.	Ld.	Lm.	R.
Bromyard	0	376	5	42	80	26
Hereford	376	0	209	713	1,776	1,166
Kington	5	209	0	6	66	79
Ledbury	42	713	6	0	52	151
Leominster	80	1,776	66	52	0	57
Ross	26	1,166	79	151	57	0

plotted on Fig. 15.9 Of particular significance is the north–south axis from Leominster to Ross via Hereford. In a planning context therefore it is this route which should be improved first. For example, if a dual carriageway should be built between these two towns which should be the first stage to be constructed? This is merely a

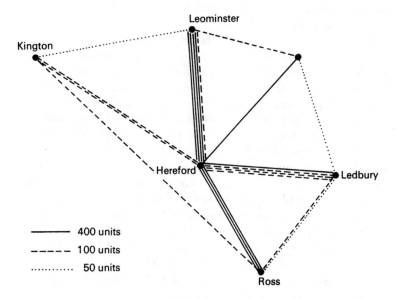

Fig. 15.9 Predicted flow of traffic between the market towns of Herefordshire

simple illustration of the gravity model being used as a predictor but it has wide application within the developing world. In regional planning of this kind a number of criteria would need to be matched to reach a satisfactory answer to route improvement programmes. A large detour index may indicate a need to improve a link yet the predicted traffic flow may not justify the cost of such improvement especially if the index relief is high as a result of the presence of a major obstacle. Can you illustrate this problem from your studies in regional geography?

Establishing a priority for road building

A good example of how geography can be truly predictive and applied in actual planning is illustrated by the work of Burton on the regional highway network in Northern Ontario. From his study he was able to predict the increased accessibility each additional link to the network would provide. This predictive quality marks a significant progression in geographical methodology beyond that of both Kansky and Garrison who measured the impact of the Inter-State Highway System upon economic activity. You are already familiar with Kansky's work and Garrison's significant paper is suggested as further reading.

Unfortunately, Burton's work is unpublished but his methodology is introduced in the context of the Italian Autostrada and you can try the method yourself on the London Underground network.

Look at Fig. 15.10 which shows the autostrada network for Italy, north of Naples. Imagine that it is proposed to build three new links to improve the network. The national budget is limited and it is necessary to establish an order of priority in building. The problem then is to discover which link or combination of links would be most effective for the network as a whole so that it may be decided which to construct first. Alternatively, by using different criteria, it may be necessary to establish which towns will benefit most from specified new links. This too may establish an order of priority for building.

The first step in solving either of the above problems is to establish the accessibility of each town in the existing network by constructing a shortest path matrix as in Table 15.11. The towns may be placed in rank order and the gross accessibility of the entire network calculated as explained in Chapter 14.

Similar matrices must then be constructed when each link is added

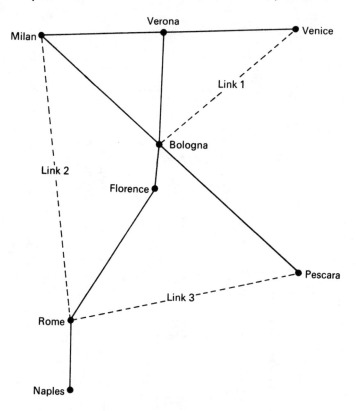

Fig. 15.10   Improving part of the Italian Autostrada

individually or in combination. This is a tedious task and is best undertaken in association with the other members of your group to divide the labour. If you are fortunate enough to have access to a computer terminal and suitable program then the task is diminished. The results of introducing the three links individually and in all possible combinations are summarised in Tables 15.12 and 15.13.

Look at Table 15.12. When all three links are added then the gross accessibility index falls from 130 to 100. You will also see that the greatest single improvement would be effected by constructing link 2 and the most powerful combination is links 2 and 3. Table 15.13 shows that whatever happens Bologna remains the most accessible place and Naples the least accessible. Rome and Milan significantly improve when links 2 and 3 are added. Any improve-

Table 15.11

Shortest path matrix in original network of autostrada in Italy

	Milan	Verona	Venice	Bologna	Florence	Pescara	Rome	Naples	Accessibility index	Rank order
Milan	0	1	2	1	2	2	3	4	15	4
Verona	1	0	1	1	2	2	3	4	14	3
Venice	2	1	0	2	3	3	4	5	20	7
Bologna	1	1	2	0	1	1	2	3	11	1
Florence	2	2	3	1	0	2	1	2	13	2
Pescara	2	2	3	1	2	0	3	4	17	5
Rome	3	3	4	2	1	3	0	1	17	5
Naples	4	4	5	3	2	4	1	0	23	8

Gross accessibility index　130
(Dispersion of network)

Table 15.12

Gross accessibility indices resulting from improvements in the network

	Accessibility index	Gain	Rank order	Gain per link	Rank order
Original network	130	—	—	—	—
plus link 1	120	10	6	10	4
link 2	114	16	5	16	1
link 3	122	8	7	8	7
links 1 and 2	108	22	3	11	3
links 1 and 3	112	18	4	9	6
links 2 and 3	106	24	2	12	2
links 1, 2, 3	100	30	1	10	4

Table 15.13

Rank order of accessibility resulting from specified linkage improvements

	Original net-work	Link 1	Link 2	Link 3	Links 1 and 2	Links 1 and 3	Links 2 and 3	Links 1, 2, 3
Milan	4	4	1	5	2	6	1	2
Verona	3	3	3	4	3	4	4	4
Venice	7	4	7	7	6	6	8	7
Bologna	1	1	1	1	1	1	1	1
Florence	2	2	4	2	4	2	5	4
Pescara	5	6	6	2	7	2	5	4
Rome	5	6	4	5	4	4	1	2
Naples	8	8	8	8	8	8	7	8

ment must depend upon economic feasibility or demand and hence the gravity model should be used in conjunction with this method. However, in this case building link 2 clearly offers the greatest single advantage and since Milan also gains very substantially, the economic motive may also justify its construction.

Summary and Concluding Exercise

Although a necessary preliminary, network analysis is not

merely discovering relationships between abstract points, it is helpful in solving problems and enables sound prediction to take place. Above all it informs the geographer of changes in spatial arrangements and expresses the dynamic nature of the human landscape. It is this appreciation and assessment of constant change which will continue to challenge and interest the geographer.

1. The London underground represents a dynamic network responding to changing demands. Figure 15.11 shows part of the

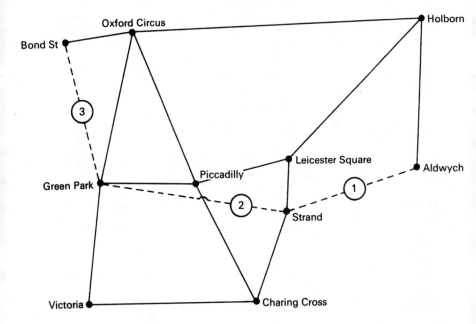

Fig. 15.11   Improving the London underground network: the Fleet Line

route of the proposed Fleet Line. Using the methods outlined above decide which of the three links should be built first in order to improve the overall accessibility of this section of the underground network.

2. Everyone faces a network problem and especially is this so in the daily journey to work. You will recall that the arrangement of residential areas adjacent to industrial ones was a feature of the urban models in Chapter 13. A study of journey to work in the Newcastle area revealed that 75% of the people travelled no more

than 3 km. in 1961. However a trend of modern society is longer distance commuting and by using the Usual Residence and Workplace Tables of the 1971 Census you will be able to discover not only where the people living in your town travel to work but also where the people working in your town live.

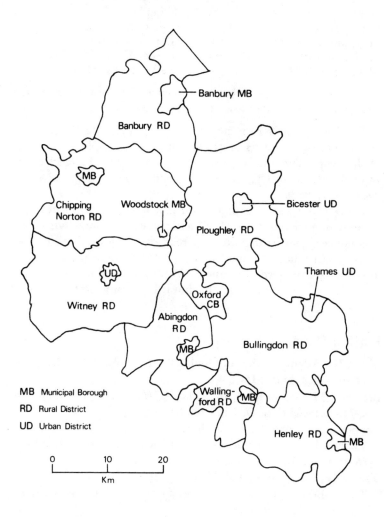

Fig. 15.12 Enumeration districts around Oxford

Table 15.14

Journeys to work around Oxford.

Into Oxford from		Out from Oxford to	
Bullingdon R.D.	1144	Bullingdon R.D.	68
Abingdon R.D.	673	Ploughley R.D.	59
Ploughley R.D.	562	Abingdon R.D.	30
Witney R.D.	312	Greater London	25
Chipping Norton R.D.	186	Abingdon M.B.	23
Abingdon M.B.	150	Bicester U.D.	16
Wallingford R.D.	100	Wallingford R.D.	11

Note: only values greater than 100 are given for inward movements and greater than 10 for outward movements.

The distributions for the city of Oxford are shown in Table 15.14. Remember the numbers are based on a 10% sample. Some 52% of the people live and work within the borough. Modes of travel to work are: car 63·6%, bus 17·7%, motor cycle 6·0% and pedal cycle 6·3%.

Using Fig. 15.12 as a base map, plot flow lines to identify the pattern of journeys to work. What particular characteristics do you notice? Look at the area in a road book. To what extent does this pattern reflect the road network? What problems arise from the scale and pattern of journeys? What information do you need to explain differences between the inward and outward movements?

Further Reading

Abler, R., Adams, J. S. and Gould, P. (1971) *Spatial Organisation*. Chapter 8. Prentice-Hall.

Bradford, M. G. and Kent, W. A. (1977) *Human Geography: Theories and their Applications*. O.U.P. Chapters 6 and 7.

Cooper, J. C. (1970) 'A graph theoretic analysis of the effect of the Victoria Line on the underground network of Central London'. *Horizon*, vol. 19, pages 19–24.

Dinkele G., Cotterell, S. and Thorn, I. (1976) *Transport*. Harrap.

Fullerton, Brian (1975) *The Development of British Transport Networks*. O.U.P.

Garrison, W. L. (1960) 'Connectivity of the inter-state highway system' contained in Ambrose *Analytical Human Geography*, pages 103–20. Longman

Goddard, J. B. (1970) 'Functional regions within the city centre: a study by factor analysis of taxi flows in Central London'. *I.B.G.*, no. 49, pages 161–80.

Kansky, K. J. (1963) *The Structure of Transport Networks.* Research Paper 84, University of Chicago.

Morgan, M. A. (1967) 'Hardware models in geography', Chapter 17 of *Models in Geography*, ed. Chorley and Haggett. Methuen.

Robinson, Roger (1977) *Ways to Move.* C.U.P.

Taaffe, E. J., Morrill, R. L. and Gould, P. R. (1963) 'Transport expansion in underdeveloped countries: a comparative analysis'. *Geographical Review*, 53, pages 503–29.

Postscript

It may seem strange that a book entitled *Human Geography* contains no chapter specifically named 'population'. Instead attention has been focused throughout upon man's actions and the patterns created by him within physical and economic parameters.

Many of the models which have been introduced may well appear dated, yet they have not been superseded. We can only build upon the work of our predecessors and the task ahead is the construction of more helpful models. Often, however, it is the appreciation of the concepts underpinning a model which can lead to generalisation and the development of 'probability norms'. Hence our need is to identify fundamental and repetitive processes associated with patterns: perhaps the most significant one in spatial terms is the tendency of certain phenomena to agglomerate, and for the intensity of this concentration to decrease with increasing distance from the centre of that agglomeration. Such an observed relationship, however, does not answer the question 'why' it occurs.

Distributions of phenomena in the landscape pose as many problems for us as for geographers in the past. We do have some advantages: there are available more sophisticated ways of identifying and portraying patterns together with more powerful analytical tools with which to discover relationships. Facilitating both procedures is the computer.

In seeking intellectually satisfying explanations for distribution patterns, progress has been accomplished in two dimensions. We have freed ourselves from subservience to the man–environment model, thus lessening the traditional bonds with the physical sciences; the key to understanding would seem to be closer to the realm of the behavioural sciences. In particular, an appreciation of the decision making environment and the psychological complexities of the decision-making process, focuses attention upon individual perception levels and motivation in conjunction with the attitudes and values of society as a whole.

The second forward move is represented by the attempt to conceive the system as a whole rather than be confined to selected elements. No longer are we obsessed with the explanation for a single set of phenomena but are equally concerned with how it contributes towards a general theory, so enabling valid prediction for the future to be made.

The sequence of description, explanation, generalisation and prediction as embodied in the scientific mode of enquiry has been exemplified. If this book leaves you with an enthusiasm to pursue geographical enquiry then it will have achieved its principal objective.

Appendix I

GUIDANCE IN THE USE OF RANDOM NUMBERS

1. Both the horizontal and vertical grouping of the numbers may be ignored. This printing arrangement is merely to facilitate use.
2. Numbers may be used in any combination: either singly, or in twos or in threes. Examples:
   (i) To establish a six figure grid reference use threes, eg. 201742.
   (ii) To choose a random sample from numbered items not exceeding 100 use two figures, eg. 20. Note in this case that 00 would represent the hundredth item.
3. Numbers may be used in sequence either vertically or horizontally provided use is consistent. For example, in establishing the grid reference one may choose either 201742 or 201744.
4. Once the direction of movement has been determined, ie. either vertical or horizontal, this must not be varied.
5. The initial choice of numbers may take place at any point in the table, eg. row 20 and column 9 would be 4. The above rules about choice of combination and sequence of movement thereafter must be observed.

Table of random sampling numbers

20 17	42 28	23 17	59 66	38 61	02 10	86 10	51 55	92 52	44 25
74 49	04 49	03 04	10 33	53 70	11 54	48 63	94 60	94 49	57 38
94 70	49 31	38 67	23 42	29 65	40 88	78 71	37 18	48 64	06 57
22 15	78 15	69 84	32 52	32 54	15 12	54 02	01 37	38 37	12 93
93 29	12 18	27 30	30 55	91 87	50 57	58 51	49 36	12 53	96 40
45 04	77 97	36 14	99 45	52 95	69 85	03 83	51 87	85 56	22 37
44 91	99 49	89 39	94 60	48 49	06 77	64 72	59 26	08 51	25 57
16 23	91 02	19 96	47 59	89 65	27 84	30 92	63 37	26 24	23 66
04 50	65 04	65 65	82 42	70 51	55 04	61 47	88 83	99 34	82 37
32 70	17 72	03 61	66 26	24 71	22 77	88 33	17 78	08 92	73 49
03 64	59 07	42 95	81 39	06 41	20 81	92 34	51 90	39 08	21 42
62 49	00 90	67 86	93 48	31 83	19 07	67 68	49 03	27 47	52 03
61 00	95 86	98 36	14 03	48 88	51 07	33 40	06 86	33 76	68 57
89 03	90 49	28 74	21 04	09 96	60 45	22 03	52 80	01 79	33 81
01 72	33 85	52 40	60 07	06 71	89 27	14 29	55 24	85 79	31 96
27 56	49 79	34 34	32 22	60 53	91 17	33 26	44 70	93 14	99 70
49 05	74 48	10 55	35 25	24 28	20 22	35 66	66 34	26 35	91 23
49 74	37 25	97 26	33 94	42 23	01 28	59 58	92 69	03 66	73 82

08 72	87 46	75 73	00 11	27 07	05 20	30 85	22 21	04 67	19 13
95 97	98 62	17 27	31 42	64 71	46 22	32 75	19 32	20 99	94 85
37 99	57 31	70 40	46 55	46 12	24 32	36 74	69 20	72 10	95 93
05 79	58 37	85 33	75 18	88 71	23 44	54 28	00 48	96 23	66 45
55 85	63 42	00 79	91 22	29 01	41 39	51 40	36 65	26 11	78 32
67 28	96 25	68 36	24 72	03 85	49 24	05 69	64 86	08 19	91 21
85 86	94 78	32 59	51 82	86 43	73 84	45 60	89 57	06 87	08 15
40 10	60 09	05 88	78 44	63 13	58 25	37 11	18 47	75 62	52 21
94 55	89 48	90 80	77 80	26 89	87 44	23 74	66 20	20 19	26 52
11 63	77 77	23 20	33 62	62 19	29 03	94 15	56 37	14 09	47 16
64 00	26 04	54 55	38 57	94 62	68 40	26 04	24 25	03 61	01 20
50 94	13 23	78 41	60 58	10 60	88 46	30 21	45 98	70 96	36 89
66 98	37 96	44 13	45 05	34 59	75 85	48 97	27 19	17 85	48 51
66 91	42 83	60 77	90 91	60 90	79 62	57 66	72 28	08 70	96 03
33 58	12 18	02 07	19 40	21 29	39 45	90 42	58 84	85 43	95 67
52 49	40 16	72 40	73 05	50 90	02 04	98 24	05 30	27 25	20 88
74 98	93 99	78 30	79 47	96 92	45 58	40 37	89 76	84 41	74 68
50 26	54 30	01 88	69 57	54 45	69 88	23 21	05 69	93 44	05 32
49 46	61 89	33 79	96 84	28 34	19 35	28 73	39 59	56 34	97 07
19 65	13 44	78 39	73 88	62 03	36 00	25 96	86 76	67 90	21 68
64 17	47 67	87 59	81 40	72 61	14 00	28 28	55 86	23 38	16 15
18 43	97 37	68 97	56 56	57 95	01 88	11 89	48 07	42 60	11 92
65 58	60 87	51 09	96 61	15 53	66 81	66 88	44 75	37 01	28 88
79 90	31 00	91 14	85 65	31 75	43 15	45 93	64 78	34 53	88 02
07 23	00 15	59 05	16 09	94 42	20 40	63 76	65 67	34 11	94 10
90 08	14 24	01 51	95 46	30 32	33 19	00 14	19 28	40 51	92 69
63 82	62 02	21 82	34 13	41 03	12 85	65 30	00 97	56 30	15 48
98 17	26 15	04 50	76 25	20 33	54 84	39 31	23 33	59 64	96 27
08 91	12 44	82 40	30 62	45 50	64 54	65 17	89 25	59 44	99 95
37 21	46 77	84 87	67 39	85 54	97 37	33 41	11 74	90 50	29 62

Each digit is an independent sample from a population in which the digits 0 to 9 are equally likely, that is each has a probability of $\frac{1}{10}$.

(Reproduced from *Tracts for Computers, No. 24*. Department of Statistics, University College, London)

Appendix II

Critical values of r_s for Spearman's rank correlation coefficient

Levels of significance

N	95% confidence level	99% confidence level
4	1·000	1·000
5	·900	·943
6	·829	·893
7	·714	·833
8	·643	·783
9	·600	·746
10	·564	·712
12	·506	·645
14	·456	·601
16	·425	·564
18	·399	·534
20	·377	·508
22	·359	·485
24	·343	·465
26	·329	·448
28	·317	·432
30	·306	

Source: Olds, E. G., in *Annals of Mathematical Statistics* (1938), vol. 9, pages 133–148, and (1949), vol. 20, pages 117–118.

Appendix III

Critical values of Chi-Square.
Source: based on McCullagh, P., *Data Use and Interpretation.*

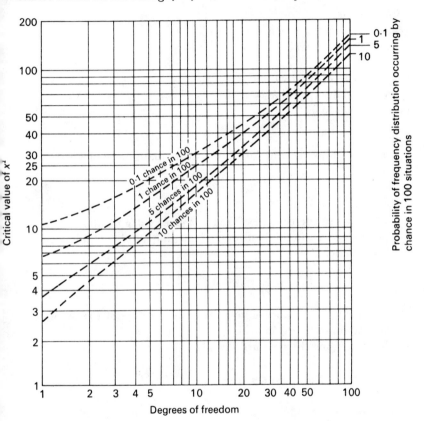

Appendix IV

USEFUL SYMBOLS AND FORMULAE USED IN THIS
BOOK

Useful symbols
$\sqrt{n}$ is the square root of n.
$(n)^2$ is the square of n.
Σ is the sum of.
$\bar{x}$ is the mean of the x values.
$(n)^{-1}$ is a reciprocal value of n.
$(2)^{-1}$ is equal to $\frac{1}{2}$.

Formulae

1. To determine the standard error in evaluating samples either

$$\text{S.E.} = \sqrt{\frac{p \times q}{n}}$$

where p is the percentage of land in a given category and q is the percentage not in this category, n being the number of points in the sample.

or
$$\text{S.E.} = \sqrt{\left(\Sigma x^2 - \frac{(\Sigma x)^2}{n}\right)\frac{1}{n} \cdot \frac{1}{n-1}}$$

where n is the number of items and where values of x represent the values of these items.

2. To determine the standard deviation.

$$\text{Standard deviation} = \sqrt{\frac{\Sigma(x-\bar{x})^2}{n}}$$

where x is the value of an item, $\bar{x}$ is the mean value of all the items, and n is the number of items.

3. Formula for Chi Square $= \sum \frac{(O-E)^2}{E}$

where O is the observed frequency and E is the expected frequency.

4. To obtain the location quotient of a square within a study area:

$$\text{L.Q.} = \frac{\text{Number of employees in square 1}}{\text{Total number of employees in area}} \times 100.$$

5. To determine the degrees of specialisation within an area:

$$\text{Index of specialisation} = \sqrt{p_1{}^2 + p_2{}^2 \ldots p_n{}^2}$$

where p is the percentage of people employed in industry 1.

6. To determine the activity rate:

$$\text{Activity rate} = \frac{\text{Number employed}}{\text{Total population of working age}} \times 100.$$

7. To determine the density of points in a study area:

$$\text{Density} = \frac{\text{Number of points}}{\text{Area}}$$

8. To calculate the expected mean in a random distribution:

$$\text{Expected mean} = \frac{1}{2\sqrt{\text{density}}}$$

9. To determine the degree of randomness of a distribution:

$$\frac{\text{Degree of randomness}}{(RN)} = \frac{\text{Observed or measured mean}}{\text{Expected mean in a random distribution}}$$

10. To determine the rank size rule relationship of town r to the primate city:

$$Pr = \frac{P_1}{R}$$

where Pr is the population of town r, P_1 is the population of the primate city, and R is the rank size of town r.

11. To determine the breaking point for retail trade between towns located in a predominantly rural area (Reilly's law of retail Gravitation)

$$\frac{\text{Distance of breaking point}}{\text{from smaller town } B} = \frac{\text{Distance } A\text{–}B}{1 + \sqrt{\dfrac{\text{Population } A}{\text{Population } B}}}$$

12. To determine the relative attraction of retail trade by towns in a more urbanised area (Urban Case of Reilly):

$$\frac{\text{Volume of } A\text{'s retail trade to } B}{\text{Volume of } A\text{'s retail trade to } C} = \frac{\text{Population } B}{\text{Population } C} \times \left(\frac{\text{Distance } A\text{–}C}{\text{Distance } A\text{–}B}\right)^2$$

13. To estimate the probability of shoppers living in centre 1 using centre 1 as opposed to other centres within the study area by applying Huff's probability model:

$$\text{Probability of C 1} = \frac{\dfrac{\text{Number of shops in centre 1}}{\text{Time taken or distance travelled to reach them}}}{\dfrac{\text{Summation of shops in the study area}}{\begin{array}{c}\text{Summation of total times taken or distances travelled}\\\text{to reach them}\end{array}}}$$

14. Formula for the Spearman rank correlation coefficient:

$$r = 1 - \frac{6\Sigma d^2}{(n^3 - n)}$$

where r is the coefficient of correlation, d is the difference in ranking, and n is the number of items rnanked.

15. To determine the shape index of an area:

$$\text{Shape index} = \frac{\text{Length of the longest axis}}{\begin{array}{c}\text{Length of the perpendicular to the boundaries}\\\text{of the area midway along the longest axis}\end{array}}$$

16. To determine the integration of a network (the beta index):

$$B = \frac{\text{Number of edges } (e)}{\text{Number of nodes } (n)}$$

17. Complete connecting is calculated by

$$\frac{n^2 - n}{2}.$$

18. The cyclomatic number is calculated by $e - n + g$ where g is the number of sub-graphs.

19. Efficiency of the network is calculated by

$$\frac{e}{\dfrac{n^2 - n}{2}} \times 100.$$

20. The alpha index is calculated by

$$\frac{e - n + g}{2n - 5}$$

21. To estimate accessibility within an area by determining an index of directness:

$$\text{Index of directness} = \frac{\text{Road distance}}{\text{Direct distance}} \times 100$$

22. To estimate the volume of movement between towns by using a simple gravity model:

$$\text{Movement } A\text{–}B = \frac{\text{Population } A \times \text{Population } B}{(\text{Distance } A\text{–}B)^2}$$

Appendix V

A SELECTION OF 'A' LEVEL SPECIMEN AND ACTUAL QUESTIONS

Section A. Agriculture

1. Show how distance from market may be expected to affect the precise use which is made of farm land. (*L*)
2. Discuss the relative merits of different techniques and measures which may be used in analysing the distribution of arable farming (*L*)
3. Discuss the criteria you would use to classify land for agricultural purposes in the British Isles. (*O and C*)
4. Examine the problems involved in classifying types of farming. (*O*)
5. Outline the main features of J. H. von Thünen's model of agricultural land uses around an isolated urban centre. Discuss any characteristics of the model which may limit its usefulness under modern conditions. (*O*)
6. You wish to make a study of the agricultural geography of an area which contains 300 farms varying widely in acreage and land use. You have time only to visit 60 farms. Give a reasoned account of ways you could use to determine which farms to visit. (*O*)
7. (a) Explain the assumptions which underlie von Thünen's concept of the 'isolated state'.

| | Livestock | | Wood | | Grain | |
Units of distance from market	Produc-tion cost per acre	Trans-port cost per acre	Produc-tion cost per acre	Trans-port cost per acre	Produc-tion cost per acre	Trans-port cost per acre
1	5	2	50	10	20	5
2	5	4	50	20	20	10
3	5	6	50	30	20	15
4	5	8	50	40	20	20
5	5	10	50	50	20	25
6	5	12	50	60	20	30
7	5	14	50	70	20	35
8	5	16	50	80	20	40

The table above lists production costs and transport costs of three commodities if they are produced at various distances from the market.

The prices obtained at the market for the product per acre of each commodity are:

Livestock	70
Wood	150
Grain	102

(b) Using the information given above draw a diagram showing the pattern of concentric 'rings' of land use which would result, according to von Thünen's model.

(c) Explain clearly how you constructed the diagram in answer to (b).

(d) Draw another diagram to show how the pattern of 'rings' you have drawn in answer to (b) might be altered by the establishment of a particularly efficient transport route in one direction from the central city.

(e) Why is it rare to find examples of von Thünen's 'rings' in present-day land use patterns? (*NUJMB*)

8. How may agricultural regions be delimited? Attempt to justify a division into agricultural regions of a large area you have studied. (*C*)

Section B. Industry

1. With reference to particular examples explain those changes which are likely to prompt an industry to shift its location. (*L*)

2. With reference to any one country or continent, examine the view that transport costs are of declining importance in the location of manufacturing industry. (*C*)

3. With reference to specific industries, demonstrate the variable effects of weight loss on the location of manufacturing. (*L*)

4. Discuss the relative merits of different techniques and measures which may be used in analysing the distribution of manufacturing industry. (*L*)

5. What types of industrial activity have spatial distributions dissimilar to that of population? Discuss, with specific examples, the reasons for this (*O* and *C*)

6. 'An area's ability to retain an industry often exceeds its ability to attract it in the first place'. Consider this statement with reference to specific industrial areas in Britain. (*O*)

7. Proximity to markets is a factor of increasing importance in the location of industry. Comment on this statement. (*C*)

Section C. Settlement

1. Discuss the techniques which can be used to delimit the sphere of influence of a town. Illustrate your answer where possible with examples based on your own fieldwork experience. (*O*)

2. Discuss the form and functions of the central business district of cities. (*O*)

3. Define what is meant by the term 'spatial interaction' and examine the factors which might affect the amount of spatial interaction between two settlements. (*L*)

4. Describe how you would set about a field-work project concerned with *one* of the following tasks:

    (a) To show the effects of site conditions on the morphology of a town.

    (b) To demonstrate the social differences that exist within the residential districts of a town.

    (c) To identify the hierarchy of shopping centres within a large town. (*L*)

5. What field evidence would you map in order to demonstrate the existence of social differences within the residential districts of a town or city? (*L*)

6. (a) Describe the main features of Christaller's central place model.

    (b) Discuss the extent to which it is helpful in interpreting geographical patterns in any specific region you have studied. (*NUJMB*)

7. Why is it that within relatively small areas of a country there may often be great variation in the size of settlements? (*L*)

8. Show how changes in methods of transport have affected retail trading patterns in urban areas. (*O* and *C*)

9. Distinguish between higher and lower order services. What relationship exists between the population size of a settlement with (a) the number of services it offers and (b) the order of services it offers. (*Scotland*)

10. Discuss the factors which you consider to have been most important in determining the location of (a) commercial areas, (b) industrial areas, and (c) high-quality residential areas within any large city you have studied. (C)

Section D. Networks
1. Patterns of communication are often more closely related to the distribution of population than to patterns of relief and drainage. Discuss. (C)
2. In the geography of transport, physical distance is often less important than other factors. Discuss (O)
3. Study the map extract provided (Sidmouth).
    (a) Draw a sketch map or topological diagram to show the network of the A and B class roads which link Honiton, Ottery St. Mary, Newton Poppleford, Sidford, and Sidmouth.
    (b) Analyse this network in terms of its density and connectivity.
    (c) Comment on those factors which appear to influence this network. (L)

Index